THE FUTURE OF
THE JUDICIAL SYSTEM
OF THE
EUROPEAN UNION

edited by
ALAN DASHWOOD
and
ANGUS JOHNSTON

Centre for European Legal Studies
University of Cambridge

·HART·
PUBLISHING

OXFORD AND PORTLAND, OREGON
2001

Hart Publishing
Oxford and Portland, Oregon

Published in North America (US and Canada) by
Hart Publishing
c/o International Specialized Book Services
5804 NE Hassalo Street
Portland, Oregon
97213-3644
USA

Distributed in Netherlands, Belgium and Luxembourg by
Intersentia, Churchillaan 108
B2900 Schoten
Antwerpen
Belgium

Hart Publishing is a specialist legal publisher
based in Oxford, England.
To order further copies of this book or to request a list of
other publications please write to:

Hart Publishing,
Salters Boatyard, Folly Bridge,
Abingdon Rd, Oxford, OX1 4LB
Telephone: +44 (0)1865 245533
Fax: +44 (0) 1865 794882
email: mail@hartpub.co.uk
WEBSITE: http//:hartpub.co.uk

British Library Cataloguing in Publication Data
Data Available

ISBN 1-84113-241-1 (hardback)

Typeset by John Saunders Design and Production, Reading
Printed and bound in Great Britain by
Biddles Ltd. www.biddles.co.uk

THE FUTURE OF THE JUDICIAL SYSTEM
OF THE EUROPEAN UNION

Contents

B. The Working Party Report

C. Documents

PART TWO: THE OUTCOME AT NICE

The Courts' Papers

Editors' Preface

The jurisdictional arrangements under which the European Court of Justice (ECJ) and the Court of First Instance (CFI) function – still with remarkable efficacy and a high level of consumer satisfaction – were made for a political and legal order very different from the European Union of today. The need for radical changes, to help the Courts cope with an increasing, and an increasingly diverse, case load, has been a topic of debate among academic friends and admirers of the Courts for a number of years. The issue got onto the political agenda, because of the challenge the impending enlargement of the Union poses for the existing institutional system as a whole, and because the Intergovernmental Conference (IGC) which completed its work in December 2000, was seen as the last practical opportunity for responding to that challenge.

The task of negotiating jurisdictional reforms within the framework of the IGC was entrusted to a group of "Friends of the Presidency", composed of government lawyers from the Member States, and working under the guidance of the Legal Services of the Council and the Commission, and of Court representatives. The "Friends" did their job so well that their proposals were seemingly accepted as uncontroversial by the Heads of State and of Government at their December meeting. The draft Treaty of Nice, accordingly, includes significant changes to the Treaty provisions on the Courts, as well as a new Protocol containing a uniform Statute which is to be annexed to the TEU, the EC Treaty and the Euratom Treaty, replacing the present separate Statutes. The changes may not go as far as some observers may have wished but, in our view, they represent a solid gain, and perhaps the IGC's most unequivocally welcome achievement.

Impetus was given to the reform process by two texts of distinguished provenance which appeared in the course of the preparations for the IGC. The earlier of these was a Paper emanating from the ECJ and the CFI themselves. This was entitled 'The Future of the Judicial System of the European Union' and contains 'Proposals and Reflections' prepared by the two Courts. It became publicly available in the early summer of 1999. The other text was the Report of the Working Party, which had been established by the Commission in May 1999, with a remit 'to review the various possible courses which may be taken in order to maintain the quality and consistency of case law in the years to come, bearing in mind the number and present duration of proceedings and foreseeable developments, in particular in the light of new jurisdiction conferred upon the Court by the Amsterdam Treaty and the forthcoming enlargement'. The Working Party (also known as 'the Group of Wise Persons'), was largely composed of former Members of the ECJ and the CFI, and chaired by former President Ole Due. It reported in January 2000. The paper on 'Reform of the Community courts', which the Commission presented to the IGC, followed up some of the proposals put forward by the Group of Wise Persons.

This volume is organised in two Parts. Part One (much the longer) is entitled, "The Debate". It presents the issues that were discussed during the run-up to the IGC, in the focus of the two key documents that were identified in the previous paragraph, the Courts' Paper and the Working Party Report. There are three Sections in Part One. Section A comprises the proceedings of a conference organised by the Centre for European Legal Studies (CELS), Cambridge on 3 July 1999, and held at the Møller Centre, Churchill College, which took as its starting point the Proposals and Reflections presented in the Courts' Paper, but ranged well beyond them: we have included a number of individual contributions, together with a synthesis of the points made in the course of the discussion. Section B of Part One consists of a commentary on the Working Party Report by its Chairman, former President Ole Due. In Section C, we have collected the two key documents in the debate, together with the final text of the latest amendments to the ECJ's Rules of Procedure (alluded to in the Courts' Paper, and since approved by the Council), and the Commission's additional contribution to the IGC on "Reform of the Community Courts" (distinctly less bold in its approach than the Wise Persons). Part Two of the volume, entitled "The Outcome at Nice", presents the concrete *acquis* of the debate, in terms of the amendments to the primary law on the Courts that will come with the entry into force of the new Treaty. Section A of Part Two offers a general appreciation of the agreed amendments, while Section B contains the annotated texts of relevant provisions.

Our purpose in compiling this volume is to provide a relatively permanent repository for a rich stock of ideas, which might otherwise disappear from view. Some of those ideas – it will be seen – found their way onto the IGC's table as proposals for the amendment of the Treaties, and ultimately into the text of the draft Treaty of Nice. However, it was unrealistic to expect the Union's judicature to be reformed root and branch by the late IGC. Radical change, so far as needed, is a project for the medium term. We are anxious that the insights generated under the stimulus of interchanges at the CELS conference, and those to be found in the Courts' Paper and in the Report of the Wise Persons, be available to enrich the future debate.

We are very grateful to the individual contributors, for the time and trouble taken in preparing their original presentations and in revising these for publication; and indeed to everyone who took part in a conference discussion of great range and depth, to which it has been a struggle in our synthesis, to do substantial justice. Special thanks are due to Advocate General Francis Jacobs, who encouraged CELS to organise the July 1999 conference, and supported it with his active participation; and to Lord Justice Schiemann, who kindly agreed to chair the conference, and kept the debate running smoothly forward. We are also very grateful to the Court of Justice and the Commission for allowing us to include the documentation relating to the reform of the Courts. Finally, our warm thanks go to the CELS Secretary/Administrator, Diane Abraham, for arranging the meeting on 3 July, and the collection and revision of conference papers, with her usual efficiency.

Alan Dashwood
Angus Johnston
Cambridge, January 2001

Part One: The Debate

A. THE COURTS' PAPER

I. Introductory Comments

Helping the Court to Function Effectively

ROSS CRANSTON QC MP
Solicitor General

As one of the Law Officers, I come across European Community matters every day. I have had to become, not an expert, but someone familiar with an area of law with which I did not have a great deal to do previously. There is no doubt that EU Law has great importance, and that the Court of Justice has a vital role in relation to our own law. In this contribution, I offer a few general comments of an introductory kind. I should say that, unlike most of those at the conference, I cannot speak authoritatively, because as a Department we do not take the lead on this matter. That is taken by the Foreign Office, and we still have not fully made our final response to the Courts' paper. There is a great deal of correspondence going back and forth between the Foreign Office and other Departments like the Lord Chancellor's Department, the Home Office and, you will be interested to hear, the Treasury, because financial matters always loom large in discussions these days.

A first point is that the United Kingdom is a friend of the Court. We value its contribution. We value the contribution it has made to the development of the European Union. And we know that it is going to have a vital role to play in the future. We have always taken (and this applied under the previous Government as well) great care about the cases that we bring before the Court, and we always put our best legal resources into fighting the cases that we do bring. As I say, we do believe in the Court.

The second point is this: we want to the Court to function effectively. The consistent application of EU Law across Member States is clearly in the interests of the Union as a whole, and it is in the interests of this country, and of institutions in this country, and of entities – businesses and citizens – too. So, we take the comments and the concerns in the Courts' Paper very seriously. As I mentioned, this is being discussed in depth at the present time. While we generally support the Courts' Paper – and, I repeat, I cannot now say what our detailed reaction will be – we are considering the precise proposals for procedural changes with care. As regards financial resources, we always have to balance many competing concerns. However, we have said that we are generally supportive of the need for additional resources for the Court, provided that the case is properly and fully argued. I would just say in passing here – this is not in my brief – that there is always a difficulty in the area of judicial administration of arguing for more resources, because over a number of years the judicial administration literature has demonstrated that the solution does not always lie in calling in more resources to deal with the problem. Often it is a matter of using the existing resources in a more efficient way; but, as I say, we generally support the need for additional resources.

The third point I would make is that changes of some sort are inevitable to meet the demands over the coming years, and the Courts' Paper is a good basis for consideration of the case for making changes. Many of the issues are not new. The UK Government has already supported greater autonomy for the Court in deciding on its own Rules of Procedure. The UK argued at the last IGC for changes to the Treaties, to allow the Courts' Rules of Procedure to be amended by a qualified majority vote in the Council, rather than by unanimity, as at present. Another concern, which will be touched on by some of the contributions to this volume, is the extended jurisdiction under the Treaty of Amsterdam. A special concern that the Home Office has, for example, is with asylum cases, and the need for very speedy resolution of such cases. To some extent it is the old adage that justice delayed is justice denied, but in cases like these that have political sensitivity, there is a special need for processing them rapidly. The Courts' Paper, of course, recognises this area of difficulty, and we have raised the matter with them.

There is clearly a lot of thinking and discussing still to be done. The contributions that follow are bold in some of their ideas and proposals for change. I would encourage that, but I would also say that there is a need to be realistic in your expectations. It is unlikely that all the changes that are desirable will be achieved. The trick will be to identify the truly essential changes.

II. Views from Luxembourg

Introducing the Courts' Paper

FRANCIS JACOBS

Advocate General, Court of Justice
of the European Communities

I think it is perhaps worth taking just a moment to try to put things into a historical perspective, because it seems to me that the judicial system of the Community has not changed essentially since the founding of the Community in the 1950s, with the single, and of course extremely important, exception of the establishment of the Court of First Instance. If one goes back to the amendments that have been made successfully to the founding Treaties, first of all in the Single European Act which provided for the establishment of the Court of First Instance, secondly in the Maastricht Treaty and thirdly in the Treaty of Amsterdam, although various changes were introduced in the jurisdictional arrangements, the fundamental functions of the Court have not changed. The Treaty on European Union, of course, introduced the three pillar structure and confined the jurisdiction of the Court essentially to the first (or Community pillar) while the Treaty of Amsterdam has modified that structure and has extended the jurisdiction of the Court to certain matters previously excluded, and has conferred certain rather substantial new forms of jurisdiction on the Court; but, as I say, with the notable exception of the Court of First Instance, the role of the Court has not significantly changed since the foundation of the Communities. The heads of jurisdiction are broadly the same: direct actions brought by or against the Community institutions; references from national courts for preliminary rulings; and certain other forms of procedure, for example, opinions on the compatibility with the Treaty of agreements which the Community proposes to conclude. The main change in the pattern of jurisdiction is that the Court of Justice has shed cases brought by individuals, which now go to the Court of First Instance, and has accordingly to handle appeals coming from that Court.

What has changed significantly in recent years is the number of cases brought before the Court, indeed before both Courts, as demonstrated by the statistics which are attached to the Courts' Paper, and also the range of subject matter to which the jurisdiction of the Courts extends; and, I would add, the increasing complexity of some of the cases, which has been a factor contributing to the increasing delays. It was in part the increase in the case load which prompted the Courts' Paper. The other main consideration was the prospect of enlargement; and the more immediate prospect of a further Inter-governmental Conference, planned to take place next year, which will be designed to amend the institutional arrangements of the European Union with a view to enlargement. Although the Inter-governmental Conference will, in political terms, probably be preoccupied with the questions of voting in the Council (that is to say the weighting of votes in the Council) and the possible extension of qualified majority voting, and with the composition of the Commission, important questions also arise in relation to the Court, including its composition. Should there, for example, continue to be a judge for each Member State? If so, how will the Court be able to function as a plenary Court? Should there be a proportionate increase in the number of Advocates General? Should an Advocate General continue to act in every case brought before the Court? Or is it conceivable that some cases could be decided without an Opinion? There is also a link between the size of the Court and its expected case load so that issues will arise, even in the context of composition, about the scope of the future jurisdiction of the Court. But the Courts' essential concern, as reflected in the Paper, is a simple one: how is it to be able to continue to function effectively both in the light of the increasing case load, including the substantial new case load likely to result from the Treaty of Amsterdam, and in the light of the enlargement of the Union? How is the Court to be able to discharge its function and to maintain the quality of its work?

Before turning to the main issues, I will mention briefly three specific changes in the judicial system recently introduced or announced. *First*, there is the provision, which is now in place, for the Court of First Instance to decide certain cases with a single judge. *Secondly*, a proposal has been put forward by the Court for certain cases brought by Member States to be heard by the Court of First Instance, which might in turn lead to other such direct actions being transferred to that Court. *Thirdly*, there are the amendments to the Rules of Procedure which were presented by the Court to the Council, seeking some procedural reforms which are perhaps overdue: under the law as it presently applies, this will require a unanimous decision by the Council.[1] Among the proposed amendments, I should like to draw your attention more particularly to that for an accelerated procedure for some references for preliminary rulings; and to that for a power to reply to some references by way of an order, without going through the full gamut of the procedure, in cases where the answer follows from the existing case law or is otherwise obvious. Other possible

---

[1] Editors' note: this proposal has since been adopted by the Council (see Part One C(1), *infra* for details).

changes, however, even of a procedural kind, will, unfortunately, need Treaty amendment. These include the suggestion in the Courts' Report for the introduction of a filter system for appeals to the Court of Justice, which would mean that there would no longer be an automatic right of appeal from the Court of First Instance. The filter system could apply in cases which have already been heard by two instances, as is already the case for trade marks appeals from the Boards of Appeal at Alicante to the Court of First Instance; and, as may be the case in the future, for staff cases to be heard first by a staff tribunal, with an appeal to the Court of First Instance (which, of course, should no longer be called the "Court of First Instance"). Further appeals to the Court of Justice from Court of First Instance in such cases might be limited to those raising a point of law of general importance, or otherwise considered to deserve further hearing.

I turn now to what is the main concern of the Court of Justice, namely the threat to the future of the preliminary rulings procedure. The Court recognises that it may be necessary to reform that system radically if the present trend of increasing numbers of references persists. This presents a very difficult problem. On the one hand, the Court is firmly convinced of the need to keep the preliminary rulings procedure open to all national courts and not just to superior courts. We believe that this is essential to guarantee effective judicial protection and the uniform application of Community Law. On the other hand, we appreciate that the continued increase in the number of cases before the Court could result in gridlock and thus effectively destroy the system. How then to achieve a situation where the Court is not asked to treat more cases than it can handle, whilst still ensuring that Community Law is interpreted by a Supreme Court whose authority is recognised throughout the European Union? The Courts' Paper breaks new ground, I think, for a document of this kind, in considering a number of possible solutions and indicating some of the advantages and disadvantages of those solutions which merit closer attention, despite their obvious difficulties. There are four possible solutions considered: first, limiting the national courts which are empowered to make references; secondly, the installation of a filtering system, which would enable the Court to decide which questions it should answer having regard to their novelty or importance; thirdly, the transfer to the Court of First Instance of some heads of jurisdiction in the area of preliminary rulings; fourthly, the creation of decentralised judicial bodies in each Member State. The Court is not, of course, putting forward solutions itself. It is simply identifying a range of possible solutions for consideration. The only thing that the Court does propose is that consideration of these possible solutions be embarked upon without delay. I would also note that the Courts' Paper speaks of the need for reflecting on these issues.

The Court has, for good reasons, not taken a position on these questions. First, I think it is doubtful whether it is the Court's role to take a position. Such radical changes should be proposed from outside, although the Court should certainly be consulted throughout the process. Secondly, I do not think one can assume that the Court would necessarily have the right answers to these problems. The skills to be expected of the Court are not those of architect or engineer, but rather those of a craftsman faced with specific problems. Thirdly, it seems unlikely in any event that the Court would be able to reach agreement on a new judicial architecture. For one thing, it is wedded to the existing design, and, for another, our numbers are too large and our viewpoints perhaps too diverse. However, it is indicative of the Courts' determination to promote debate that we have reached agreement on this Paper among the 24 Members of the Court of Justice and the 15 Members of the Court of First Instance.

We have all agreed, moreover, and no doubt most of those who participated in the conference would agree, that there are certain fundamental requirements: the need to secure the unity of Community law by means of a single supreme Court; the need to ensure that the system is transparent and accessible to the public; and the need to dispense justice without unacceptable delays. But how are we to achieve this? Well, we expect input from a number of sources. The Commission has established a group of experts, including several former Members of the Court, one of them Lord Slynn of Hadley, which has now reported (as of February 2000). We may see proposals emanating from the Governments in the context of the Inter-governmental Conference. I might add that in the recent past one or two governments might well have come forward with rather radical proposals for alleviating the burden on the Court by limiting its jurisdiction in substantial respects, although such proposals would no doubt have been resisted by other Governments. In the current climate we have the impression that the Governments generally are extremely supportive of the Court's concerns and, indeed, in very recent developments in the Council, we have even had some support in respect of our budgetary problems. It seems correspondingly less likely that the Governments will come up with radically limitative reforms to the judicial system on their own initiative. We hope also to have input from informed circles outside the institutions and outside the Member States, and that is why it seems to me very valuable that initiatives like that the instant conference have been taken. There will be a number of conferences in coming months where the problems raised by the Courts will be discussed, but I think that this was the first. In my view, informed academics, practitioners and officials, with experience of the Court's working, have a special role to play, and I hope and expect that this volume will carry forward the Courts' process of reflection.

The Court of First Instance:
Meeting the Challenge

PERNILLA LINDH

*Judge, Court of First Instance of
the European Communities*

The most important word in the title I have been given is the word, "challenge". I say this because it is clear to those sitting in the Court of First Instance, to those appearing before us, and to informed opinion generally, that we now face serious problems. It is getting more and more difficult to cope with the volume of work, and this has given rise to criticism in the press that parties have to wait too long for justice. Criticism is usually unwelcome, but here I have to say it is to some extent justified; and it is a thoroughly good thing that those involved are talking about the problems and that the point is being made at governmental level that something has to be done. Nor should we be concerned only with the immediate situation, but with how matters will stand in the years to come. In my view, it is absolutely necessary to do something, and indeed something radical. The system has functioned well so far and must continue to do so, but to achieve similar success in the future, it will be necessary to make changes.

I was very glad to accept the invitation to address the conference, not so much because I thought that I could inform you further, since my own ideas have found their way into the Courts' Paper, which is already available, but because I felt sure that the participants, who have worked on these questions much longer than I have, would have some very good ideas that I could carry back to Luxembourg. My particular focus here is the Court of First Instance, with its increasingly wide jurisdiction, and in an enlarged European Union; but of course that Court cannot be considered in isolation. Everything that happens to the Court of First Instance will be connected with what happens in the future to the Court of Justice itself, in particular so far as concerns the transfer of heads of jurisdiction from one Court to the other. As Advocate General Jacobs has said,[1] our point of departure must be to ensure the unity of Community Law by means of a Supreme Court. I use the term "Supreme Court" advisedly. The

---

[1] See p. 12, *supra*.

Court of Justice should not have to deal with all kinds of things that could as well be handled by other Instances, but it should very precisely be a Court that has the last word, and one with the job of telling other Instances how they should determine questions in the future.

So it is very clear that the Court of Justice has to dispose of some classes of case, and the question is then: to whom? As far as preliminary rulings are concerned, could these be handled by national supreme courts? Or should it be by the Court of First Instance? Or perhaps by specialised Courts? As is widely known, the Court of First Instance is in the position that it can be enlarged whenever the Governments of the Member States so wish. We do not have the same problem of ensuring coherence as the Court of Justice. We sit in Chambers of three or five, practically never in plenary. Also, for our cases, there is the possibility of recourse to the Court of Justice to tell us whatever the correct interpretation might be. As Advocate General Jacobs pointed out, the Courts' Paper, in its last section, puts forward ideas for reflection, not concrete proposals. It is probably as true of the Court of First Instance as of the Court of Justice that there are as many opinions on the future judicial architecture as there are Members. My personal view as far as preliminary rulings are concerned is that I am rather hesitant about the idea of transferring them to the Court of First Instance. There are various reasons for this. In particular, if jurisdiction were transferred only in respect of references on certain matters, for instance agriculture or social policy, there would be a serious demarcation problem. All kinds of issues of principle have arisen in cases relating to those fields, and I fear that, if the aim is to reduce delays, the effect would be the opposite, owing to the necessity of some kind of appeal to the Court of Justice. I suppose a possible solution in that regard would be to limit appeals to matters of general interest. However, to revert to the second principle mentioned by Advocate General Jacobs, the system must be transparent and accessible, and that would be compromised if matters were being dealt with by different Instances and with different appeal procedures. That is not the only problem. In my view, there is also the problem of legitimacy – of acceptance by the national courts. I, for one, do think that acceptance is more likely to be forthcoming for rulings given by the Court of Justice. Why not, then, as suggested in the Paper, require the national courts to work a bit harder themselves, for example by proposing an answer to the questions that they refer? The other suggestions, such as filtering references or disposing of them by reasoned orders, should also be tried out. Only if we find these things do not work, should the transfer of the preliminary rulings jurisdiction to the Court of First Instance be considered.

So far as direct actions are concerned, a proposal has been put to the Council that some cases brought by Member States should be dealt with by the Court of

First Instance instead of by the Court of Justice. That would be in areas such as state aids, some aspects of competition policy, transport policy and measures concerning the structural funds. It has rightly been said that the aim of the proposed change is not to relieve the Court of Justice of work but to ensure the better administration of justice, by preventing parallel proceedings from being brought in the two Courts, and personally I regard this as a very good proposal. Here, once again, there is room for discussion as to whether more might be done in view of the fact that the proposed change would affect only proceedings relating to decisions, not to normative acts; nor would it cover failures by Member States to comply with their Community obligations. So we should, perhaps, regard this as a first step. The view has been taken that non-compliance with Community obligations by Member States should not be dealt with by the Court of First Instance because this is a constitutional matter. The latter point is certainly true, but we do already deal with institutional questions in actions for annulment relating to normative acts. On the issue of non-compliance with Community obligations, I should like to add a further reflection to those in the Paper. Why not allow the Commission itself to decide that there has been an infringement in straightforward cases, such as those concerning total failure to implement a directive? Of course if the matter is more complicated, the case should be referred to the Court; but in the kind of case I have mentioned, the Commission could make a finding of non-compliance, which could then be appealed against.

Whether or not the Member States decide to transfer further matters to the Court of First Instance, our jurisdiction has already been extended, for instance to trademark proceedings. As you know, there is an Office in Alicante that deals with applications for the registration of Community trade marks. There are at present three Boards of Appeal, and a fourth Board is to be established before the end of this year, to review decisions of the Office; with a right of appeal from the Boards to the Court of First Instance. Last year the Office had received 100,000 applications, and it is estimated that the four Chambers could deal with 1,000 appeals per year. That means, in my view, that we are being very modest when we say that the number of Community trade mark cases coming to the Court of First Instance could be some 200-400. Even so, knowing that the Court of First Instance deals with some 250 cases per year, the outlook is somewhat alarming. It may be that such cases are relatively straightforward by comparison with competition cases, for example; nevertheless, especially at the beginning, there are bound to be issues of principle to be determined; and, even if a case is simple from a legal point of view, there will still be documents to be translated and the proceedings are bound to be time-consuming. A peculiarity of Community trademark proceedings is that a matter will be dealt with first by the Office, then by the Boards of Appeal, then there may be an Appeal to the Court of First Instance, and finally, an appeal, on a point of law, to the Court of Justice. By contrast, in competition proceedings, there are only three possible stages, and it is legitimate to wonder whether trademark cases need to be dealt with in such a thorough way. As underlined in the Paper, the success of the Community trademark depends crucially on being able to act speedily. At the same time, the Court of First Instance cannot give such cases priority over other cases. We have therefore asked the Council to create posts for another six judges, making it possible to establish two new Chambers; and we hope this will be given a fair wind. The case for giving more resources to the Community Courts seems to me to be unanswerable, though doubtless it will take time – posts for six judges cannot be created from one day to another. Meanwhile, we have asked for more legal secretaries to help prepare all these cases. We have not yet felt that there is need for specialisation, though we have allocated the trademark cases to particular Chambers (at the moment the Court of First Instance has five Chambers). We shall simply have to get used to handling these cases that are rather different in their content from those to which we have become accustomed.

We have also lately acquired jurisdiction in other areas. One such area is that of access to documents – we have had a number of cases, even before the new provision in the Amsterdam Treaty, and we expect such proceedings to become more frequent. These, too, are cases that need to be disposed of rapidly. Among the proceedings so far, we have had a case with somebody asking for a certain document who only got his answer two years later. You cannot help wondering whether that is really efficient: if you go to a Court, you ought to get an answer from it that comes soon enough to be useful. A few months ago, we had a case concerning access to a document, and to speed up the proceedings, the applicant refrained from lodging a Reply to the Defence. Then within the three-month time limit prescribed, a Member State asked to intervene and one had to add the wait for observations by the parties and to give the intervenor an opportunity to submit its comments. So, in the event, the attempt to speed up proceedings was frustrated; and here I really do think that there are improvements that could be made, in small but important ways. It seems to me that the Court ought to be able to adapt its rules to the circumstances of particular cases; there should be more flexibility to make the remedies available to litigants more effective.

I should briefly mention other new fields of jurisdiction. These comprise the following areas: proceedings arising out of the exercise of certain new competences of the Court of Auditors; actions in respect of sanctions imposed on undertakings by the European Central Bank; staff cases brought by officials of the European Central Bank and of Europol; and actions in the field of the fight against fraud. None of those fields seems to be very different from the matters with which we already deal. However, it has been suggested that the Court of First Instance might be given jurisdiction in proceedings relating to Community patents, and there I do think we would face types of problem that require a very particular expertise. In my opinion, careful consideration should be given to the question of whether patent cases ought to be dealt with by a separate tribunal, on the same level as the Court of First Instance, with the right of appeal to the Court of Justice. Or, if it were decided to give the jurisdiction to the Court of First Instance, the possibility should be considered of having experts to sit with the Judges. Looking ahead to a time when the European Union has been enlarged, it may well be that the Court of First Instance would have to deal with a huge variety of subjects, some of which are rather specialised in their content, and then I think it might be appropriate to establish specialised Chambers, with a certain rotation among the Judges. However, we have not reached that point yet.

If the Court of First Instance is given a range of new cases to handle, it ought to be able to dispose of some of those that it already has, and here I am thinking more particularly of staff cases. Obviously such cases have to be considered at some point in time by a judicial body, but I do wonder if it is right for the Court of First Instance to have to examine officials' annual reports to see whether it was right to give three "excellents" and two "very goods", or to decide whether a certain reorganisation of officials was in the interests of the service, or whether there may have been an abuse of the employing Institution's powers. It certainly may happen in a very big administration that officials are maltreated and need a remedy, but could there not be another body to deal with such questions, at least at an initial stage? It is suggested for reflection in the Paper that a kind of inter-institutional Appeal Board be created to deal with staff cases in the first instance. Something, too, might perhaps be done about the pre-contentious procedure, which is presently rather cumbersome and means that a long time may elapse from the date when the event complained of occurred until the case comes to Court. If some kind of Appeal Board were established, it would be for discussion whether it should be staffed by judges or by individuals enjoying the confidence of the parties and chaired by a judge. One possibility would be for the Board not to give an actual judgment, but simply to make a recommendation, with an appeal to the Court of First Instance if the recommendation were not followed. Here, as in the case of trademark proceedings, there should at least be a stringent filtering system for appeals to the Court of Justice. I do not think the Court of Justice should normally have to deal with staff cases which have already been twice considered, except perhaps on issues of fundamental principle.

I should also like to say a few things about procedural matters. We really are constantly looking for ways to make our procedures more effective and to reduce delays. Thus, although this has not yet found its way into our formal Rules, we have instituted a type of fast track procedure where, once the Defence has come in, we say to ourselves, "Is this is a case that could be dealt with immediately?" If so, we then ask Applicants whether they are willing to refrain from lodging a Reply in such cases, and if they agree, we indicate a date for the hearing. That allows the procedure to be expedited and also, if I may say so, it may provide an incentive for lawyers to structure their applications better, knowing that there may well be no second round to fill in gaps. We are also very conscious that in some cases it may be necessary, as early as after the Defence has been entered, to organise an informal meeting to discuss matters – this has happened several times in my Chamber in recent months. Also, after 26 months in the Council, there is now at last the possibility of having a single judge sitting, and we recently sent our first letters to the parties in various cases asking for their observations as to whether this should occur. I fully recognise that the change is not a vast one, but it could lead to better use of resources. In addition, we try hard to see, once the Defence is in, if we can already at that stage put written questions to the parties, to try to ensure that certain aspects of the case are better focused in the second round of pleadings. That kind of structuring may help to shorten the delay between the close of pleadings and the hearing. So genuine progress is being made. No doubt we could do more, but we are all certainly very conscious of our present predicament and fearful of what may happen in future if things do not change.

To round off my contribution, may I say that we ought not to duck the language question. I find it hard to see why all judgments (except for staff cases and possibly also trade mark cases) should be translated into all the official languages. I know that is a very political question but it needs to be faced by those responsible for fashioning the new judicial architecture.

CELS is to be congratulated for having organised this seminar so speedily after the Courts' paper. The most important thing right now is that these matters be discussed – not least since this has given the group of Wise People a broad range of fruitful ideas for their report – and so that finally the Member States, who bear the final responsibility for an efficiently-functioning judicial system of the Union, can take their decisions.

III. Views from Member States

Thoughts from the Finnish Presidency

PEKKA NURMI

Director General, Law Drafting Department,
Finnish Ministry of Justice

I should like to begin by saying that we in Finland have the habit of abiding by the rules in force. Similarly, we are fortunate in being able to look to an independent judiciary to enforce our rights under those rules. Accordingly, it is quite easy for us Finns to accept the European Court of Justice as a competent Court in matters relating to the enforcement of EU law. However, by the same token, we expect the Court to function, both structurally and operationally, at a level that, at the very least, does not fall short of the acceptability or reliability of our national judiciary.

Next, some points need to be made about the official discussions that are going on. As is widely known, the Paper presented by the European Courts was the subject of a preliminary discussion by the Justice and Home Affairs Council in Brussels last May. On that occasion, the Finnish Minister of Justice, Mr Johannes Koskinen, referred to three important principles. First, he cited the efficiency of the operation of the European Court of Justice. Secondly, he emphasised the need to ensure the acceptability of the ECJ's rulings throughout the Union. Thirdly, the transparency, openness and intelligibility of proceedings in the ECJ for citizens of the Union were recognised as central issues. More concretely, Mr Koskinen stressed the importance of the translation service of the ECJ and the need to provide it with adequate resources. In addition, the Minister considered it quite possible that the amendments that were necessary to the Rules of Procedure could be carried out with appropriate speed; on the other hand, any alterations to the structure of the Court will require thorough discussion and research. Issues relating to the structure of the Court should, according to Mr Koskinen, be studied and clarified before they are put on the agenda of an Inter-Governmental conference.

It is also common knowledge that the Council's ad hoc Working Party on the Court of Justice has been discussing the performance of the judicial system. It also, at its last meeting, briefly considered the Paper presented by the European Court. It was noted, too, at the Working Party's last meeting, that the Court itself will come up with an official draft proposal for the amendment of the Rules of Procedure.[1] In addition, the European Commission set up a Group of Wise Men to consider the development of the Community's judicial architecture.[2]

I would now like to turn to a consideration of the Finnish Presidency of the Council in this connection. During our Presidency, the ad hoc Working Party will be discussing a draft proposal for the extension of the competence of the Court of First Instance, as well as a proposal for an increase in the number of Judges serving in that Court (the proposals mentioned by Judge Pernilla Lindh above).[3] Naturally, the Working Party will begin with the discussions of amendments to the Rules of Procedure as soon as the Court's detailed draft proposal has been submitted. Depending on the timing of the proposal and since any changes to the Rules of Procedure require unanimity in the Council, it may be that the discussions on these matters will continue beyond the Finnish Presidency. When it comes to the structural reform of the judicial system, there is good reason to wait for the findings of the group of Wise Men. The report will probably not be available for discussions during the Finnish Presidency. In addition, Finland appears to be showing little inclination to put the future of the judicial system on the agenda of the next Inter-Governmental Conference. Our view is that the scope of that agenda should be restricted, and that only the fundamental issues left unresolved in the Treaty of Amsterdam should be included on it. Any structural reform of the judicial system really does require in-depth analyses and much debate, and this makes it impossible to carry out such a reform in a hurry. Nor does there appear to be any justification for including these matters on the agenda of the special European Council in Tampere in October 1999. So, as the schedule stands, Finland will not have much chance of furthering the more structural development of the European judicial system in its capacity as holder of a six month of Euro-Presidency. However, as I have said, a well-functioning judicial system for the EU is considered essential in Finland. Therefore we must be prepared to play our part in ensuring that this is achieved in the future. And that is why it is very good that we have this kind of conference where we can present and develop our ideas, even if the official procedure goes more slowly. We must ensure that we are well prepared to express our views as the official proposals are put forward.

Finally, I should like to make some specifically Finnish points. As I have said, no official position has been taken, but there has been some discussion inside the Ministry of Justice, so the points I am going to make here represent a mixture, partly of my own views and partly of views expressed with the Ministry. When I referred to Mr Koskinen's speech at the Justice and Home

[1] Which has now been submitted and approved: see Part One C(1), *infra*.
[2] This Group reported at the end of January 2000: see Part One C(3) of this volume, *infra*.
[3] See pp. 15–16, *supra*.

Affairs Council, I said that we consider the acceptability of the rulings of the Court of Justice to be of vital importance. This, in turn, reflects on the composition of the Court and on its language regime. It has been, as a starting point, almost self-evident, that every Member State must be represented among the Judges. Officially the position is that every Member State should be represented. As to the language regime, clearly something has to be done to strengthen further the operational capability of the translation service.

It may well be thought that the structure and activities of the different institutions of the European Union are far from clear and comprehensible to the public and to ordinary citizens; and in the development of the judicial system, too, we should try to achieve more transparency, whether by structural or by operational reforms. When we consider structural issues, the first point is the division of competences between the Court of Justice and the Court of First Instance. It should be the task of the Court of Justice to determine institutional cases and cases that relate to the foundations of Community law – one could call them constitutional cases. In this context, the preliminary ruling procedure is, of course, very important. In contrast, the Court of First Instance should operate more as an administrative court of justice, dealing with the judicial review of acts adopted by the EC institutions. The general principle should be that cases of the same type would always be heard in proceedings of the same type. If the Court of First Instance is considered as an administrative Court, it can be seen that there is scope for many detailed improvements. An increase in the number of judges sitting, and specialisation according to the type of case are options to be examined seriously, as is the idea of setting up an inter-institutional tribunal to deal with staff cases. As a comparative point, I would mention that in Finland many administrative matters are first re-examined under procedures that are internal to the authority in question, with a possible appeal to the courts for judicial review. On the alternatives outlined in the Paper of the European Courts, I would take a cautious stand as regards the radical alteration of the preliminary rulings procedure. From the point of view of national courts, it is very important that an authoritative ruling by the Court of Justice be available at an early enough stage in the domestic proceedings. In addition, the Court of Justice should not become a new, hierarchically superior court. In principle, I feel that the current system, which is based on co-operation between courts, is a balanced and commendable one.

The reform proposals contained in the Paper of the European Courts are grouped in accordance with the type of amending legislative act that is needed to carry them out. In my opinion, the hierarchical streamlining of the rules governing the judicial system should also be made a more general priority. We should decide what sort of things ought to be governed by provisions found at a given hierarchical level: in Treaties, in Statutes or in the Rules of Procedure. For instance, the Rules of Procedure of the European Court of Justice contain numerous provisions on matters which, at least in Finland, would be governed by Acts of Parliament: they could not be left for the judiciary itself to decide. In contrast, many of the more technical provisions could very well be left to the European Courts; or at least it could be provided that those kinds of rules should not require the unanimous approval of the Council for their amendment.

As to the immediate amendments to the Rules of Procedure presented in the paper, the proposals go in the right direction. They are not, however, precise or detailed enough to make it possible for a clear position to have been taken so far at national level – certainly not in Finland. However, concern has been expressed as regards the accelerated procedure: questions have been raised, such as which part of the procedure could be omitted, and the status of the oral procedure needs further examination. An official proposal has actually already been submitted on part of the ECJ.[4] Consequently, the work can be started in the autumn in the Council's Working Party. I note this with content.

In concluding, Mr Chairman, I would like to say that the Court should be given a relatively free hand in the practical management of its business. For instance, any communication with the parties to the case should be simple and flexible. There are many existing rules of procedure, and some of the proposals by the Courts in their Paper which, from a Finnish point seem totally self-evident, present no problem at all. One would say that the Courts could themselves be made guarantors of the transparency, openness and approachability of their operations and their procedures. They should, and would be able to, assume responsibility for their own procedures.

---

[4] See Part One C(1), *infra*.

A United Kingdom Perspective

MIKE THOMAS
Cabinet Office Legal Adviser

As a preliminary point, I should say that Government policy in this area is still in evolution; so I shall, where necessary, distinguish between ideas that are being considered at official level and matters on which I am expressing some personal thoughts. May I also say that, whatever the position may have been in previous years, the attitude of the present Government is one of attributing great value to the work of the European Courts. There is support for strong judicial institutions in the European Union and a readiness to support, in principle, measures to improve efficiency and effectiveness. So that is the UK's official starting point.

I thought it might be useful just to go over some of the lines of thinking which have prompted us within Whitehall to look at this whole area under discussion today, because of course we did not just start last week because this conference was on the agenda. Thinking has been going on for some time within Whitehall, and it was prompted in recent times by four or five considerations of policy. The first (which has been mentioned already and is very obvious) was concern about the duration of proceedings in the Luxembourg Courts. The historical trend does not give any reassurance, and there is a general feeling that the average length of proceedings, which is now something like 23 months, just will not do. Secondly, there was the special need for speed of deliberation in certain urgent cases. What we particularly had in mind, at one stage, was violent resistance to free movement of goods within the internal market. The Court's decision in *Commission* v. *France*, known in Whitehall as the *Spanish Strawberries* case, provides an instance.[1] The case concerned the French Government's action, or rather inaction, in the face of citizens' impeding the importation of fruit and lamb. The second kind of case requiring speedy disposal is in the area of Justice and Home Affairs. There is considerable worry in the Home Office that, if not now then in the future, for Courts having jurisdiction in areas particularly affecting individual rights, family matters, and so forth, two years on a reference, again, simply will not be good enough. That is a major consideration in

---

[1] Case C-296/95 *Commission* v. *France* [1997] ECR I-6959.

looking at how much participation the UK will have in the Justice and Home Affairs area of Schengen.

Other strands should also briefly be considered, such as the flood of trade mark cases which is anticipated. Obviously, we are also interested in the problems that enlargement will bring. Of course, throughout this, we were aware of similar concerns in other Member States, at the Courts themselves, in the Commission and amongst practitioners, and, dare I say it, amongst academics, so we thought that we were in good company. Our initial discussion was in the nature of a brainstorming, and produced a crop of ideas for none of which we would claim any great originality, but we attempted to structure them under four main headings: the demand side, that is, the demand on the Courts; efficiency, in a neutral sense; resources; and structure. It will be useful briefly to run down this list.

On the demand side, we should like to see an improvement in the quality of preliminary references, with perhaps further guidance from the European Court for national courts, going even further than the recently produced up-to-date guidance. Perhaps, also, a tougher approach needs to be taken regarding inadequate references. Secondly on the demand side, the possibility of systems of leave under the various jurisdictions needs to be considered.

Under the heading of efficiency, again in no special order, we favour further transfers of jurisdiction to the CFI, making better use of judicial time. So we welcome the single judge procedure which has recently been introduced and also the possible use of specialist Chambers. Improved efficiency would also call for an examination of the role and procedure concerning Advocates General. This brings us into difficult territory, and at this stage it should just be pointed out as a possible area for examination. An idea that has been talked about already is the Courts being given more power to decide on their own procedures, either without reference to the Council or with an easier procedure for making changes. Finally on the efficiency point, there is the possibility that some of the translation work might be, as it were, privatised – that is to say, left to the parties and not to the Court. Under the heading of resources, there is the perennially difficult issue of the Council providing more money; but another thought that may be worth putting on the table would be the possibility of the Courts charging fees, as national courts routinely do.

Then, finally, we need to consider structure. We need to move towards a situation where the Court of Justice can fully assume its role as a constitutional Court. I am not sure if it is right to regard this as a matter of structure. What seems to be needed is simply more judge power in the Court of First Instance.

This volume is mainly concerned with the Courts' Reflections Paper and I will deal with that in a moment. However, I think that it is worth just mentioning the UK Government's approach to the other three Papers which have been presented in pretty rapid order by the Court in recent times. First, there was the Paper proposing further transfers of jurisdiction from the Court of Justice to the Court of First Instance, particularly with a view to reducing overlap and parallel cases. The Government supports that proposal. We think that the Court of First Instance is particularly well suited to the kind of case it is proposed to transfer. This should lead to a useful reduction in the case load of the Court of Justice. Looking at the matter selfishly, if you like, from the point of view of the Government, we do not see any difficulty for Member States' participation in litigation arising from that proposal. So there is clear support for that proposal from the UK side. A second Paper concerns intellectual property cases. Here, the Government approach is, as the Court itself has indicated, that timely disposal of cases in the intellectual property area is essential for the credibility of Community policy on intellectual property, more particularly the Community trademark. We think the Court's bid for additional resources, and specifically for additional judge power, is well-reasoned and based on realistic assumptions, and we are of the opinion that an increase in the number of Chambers, which is what the CFI is asking for, is justified right away. We are also sympathetic to the notion of a filter mechanism for appeals. There are far too many stages in the process of appeals as it presently stands. Furthermore, the proposals would clearly be consistent with the UK policy in favour of speedier resolution. The third of the additional papers deals with the budget for the Communities and for the Court next year. Ministers are still considering this, and inevitably it forms part of the Government's approach to the wider budgetary settlement for the EU for the year 2000, but it can safely be said that sympathetic consideration is being given to the Courts' budgetary bid, because of the pressures the Courts face, although there is a natural inclination (and if we forget it, the Treasury reminds us) to ensure that additional funds are demonstrably well targeted and well-spent.

Finally, I would like to move on to the Reflections Paper, and again I can take it fairly shortly, I think. So far, Ministers have only given very preliminary views on this Paper. It is essentially before them at the moment but Whitehall lawyers have looked at the Paper under the usual governmental co-ordinating processes, and we believe at official level that the Paper should be welcomed (as everyone at the conference acknowledged) as a thoughtful foundation for considering ways of improving the judicial system, to the general benefit. We think we should support the thrust of the proposals. We want to see them discussed constructively in the Council, with a view to making early progress on any measures that command general support. My own view is that we ought to get on with this, frankly, and while I am all for research, and I do not doubt that full consideration needs to be given to this, I would be in favour of pushing this on apace, because we all recognise that something must be done. The analysis of the problems in the Reflections Paper is actually very similar to our own, and I do not propose to say anything more about that. In relation to the specific ideas, the general approach is one of support, so perhaps I can give that as our general line and just pick out a couple of matters, where our support is, as it were, diluted in some way. One area where we foresee problems is in the notion of more restrained use of the oral hearing. I am quite sure that we need to look at this, but it is not a straightforward area, and perhaps it is less straightforward for those of us who are used to a common law and oral tradition. The other area at which I do not think we have looked in any great depth is the essential structure point, the composition of the ECJ/CFI. The key issue is whether or not one should build up the CFI into something grander, and therefore reduce the load on the Court of Justice. My view on this is that the only way we will actually sort this out is to turn the ECJ into a true constitutional court, which probably means taking away all of its original jurisdiction and having that dealt with at the level below. That is my personal view, not a Whitehall view necessarily.

Finally, having given you my personal notion about the essential structure, the other thing that seems to me to be absolutely basic to all of this is the usual subject: money. Frankly, although lots of the ideas discussed in this volume and which are in the Paper are valuable, they are in the nature of the normal upgrading of the system. What we are actually looking for is more computing power, and at the end of the day that costs money.

IV Futurology of the Judicial System

Problems and Prospects

HENRY SCHERMERS
Professor, University of Leiden

I think the Courts' Paper is a very interesting contribution to the debate and certainly well worth discussing. I should like to make eight comments upon it.

There is only one issue on which I really disagree with the Paper, and that is the very last statement on page 29 – that it is not necessary to do anything before the expansion of the Community. Once you say that it is not necessary to do something, Governments will immediately drop the case, and this will slow everything down too much. For my part, I think it is essential to make changes before the enlargement, because the new Member States want to know what they are entering into, and also the present Member States would do well to have some experience of a new system before we expand the Community. So, in my opinion, it would be useful to stress that it is urgent to change things well ahead of the expansion.

I agree that a single court should cover the whole Union – a single court composed of the Court of Justice and the Court of First Instance. I am a bit afraid of too many specialised courts for specialised issues, except for civil servants' cases. I agree with the widely held view that staff cases should go to another tribunal. This has been discussed almost from the beginning of the Communities, and there has always been a divergence of opinion on the question of what kind of court it should be: should it be a tribunal of officials, or should it be a tribunal of judges? In the early years of the Community, no-one could ever agree on this, but we may now have reached a stage where it is possible to set up a special court for these staff cases.

My third remark concerns the composition of the Court. I think that it is essential to have one judge for each legal system in the Community. As the legal system of every Member State diverges, in at least some fields, from the other legal systems, each Member State wants to be certain that its legal system will be taken into account by the Court of Justice. I also think that a large Court may have its advantages. The European Court of Human Rights, now composed of 41 judges, sits in Chambers (each of 7 judges); we shall have to wait and see how that works out. The Dutch Supreme Court also sits in Chambers: we have a Chamber for tax law, for criminal law and for commercial law, for example, but these are not fixed. A judge will move from one Chamber to another, will sit there for about two years, and during those two years will become a specialist in (say) tax matters, but there is no separation of the Chamber from the full Court because of that rotation of Members. I am also of the opinion that the Court of Justice probably could also operate in different Chambers. Advocate General Jacobs feared that this would affect the unity of the case law of the Court, and in this area we may also look at the European Court of Human Rights, which has, for important cases, a Grand Chamber. This Grand Chamber is composed of less than half of the Members of the Court, so it is not really a plenary, but it is a more of a "heavy" Chamber: it is larger and composed of the Presidents of the Chambers, and the most experienced Judges. One could think about special-isation, if there were a number of Chambers (of say 7 judges). To preserve the unity of the law, there could be an enlarged Chamber, in which for instance the 10 or 15 most senior judges of the Court of Justice would sit: it would not be absolutely necessary that everyone sit there.

Often a small Chamber will work well, and I would take the *Turkey Tail* case as a useful example. Is the turkey tail edible offal of poultry, or is it a part of the turkey? That makes an enormous difference to the customs duty the importer has to pay, so for him it is an important question. For the German Judge, too, who has to settle this problem, the question is important. Yet for Community law as such, this is probably an extremely unimportant question. How do you solve this kind of customs classification problem, many of which come before the Court of Justice? In practice, as far as I can see, the Court follows the proposals of the Commission. The Commission always intervenes in these cases and they explain how the Common Customs Tariff is constructed and why a turkey tail is actually edible offal of poultry and not part of the turkey. If it is true that such questions are largely determined by the Court on the advice of the Commission then surely it should be possible for the Court to decide cases of this kind in a very small composition – the decision might even be entrusted to a single Judge. That would be so, even though the proceedings were on a reference for a preliminary ruling, and even though the matter is significant, because if the decision were left to the national judiciaries, and if the German courts were to say this is part of the turkey (hence a high duty) and the Dutch court were to say it is edible offal (hence a low duty), that would result in the diversion of trade from Hamburg to Rotterdam. That result should be avoided, so a unified answer in all these customs duties cases is essential; however, the decision does not need to be taken by a large court. Now, there is also a question as to the form of judgment in cases of this kind. Would it not be possible to have summary judgments here, as the European Commission of Human Rights used to have, with the reasoning in unimportant cases being one or two pages, rather than stretching to between 25 and 50. In a case like the *Turkey Tails*, is it really necessary to have a long statement of the facts, the arguments of the parties and the intervention of the Government concerned? Could you not, in just a page, give the decision of the court? Perhaps that should be described as "a reasoned order", but I should prefer to call it a summary judgment in which the Court gives the ruling: turkey tails are edible offal of poultry. If it were possible to give such rulings in a couple of pages, that would save an enormous amount of translation work, thus helping to overcome one of the Courts' translation problems. I should add that, in the European Human Rights Commission, these summary judgments for unimportant cases actually worked quite well.

A remark should also be made upon flexibility. I think it is important to have a flexible system, allowing the Court itself to make rules about hearing or not hearing, about urgent cases, about dropping particular stages of the proceedings in event of urgency and so on. Therefore, I would like to support the suggestion that rules that can be amended only with the approval of the Council should be incorporated into the Statute of the Court. One could well conceive of a system where the Statute of the Court could be amended only with the approval of the Council, while the Rules of Procedure of the Court could be amended by the Court itself.

So far as hearings are concerned, here again flexibility is the most important aspect. *Turkey Tails* is, once more, a good example, where it makes no sense to have a hearing. The importer, of course, wants the cheaper customs duty, while the German Government in that case wanted a higher duty. Both sides can explain that in writing and there is no real justification for an oral hearing, since these always take a considerable amount of time. Judge Lindh suggested that the rules be adapted, according to the kind of case concerned: you do, of course, need rules so that people know what the system applicable to them is, but I think that here we could leave the necessary flexibility to the Court itself.

Then, my seventh point is on preliminary rulings. I agree that all courts should be allowed to make references for preliminary rulings. The preliminary rulings system is the crown jewel of Community law and it makes no sense to force an applicant to go up to the Supreme Court if it is clear from the beginning that the case turns on a particular question of Community law. It is more economical that the lower court should have the right to make the ruling. As for the suggestion of asking the national court to include a proposal for a reply, that is the system which exists in Germany when a lower court requests a ruling from the German Constitutional Court and, as far as I know, that system works well. In early cases on European Community law, the German courts, which were used to this system, often gave their own suggestion as to how the Court of Justice should reply. If that approach still works well in Germany – and that is one of the aspects of a comparative study that it would be useful to make – consideration should be given to requiring the national court, when making a reference for a preliminary ruling on interpretation, to suggest what this interpretation should be. Also, as to the possibility of having a sole Judge, or summary judgments, I should prefer either of these to a filtering system. The Court of Justice, particularly in the early days, was very keen on creating a system of cooperation. There was a certain fear in the very beginning that national courts would simply ignore the Court of Justice and that they would not ask for preliminary rulings. Indeed, it took some time before the first preliminary rulings came. The Court of Justice did its utmost to build an atmosphere of co-operation: they said over and over again "we are not superior. We are a specialised court. We co-operate with the national judiciaries." If the national supreme court were to seek a preliminary ruling which was subsequently filtered away as not being good enough, that would probably upset such co-operation. So I would rather look to smaller Chambers, summary judgments and other mechanisms, rather than filtering.

My last observation concerns the use of languages. For legislative acts it will always be necessary to have translations in all languages of the Union. It is impossible to bind citizens to laws that they cannot read. Also, in the European Parliament it should probably be possible to use all languages of the Union. The freedom of election would be hampered if only people who speak foreign languages could be elected. The "Party of Simple People" and the "Party of Uneducated Labourers" would be discriminated against. However, totally uneducated parliamentarians could not be effective anyhow. Some knowledge of the European Union and of the issues treated will always be necessary. Someone who speaks, for example only Hungarian, would be totally isolated in the lobby and could hardly be an effective parliamentarian even if all official texts are translated into Hungarian. In the case of the staff members of the Union and of most working parties of civil servants, restrictions to only a few working languages should be possible. Normally, the persons involved will be able to communicate in one or more of the larger languages of the Union.

However, a limitation to a few working languages will be an enormous sacrifice for those who speak none of these languages. Thus imagine how effectively delegates could have participated in the conference that led to this volume if they had had to speak only German (the language most used in the European Union) or French (the official language of three Member States). As official translations will anyway continue to be necessary amongst the working languages, into all other languages for the official legislation and out of other languages for at least some speakers in parliament, there will always be considerable costs of translation. It seems only fair to have these costs fully paid by the States whose language is used as a working language. This would be a small compensation for the Member States that cannot freely use their own languages.

Amsterdam and Amendment to Article 230: an opportunity lost or simply deferred?

DR ANGELA WARD

Reader in the Law of the European Union
University of Essex

One of the disappointing outcomes of the Amsterdam IGC was the absence of improvement of access to the Court of First Instance for private parties seeking judicial review Community legislation. While private parties, or individuals, as the Court of Justice and the Court of First Instance have termed them, have long been entitled, as a matter of Community law, to ask national courts to ensure the availability of an "effective remedy" when *Member States* fail to comply with directly effective Community rules, much more lethargic case law has evolved in the parallel field of challenge by private parties to the legality of acts of *EC institutions* before the Community judicature. In the latter context, the key barrier to judicial scrutiny of allegedly unlawful legislative measures has been a rigorous *locus standi* test, which is housed in Article 230, and which has been interpreted restrictively. Before private parties will be granted standing to sue with respect to EC measures of a legislative character, they must prove that the measure in question is of "direct and individual concern" to them. This has resulted, in almost all actions brought by private parties for the annulment of legislative measures, in a refusal to review the merits of the case, no matter how cogent the complaint, on the ground that the applicant lacks *locus standi*.

The failure of the Amsterdam IGC to address this problem is all the more surprising when it is recalled that, prior to the Maastricht IGC, the European Court of Justice made an express call for amendment to Article 230. The Court took the view that private parties should be granted standing to sue in cases concerning alleged breach by Community institutions of fundamental rights recognised in the Community legal order. As the law stands at present, even the most egregious abuse of fundamental rights by a Community institution cannot be challenged under Article 230 by individuals if they fail to prove that the measure in question was of direct and individual concern to them. Indeed, the

Amsterdam review, in some respects, attenuated the access of individuals to legal remedies afforded by the Community judicature.

Under the arrangements for incorporating the *Schengen acquis* into the European Union legal framework, Member States retain an absolute discretion on whether to introduce an Article 234 style mechanism with respect to EU measures concerning Police and Judicial Cooperation in Criminal matters, while only national courts against whose decision there is no judicial remedy will be entitled to make a reference to the Court of Justice on the validity and interpretation of EC initiatives pertaining to visa, asylum, and immigration policy. Further, there are certain derogations in both areas in which the jurisdiction of the Court of Justice is entirely excluded. In addition, the Article 230 "direct and individual concern" standing test will operate with respect to direct challenge before the Court of First Instance of laws promulgated within the rubric of visa, asylum and immigration policy, while the position is even worse with respect to acts concerning Police and Judicial Cooperation in Criminal matters. There is no possibility for private parties to have such measures reviewed directly by the Court of First Instance, leaving challenge to implementing measures via national courts as their principal avenue of redress.

Somewhat ironically, these developments seem to have enjoyed the recent support of the Court of Justice, despite its abovementioned pre – Maastricht stance on Article 230 standing problems and fundamental human rights. In the Courts' Paper the view is expressed that "the specific nature of the rules contained in Title IV of the EC Treaty (visas, asylum, immigration and other policies related to the free movement of persons) and of the Conventions adopted by the Council under the third pillar (justice and home affairs) justified derogations in the Treaty of Amsterdam from the principle that all courts and tribunals are to have the power to make references to the Court of Justice".

It is submitted that "access to justice" problems, in the context of Article 230 review, are becoming more self-evident, and more pressing, for two reasons. First, there exists an increasing body of EC legislation that affects the interests of private sector actors. From directives regulating the advertising industry, to environmental controls, to EC initiatives concerning labour and industry, to name but a few examples, the political activities of the Community have long since moved from pre-occupation with governance of *Member State* activities, and increasingly carry dramatic impact on the affairs of private sector actors. It is essential to the legitimacy of the EC polity that there exists a system of judicial review guaranteeing compliance by Community institutions with general principles of law and fundamental rights recognised within the legal traditions of the Member States. Declining to hear cases on grounds of *locus standi* and *locus standi* alone does little toward the propagation of an impression that the

Community judicature presides over a mature system of administrative and constitutional review, or a commitment to binding EC institutions to the same standards demanded of Member State governments. Second, an increase in the number of joint initiatives by the Commission and national authorities will inevitably expose the disjuncture in standards of judicial review when misconduct on the part of Community institutions, as opposed to Member State governments, is in issue. This was starkly illustrated by the *Stichting Greenpeace* case[1] in which applicants were denied *locus standi* under Article 230 to contest compliance of an act the EU Commission with Community environmental law, partly on the ground that an adequate judicial remedy was available to them *against Spanish government authorities,* via the Spanish courts, with respect to their involvement with the allegedly unlawful act.

Finally, a word might be said about the system for challenge to the validity of EC measures via national courts. Could it not be argued that this mechanism adequately ensures that Community institutions adhere to fundamental legal principles, given that the Court of Justice retains jurisdiction to declare invalid any and all EC measures, even if Article 230 standing requirements would not have been satisfied? Is this not a manifestly appropriate route for the protection of the interests of private parties, thereby rendering defunct, for all practical purposes, difficulties associated with Article 230 review? There are several problems, however, subsisting under the action for validity, principal among which relate to delay.

National courts are not entitled, under the so-called *Foto-Frost* principle,[2] to declare Community acts invalid. If they entertain a serious doubt as to the validity of an EC measure, they are obliged to refer an Article 234 question to the Court of Justice. At the very most they are entitled, but are not bound, to award an interim order temporarily suspending the impugned EC measure. The test, however, for the award of interim orders, is extremely difficult for private parties to satisfy given that, among other things, national courts are bound to consider "the Community interest" before issuing a suspension order. Given the length of time for the return of Article 234 references, the road to justice for challenge to validity can be arduous indeed. This delay is exacerbated by the fact that private parties are not entitled to contest the validity of Community measures, in and of themselves, before national courts. Rather, they are obliged to wait for the promulgation of a national implementing measures, and ground their challenge before Member State courts on this latter rule, with the validity of the parent Community norm being subject to collateral challenge only.

---

[1] Case C-321/95 *Stichting Greenpeace and Others v Commission* [1998] ECR I – 1651.
[2] See case 314/85 *Firma Foto-Frost v. Hauptzollamt Lübeck Ost* [1987] ECR 4199.

At this juncture too, therefore the standards of judicial review applicable when private parties challenge the legality of EC rules, as opposed to the compatibility of Member State laws with (lawful) Community measures, compare unfavourably. In the latter context, a quick remedy is more likely to be available given that national courts are indeed vested with jurisdiction to disapply domestic laws that fail to meet up to directly effective Community obligations. No reference to the Court of Justice is necessary. Further, even if a reference were made, one might expect an interim order to be obtained more easily, given that "the Community interest" would militate in favour of temporary disapplication of the allegedly unlawful Member State rule.

Judicial Architecture or Judicial Folly? The Challenge Facing the EU*

ANTHONY ARNULL

Wragge Professor of European Law,
University of Birmingham

INTRODUCTION

It is relatively easy to draw up a blueprint for reform of the Union's judicial system which looks fine on the back of an envelope. It is much more difficult to devise one that will work in practice. The genius of the authors of the Treaty of Rome lay in doing precisely that. The framework which they laid down was skilfully exploited by the Court of Justice in order to create a Community firmly based on the rule of law in which the uniformity on which the proper functioning of the common market depended was protected. That trick needs to be replicated now in the vastly different circumstances of today's Union. Then there were six Member States, relatively homogeneous in terms of politics, economics and legal systems. Now there are 15. The political and legal homogeneity of the original six has been lost. The remaining degree of economic homogeneity will be shattered when the next enlargement takes place. The material scope of the Treaties is now much wider. European law is no longer confined to the realm of trade and commerce, but reaches into the nooks and crannies of national life.

Moreover, *fin de siècle* Europe bears little resemblance to the Europe gripped by the Cold War in which the founding Treaties were drawn up. The difference is not just political and economic but also sociological. There has been an erosion of deference that has made people less willing to accept government by unaccountable élites. Political and legal institutions have become the subject of an increasing level of critical scrutiny; people have become more litigious. These pressures erupted during the Maastricht ratification process, when it became clear that the elaborate edifice painstakingly constructed over the previous 40 years or so enjoyed only a limited degree of social legitimacy. The failure of the

* An earlier version of this chapter can be found at (1999) 24 E.L.Rev. 516. We are grateful for permission to include it here.

Commission to recognise the change in climate led to its collective resignation in March 1999. The mood now is one in which accountability, transparency and probity are as important to the Union's legitimacy as the substance of what it does.

THE COURTS' DISCUSSION PAPER

It is against that background that the Community Courts' discussion paper on the future of the judicial system of the Union needs to be assessed. The paper is one of a series of documents that might in time lead to profound changes in the Union's judicial architecture.[1] So far as can be ascertained, none of these documents contains anything which could legitimately be regarded as confidential, yet remarkably only the discussion paper seems to be available on the Court's Web site.[2] Even that was only posted there belatedly. This is hard to reconcile with "the need to ensure that the judicial system is transparent, comprehensible and accessible to the public", described by the Courts in the discussion paper[3] as a fundamental requirement.

Be that as it may, the substance of the Courts' discussion paper is refreshingly open-minded. There will be widespread agreement with some of the detailed changes they propose. These include: (i) introducing an accelerated procedure to enable the Court to deal with certain cases under a special regime derogating from the general rules normally applicable;[4] (ii) permitting the Court to ask the national court for clarification in reference proceedings, a suggestion made by several commentators;[5] (iii) permitting the Court to respond to simple references by reasoned order;[6] (iv) permitting the Courts to adopt their own Rules of Procedure;[7] and (v) establishing so-called inter-institutional chambers composed

[1] See also the proposal for the CFI to be given jurisdiction in certain annulment actions brought by Member States, discussed in the editorial at (1999) 24 E.L.Rev. 213, and the set of proposals for dealing with the new intellectual property cases presented to the Council on April 27, 1999.

[2] See http://europa.eu.int/cj/en/pres/aveng.pdf.

[3] See p.18.

[4] At present, the Rules enable the President to order that a case be given priority over others but not to dispense with any procedural steps: see Art. 55(2).

[5] See e.g. Barnard and Sharpston, "The changing face of Article 177 references" (1997) 34 C.M.L.Rev. 1113, 1167-1168; O'Keeffe, "Is the spirit of Article 177 under attack? Preliminary references and admissibility" (1998) 23 E.L.Rev. 509, 533.

[6] Cf. Art. 104(3) of the Rules of Procedure of the Court of Justice, which permits the Court to give its decision by reasoned order only "[w]here a question referred to the Court is manifestly identical to a question on which the Court has already ruled."

[7] At present, the Rules of Procedure of both Courts require the unanimous approval of the Council: see Arts. 245 (ex 188) and 225(4) (ex 168a(4)) EC. The Courts ask "at the very least" for this requirement to be modified so that the Rules require Council approval by qualified majority only: see p.15 of the discussion paper.

of an independent lawyer and lay assessors to deal with staff cases, subject to a right of appeal to the CFI. The Courts also contemplate – though without necessarily advocating – a number of more far-reaching changes to the judicial architecture of the Union, such as the filtering of certain types of case and the decentralisation of jurisdiction in reference proceedings. These ideas will inevitably prove more controversial for they touch on two fundamental issues, which lie at the heart of any reform, namely the role of the CFI and the treatment of preliminary rulings.

(a) *The role of the CFI*

The CFI was originally conceived as a court with special expertise in dealing with cases whose factual background was particularly complex. That conception of the CFI has influenced the categories of case it has been given jurisdiction to deal with and is evident in the Court's request, mentioned above, for the CFI to be given jurisdiction in certain actions brought by Member States. Thus, the Court excludes from its request "actions against normative acts of general application". It does not extend to disputes between institutions and actions against Member States for failure to fulfil their Treaty obligations because "as a general rule they are institutional in character". Actions by Member States against decisions addressed to them in the field of competition law are also excluded because they are "more liable to raise institutional questions" than actions by Member States against decisions addressed to undertakings.

It is submitted that this conception of the CFI is preventing its full potential from being exploited and should be abandoned. Bearing in mind the appellate jurisdiction of the Court of Justice and the CFI's impressive track record, there is no longer any compelling reason why the CFI should not deal with institutional issues. The Member States seemed to accept this at Maastricht, when Article 225(1) (ex 168a(1)) EC was amended to permit actions brought by the Community institutions as well as the Member States to be transferred to the CFI. It therefore seems inevitable that the CFI will in due course become the first instance tribunal for all direct actions, regardless of the status of the applicant. That would represent a desirable development.

The Courts point out in the discussion paper that appeals are now brought against 20 to 25 per cent of the CFI's decisions, a percentage which they say is rising. This leads them to suggest that the right to appeal in trade mark cases,[8] and possibly also in staff cases, should be subject to the grant of leave by the Court of Justice (what the Courts call a "filtering procedure"). This would be a

---

[8] That is, challenges to the decisions of the Boards of Appeal attached to the Office for Harmonisation in the Internal Market (OHIM) set up under Reg. 40/94 on the Community trade mark, [1994] O.J. L11/1.

welcome innovation, which might in time be extended to all appeals to the Court. The test of whether leave should be granted should be something like whether there is a point of law of general Community interest at stake in the case.

It is not envisaged that the power to grant leave to appeal to the Court should be extended to the CFI. On balance this seems sensible: such an extension would reduce the ability of the Court of Justice to control the flow of cases and represent more of a departure from the civil law tradition, with which the very idea of leave to appeal is inconsistent. There is, however, a case for making the right to bring some proceedings before the CFI itself subject to a similar filter. An example would be cases that have already been considered once by a quasi-judicial body, such as the Boards of Appeal set up under the trade mark regulation. This is a possibility that might be explored once experience of the operation of a filtering procedure at the CFI/Court of Justice level has been acquired.

(b) Preliminary rulings

The preliminary rulings procedure poses some of the most intractable problems for the proper functioning of the Union's judicial system. According to the discussion paper,[9] references from national courts now account for more than half the new cases brought before the Court. Astonishingly, the number of references made in 1998 was 85 per cent higher than the number made in 1990. The main reason for this growth in the volume of references is simply that the Union is getting bigger. In addition, there have since 1990 been important extensions in the scope of the EC Treaty. The increasing volume of references shows no sign of abating. Indeed, several conventions concluded between the Member States under the old Article K.3 of the TEU confer on the Court a preliminary rulings jurisdiction.[10] Moreover, the Court's jurisdiction to give preliminary rulings was extended by the Treaty of Amsterdam.[11] The preliminary rulings procedure is of course an essential guarantor of the proper application of Community law in the national courts. Nevertheless, some references are not of sufficient importance to require detailed consideration by the Court. Could the way in which references of that nature are dealt with be altered?

The Community Courts canvass several possibilities: (i) limiting the national courts which are empowered to make references; (ii) introducing a filtering

---

[9] See p. 5.

[10] See e.g. the protocol on the interpretation by the Court of Justice of the Convention on Jurisdiction and the Recognition and Enforcement of Judgments in Matrimonial Matters ("Brussels II"), [1998] O.J. C221/20. The others are listed in an annex to the discussion paper.

[11] See Art. 68 (ex 73p) EC and Art. 35 (ex K.7) TEU.

system to enable the Court of Justice to decide which questions referred to it need to be answered having regard to, for example, their novelty, complexity or importance; (iii) giving the CFI jurisdiction in reference proceedings; and (iv) designating in each Member State decentralised bodies responsible for dealing with references from courts within their area of territorial jurisdiction. The Courts note that, in its 1995 report on the application of the TEU,[12] the Court of Justice stated that "to limit access to the Court would have the effect of jeopardizing the uniform application and interpretation of Community law throughout the Union, and could deprive individuals of effective judicial protection and undermine the unity of the case-law." The Courts therefore reiterate the need for all courts and tribunals to retain the right to refer questions to the Court of Justice, a view with which few objective observers would disagree. The new Article 68 EC, which confines the right to refer questions arising under Title IV of the Treaty to national courts of last resort, represents in this respect a step in the wrong direction. The idea of introducing a filtering system that would enable the Court to decide which questions to answer is also unattractive. Where a question is relevant and the background to the case has been properly set out by the referring court, a refusal by the Court of Justice to answer would risk serious damage to the spirit of co-operation on which the procedure depends. Even less appealing is the idea of decentralised judicial bodies with responsibility for dealing with references made by courts in particular areas of the Union. Leaving aside the expense of such bodies, they would present an almost insurmountable obstacle to the uniform application of the law. As the Courts put it in the discussion paper, "[j]urisdiction to determine the final and binding interpretation of a Community rule, as well as the validity of that rule, should therefore be vested in a single court covering the whole of the Union."[13]

The solution to the problems posed by preliminary rulings must therefore be sought in the way in which they are handled on the Kirchberg. As mentioned above, the Courts propose that the Court of Justice should be permitted to give preliminary rulings by way of reasoned order where the questions referred are simple and they do not raise any new issues. The Court has made that proposal before. It is to be hoped that this time it meets with a more positive response from the Member States. But a way needs to be found of dealing with references that, although raising new issues, do not merit the full majesty of the Court's procedures.

[12] See "The Proceedings of the Court of Justice and Court of First Instance of the European Communities", May 22 to 26, 1995 (No. 15/95); Arnull, 'The Community judicature and the 1996 IGC' (1995) 20 E.L.Rev. 599.

[13] See p.28. The Courts go on to discuss ways of reducing the risks inherent in a decentralised system.

A simple possibility would be to permit straightforward references to be assigned to a three-Judge chamber sitting without an Advocate General. Another possibility broached in the discussion paper would be to involve the CFI. If this is to be done, it must be accepted that the CFI will have the last word. The referring court and the parties to the main action cannot be expected to wait while both Community Courts look at the case. The difficulty would be to determine which particular cases the CFI should deal with. It would not be feasible to give the CFI responsibility for dealing with certain pre-defined categories of reference: neither the subject-matter – and references may cut across several areas – nor the status of the referring court is a reliable guide to the importance of the issues raised. The only solution seems to be to permit the Court to delegate references to the CFI on a case-by-case basis. The decision to delegate a case would have to be taken at an early stage in the procedure, for example once the written observations had been translated into French.

There seem to be two main objections to a reform of this nature. Some would say that it would be incompatible with the principle of the *juge légal*, according to which the jurisdiction of courts of law must be settled in advance in abstract and general terms.[14] Although that principle is not universally recognised in the Member States and its applicability in the Community legal order may be doubtful, there is no doubting its resonance in some Member States. However, it needs to be borne in mind that the CFI is not a separate institution but is, according to Article 225(1) EC, "attached" to the Court of Justice. A more substantial objection is that the full significance of a reference might not become apparent until later in the proceedings. One might envisage giving the CFI a power to refer a case back to the Court in these circumstances, but that would risk reducing the proceedings to the level of farce and lengthening them still further, particularly if procedural steps had to be repeated. It would have to be accepted that the number of cases in which the Court's initial assessment of a case turned out to be misconceived would probably be small and that the CFI could safely be trusted to deal with them.

Should the national courts be encouraged to take more responsibility for resolving questions of Community law for themselves? Some national courts, which have in the past been regular users of the preliminary rulings procedure, could undoubtedly be trusted to do more but many others, particularly at the lower end of the judicial ladder and in the newer Member States, continue to rely on the assistance of the Court of Justice. Indeed, it may be thought ironic that Article 68(1) EC confines the right to refer to the courts which in this

---

[14] See the Court's report on the application of the TEU, supra; British Institute of International and Comparative Law, *The Role and Future of the European Court of Justice* (1996), pp. 57-58.

respect need it least, those against whose decisions there is no judicial remedy under national law.

In *Wiener* v. *Hauptzollamt Emmerich*,[15] a customs classification case, Advocate General Jacobs suggested that a reference should generally be considered inappropriate "where there is an established body of case-law which could readily be transposed to the facts of the instant case; or where the question turns on a narrow point considered in the light of a very specific set of facts and the ruling is unlikely to have any application beyond the instant case." Where a reference was made in such a case, the Advocate General argued[16] that the Court should merely recall the principles and rules of interpretation developed by the previous case law, leaving it to the national court to decide the particular issue with which it was confronted. That approach undoubtedly has its attractions, which may outweigh the dangers to which it would give rise. One is that the delivery of what might be perceived as unhelpful replies might have a generally discouraging effect on the willingness of national courts to refer. A second is that if, as Advocate General Jacobs suggested,[17] national courts of last resort were to be considered absolved of the obligation to refer in cases where a reference by a lower court would be inappropriate, there would be no safeguard against misunderstanding by superior courts of the extent of their duty to refer.

Another possibility would be to extend Article 68(3) EC beyond the confines of the new Title IV. Article 68(3) permits the Council, the Commission and the Member States to ask the Court to rule on questions of interpretation arising under Title IV. If its scope were extended, it might be possible to remove the obligation to refer questions of interpretation – though not validity – which is currently imposed on national courts of last resort by the third paragraph of Article 234 (ex 177) EC. That paragraph might no longer be considered necessary "to prevent a body of national case-law not in accord with the rules of Community law from coming into existence", which the Court has described as its purpose.[18] Removing the obligation to refer from courts of last resort would send a powerful signal to the national courts that they were expected to play a greater role in the application of Community law in the Member States.[19]

---

[15] Case C-338/95 *Wiener* v. *Hauptzollamt Emmerich* [1997] E.C.R. I-6495, 6502.

[16] At p. I-6503.

[17] See p. I-6513.

[18] See Case 107/76, *Hoffmann-La Roche* v. *Centrafarm* [1977] E.C.R. 957, para. 5; Joined Cases 35/82 and 36/82, *Morson and Jhanjan* v. *The Netherlands* [1982] E.C.R. 3723, para. 8.

[19] One might wish to retain the obligation imposed on courts of last resort by Art. 68(1) since they are the only national courts that can make references under Title IV.

OTHER POSSIBLE CHANGES

The social and political climate referred to above in which any process of reform will take place has certain implications for other changes that might be envisaged. Three are perhaps worth mentioning here.

First, it now seems to be generally accepted that there is a continuing need for one Judge in the Court of Justice from each Member State. The managerial gains from reducing the number of Judges would be outweighed by the loss of legitimacy in States without a Judge of their own. However, the quorum for the full Court, which was raised to nine at the last enlargement,[20] should be left where it is at the next enlargement (and probably the one after that too). Assuming that the full Court did not in practice sit with fewer than 11 Judges, it would in due course be possible for two plenary formations to sit simultaneously. The threat to consistency would be small: the composition and presidency of each plenary formation could change on an annual basis, and each formation would, of course, be assisted by an Advocate General. If necessary, a grand plenum consisting of more than 11 Judges (but less than the total number) could sit to iron out difficulties.

Secondly, the present system for nominating Judges and Advocates General exposes the Community Courts to criticism – however ill founded – that members are being appointed for political reasons. That criticism could be neutralised by distancing the selection of members from the domestic political process and making it more transparent. The British Government's decision to advertise the vacancy at the CFI occasioned by the departure of Judge Bellamy is therefore to be welcomed.[21] However, the matter should not be left entirely to the discretion of the Member States. One way forward would be to set up some form of judicial appointments panel.[22] Such a panel might consist of senior national judges and present and former members of the Court itself, with the task of choosing from a shortlist drawn up by the Member States. However, it would not be right to require the assent of the European Parliament to nominations[23] because of the frequency with which the Parliament is now involved in proceedings before the Court. The system for appointing the Courts' temporary

[20] See Art. 15 EC Statute.

[21] See *The Times*, April 20, 1999.

[22] See Koopmans, "The future of the Court of Justice of the European Communities" (1991) 11 Y.E.L. 15, 26; Professor Dashwood's evidence to the House of Lords Sub-Committee on the 1996 IGC (Session 1994-95, 18th Report), p. 259. For the view of the Sub-Committee, see Session 1994-95, 21st Report, para. 260.

[23] See the European Parliament's resolution of May 17, 1995, on the functioning of the TEU, [1995] O.J. C151/56, point 23(ii).

staff, particularly those who work in the members' chambers, is also vulnerable to criticism for its lack of transparency. The Courts might consider the systematic publication of vacancies and drawing up a list of the criteria which prospective appointees are expected to satisfy.

Thirdly, important judgments should continue to be published in all languages simultaneously. It is essential to avoid a return to the situation of a few years ago, when judgments in the language of the case and in French were available some considerable time before the other language versions, even in important cases. The Court refers in the discussion paper to "the crisis resulting from the lack of resources for its translation service"[24] and it goes without saying that the Courts should be provided with the translators they need. However, the time may have come for the Courts to be more selective in the decisions they publish. An experiment several years back with the summary publication of judgments had to be abandoned after objections from some Member States. However, staff cases are no longer systematically published in full in all the official languages of the Communities. Moreover, the recent judgments of the CFI in the 'Beams' cases are not being published in full. One judgment, which is considered representative, is available in all the languages,[25] but the others are available only in the language of the case, with abstracts being published in the other languages. Very few national systems would seek to publish every court decision even without the translation problem. One possibility would be for all judgments to be published on the Internet in the language of the case and whichever language has been used as the working language. Publication in all the languages might be confined to cases that are considered sufficiently significant by the formation of judgment. As with staff cases, the Reports of Cases before the Courts might contain the judgment in the language of the case, along with abstracts in the other languages, in cases that are not being translated in full.

Intellectual property cases perhaps merit special consideration in this respect. The Community Courts mention various options in their proposals regarding those cases: "publication in full of all judgments in all the Community languages; publication, save for the most important judgments, of the full text solely in the language of the case and a summary in the other languages; and finally, full publication in the five languages of the Office [for Harmonization in the Internal Market]", i.e. English, French, German, Italian and Spanish.[26] Precisely because the Office only operates in five languages, the third of those possibilities seems unacceptable: it would compound the prejudice suffered by

---

[24] See p. 9.

[25] Case T-141/94, *Thyssen Stahl AG* v. *Commission*, judgment of March 11, 1999.

[26] See Art. 115(2) of Reg. 40/94, supra.

other languages. However, the likely volume of judgments means that attempting to publish them all in all the languages would probably be over ambitious. The second option seems adequate, it being understood that in the early years the proportion of judgments considered important enough to merit publication in full in all languages might be fairly high.

One final suggestion for reducing the translation burden may also be worth considering, although it might not produce a dramatic difference. This is that Member States, which are at present entitled to use their official languages when intervening in a direct action or submitting observations in a reference for a preliminary ruling,[27] should be required to supply translations of their written pleadings into the language of the case.

THE JUDICIAL ARCHITECTURE OF THE UNION IN 2025

So what will the Union's judicial architecture look like in, say, 2025? At the considerable risk of offering a hostage to fortune, something like the following might be suggested.

(i) Members of both Community Courts will be appointed by a judicial appointments panel from shortlists drawn up by the Member States.

(ii) The Court of Justice will consist of one Judge from each Member State and 12 Advocates General. It will have the power to adopt its own Rules of Procedure. The quorum for a full Court will remain at nine, enabling two *petits plena* of 11 Judges to sit simultaneously. A grand plenum of 15 Judges will occasionally sit to maintain consistency in the case law and to decide the most important cases. The Court's main tasks will be dealing with requests for opinions on the compatibility with the Treaty of proposed international agreements, appeals from the CFI and references for preliminary rulings. It will have the power to ask a national court for clarification where an order for reference is unclear and to respond to simple references by reasoned order. Some references will be dealt with by three-judge chambers sitting without an Advocate General or delegated to the CFI. National courts of last resort will no longer be obliged to refer questions of interpretation, but the Court will be called upon to deal with a small number of references on such questions made by the Council, the Commission and Member States.

(iii) The CFI will consist of two Judges from each Member State. Its Rules of Procedure will be drawn up with the agreement of the Court of Justice

---

[27] See Art. 29(3) of the Court's Rules of Procedure.

only. The CFI will have become the Union's *juridiction de droit commun*, dealing at first instance with all direct actions, whether brought by a Community institution, a Member State or a private applicant. It will also deal with challenges to decisions of a separate staff tribunal and bodies such as the Boards of Appeal set up under the trade mark regulation. Before such challenges can be brought, the leave of the CFI will be required. All decisions of the CFI will be subject to appeal to the Court of Justice on points of law. Such appeals will require the leave of the Court.

(iv) Significant judgments and orders of the Community Courts will be published in full in all the official languages on the day they are delivered. Others will only be published in the language of procedure, with abstracts being issued in the other languages. A text in the language used by the Court concerned as its working language will be available on the Internet.

V Synthesis of the Debate

Synthesis of the Debate

PROFESSOR ALAN DASHWOOD
Sidney Sussex College,
Cambridge

ANGUS JOHNSTON
Trinity Hall, Cambridge

1. INTRODUCTION

This chapter has grown out of the summing up given by one of the authors at the conference itself. We have tried to provide a fair reflection of the depth and breadth of the discussion of the numerous issues raised during the conference, and in so doing we have drawn on the transcript of the proceedings and the individual papers. That discussion was wide-ranging and full of interesting and often novel contributions, and we can only hope that this report has done them justice.

The report that follows is divided into a number of sections. Underlying the whole debate are the fundamental challenges facing the European judicial system in the future, so this topic is covered first. Thereafter, the possible juris-dictional structure of the system is discussed at some length, reflecting the serious attention paid to the subject during the conference and its potential impact upon the other areas under consideration. There then follows coverage of the structure and procedure of the Courts, as well as comments on some of the practical questions that future developments will pose.

One other element should be highlighted at an introductory stage, as it became increasingly apparent at the conference that it could well play a major role in any reform proposals. The comparative law dimension of the discus-sion is a difficult and yet vital one, as many of the proposals made for reform draw extensively on ideas and experiences from particular national situations. It seems that this trend in European legal thinking in general, as well as its particular application to the matter of the judicial system, will not be denied. The key to its successful use will no doubt be to harness its potential to teach us valuable lessons, without becoming over-reliant upon it as the fount of all wisdom and knowledge, especially in the very particular and evolving context of the European Union. We hope that the discussion that follows exhibits precisely this balanced approach to matters comparative.

2. THE CHALLENGES FACING THE EUROPEAN JUDICIAL SYSTEM

The challenges facing the judicial system of the Union at the moment are well set out in the Paper prepared by the two Courts.[1] It seems that these challenges are essentially of three kinds.

There is, first and foremost, the challenge of the workload facing the two Courts. The point is well made in the Paper that the workload has reached a level that threatens the well-functioning of the system, and something really must be done about that. At its outset, the Paper provides some very telling statistical evidence, which was discussed at the conference – most notable is the fact that references for preliminary rulings increased by 10% between 1997 and 1998, and by as much as 85% between 1990 and 1998.[2] Evidently then, there has been an exponential increase in the business of the Court. That is due to, and we can expect things to get worse for, a variety of reasons. One such reason is the almost casual way in which the competence of the European Community has been extended, without, one suspects, any thought being given to the impact on the work of the Courts. The authors are certainly not aware, during the negotiations that led to the Maastricht Treaty, of any consideration being given to the fact that the establishment of economic and monetary union, in particular, might lead to a considerable increase in the Courts' business; nor that the legislation that would be needed to bring the third stage of EMU into effect would have a similar consequence. It is also doubtful whether much thought was given to this matter in the context of the Amsterdam negotiations. An exception can be found in relation to the new Title IV of Part Three of the EC Treaty, where the restriction of the preliminary rulings procedure to Courts of final resort was, as we understand, intended to avoid a flood of references by lower courts to the Court of Justice. There will also be a considerably increased burden for the Community judicature under the reformed Third Pillar, which now relates to Police and Judicial co-operation in Criminal Matters, as also under the Rome and Brussels Conventions. Furthermore, the first appeals from the Office for Harmonisation in the Internal Market are now arriving at the Court of First

---

[1] The Future of the European Judicial System (Proposals and Reflections) (1999), Ch 1 (hereafter '*The Courts' Paper*' – see Part One C(2) of this volume, *infra*).

[2] *Ibid*, p. 5 and cf Annex I.

Instance and the Courts themselves are extremely concerned at the sheer volume of work this may create.[3] So, the workload of the Courts is set to go on increasing.

A second challenge, which perhaps came out better in the discussion at the conference than it does in the Courts' Paper, is the difference in the kinds of work which the Courts are called upon to do. The Paper does mention urgency. It has always been a problem that the Court, with its steadily increasing workload, has found difficulty in giving judgment as soon as justice requires; but that is of particular concern in the matters relating to treatment of third country nationals under the new Title IV of Part Three of the EC Treaty, and under the Brussels II Convention on Jurisdiction and the Enforcement of Judgments in Matrimonial Matters.[4] So urgency is now something that is structural to the Courts. As was commented upon at the conference, there has also been an enormous extension of the range of subject-matter which the Courts have to deal with. That is simply because of the scope of the legislation, which has had to be developed for the purposes of the internal market and flanking measures. Indeed, the increasing complexity of the matters brought before the courts of the Union, as adverted to by Advocate General Jacobs in his chapter,[5] has also contributed to an overall increase in workload. This complexity can be traced in no small part to the ever-maturing Community legal system and its growing body of secondary, implementing legislation.

And, of course, looming over all of this is enlargement. We do not yet know quite how much that is going to entail, but we know that it will be a substantial amount, both in terms of the Courts' workload and in terms of adaptations to its structure. This may be of particular concern in accommodating the national judiciaries of new Member States, which in the early years of membership will be relatively inexperienced in dealing with the kinds of cases and issues to which the application of Community law will give rise. So, one of the key questions in the future of the European judicial system is undoubtedly how the roles of the national and European judiciary can be both safeguarded and utilised to ensure the optimum functioning of that system. It is to such issues that the discussion will now turn.

---

[3] Indeed, this has led them to highlight an urgent need for an increase in the number of judges in the Court of First Instance. See http://www.curia.eu.int/en/txts/propositions/intelcourt.pdf for the text of this proposal.

[4] [1998] OJ C 221, signed on 28 May 1998.

[5] See p. 9, *supra*.

3. JURISDICTIONAL STRUCTURE

In any judicial system, one of the most interesting questions is how the various courts within that system relate to and interact with one another. This interest can only be heightened when those issues are examined in the context of the European Union and its unique legal arrangements. How do the ECJ and the CFI interact with each other, and how should the relationship of the Community judicature with national courts be characterised? These seemingly straightforward questions cover many of the most difficult issues facing any would-be reformer of the judicial system of the EU.

(1) Hierarchy or co-operation?

The way in which the ECJ has developed Community law and the impact that this development has had upon national courts have been matters of some controversy. One certainly cannot deny that there does exist a hierarchy of *legal orders*: over the years, the concepts of direct effect[6] and the supremacy of Community law[7] have been applied so as to make that plain, and the more recent development of Member State liability in damages under the *Francovich/Brasserie du Pêcheur* line of case law[8] has only served to underline this. National courts, when applying Community law, are ultimately required to defer to the rulings of the ECJ: the ECJ has the final word on the interpretation and validity of EC provisions.[9]

Nevertheless, this clear hierarchy of legal orders does not necessarily require that the *courts* applying the rules belonging to these different orders should be in an hierarchical relationship. Each 'side' has its own particular task in matters concerning Community law: the national court must decide any relevant questions of fact and national law, as well as giving the final ruling on the application of Community law in the national context, while leaving the definitive determination of the meaning of points of Community law for the ECJ. In such cases, neither side can perform its proper function effectively without the input of the other. This fact lends great credence to the co-operative analysis of the

---

[6] Cf Case 26/62 NV *Algemene Transporten Expeditie Onderneming van Gend en Loos* v. *Nederlandse Administratie der Belastingen* [1963] ECR 1 and its progeny.

[7] Case 6/64 *Flaminio Costa* v. *ENEL* [1964] ECR 585 and its developments.

[8] Cases C-6 and 9/90 *Francovich and Bonifaci* v. *Italy* [1991] ECR I-5357 and Cases C-46 and 48/93 *Brasserie du Pêcheur SA* v. *Germany* and R v. *Secretary of State for Transport*, ex parte *Factortame Ltd and others* [1996] ECR I-1029.

[9] See Case 66/80 *International Chemical Corporation* v. *Amministrazione delle Finanze dello Stato* [1981] ECR 1191 and Case 314/85 *Firma Foto-Frost* v. *Hauptzollamt Lübeck-Ost* [1987] ECR 4199.

relationship between national courts and the Community judicature. Although there have been some instances where the ECJ might seem to have overstepped the line in this relationship, seeming effectively to have *decided* the outcome at national level as well,[10] these cases are much more the exception than the rule and national courts are not slow to emphasise their prerogatives on their side of the line.[11]

Indeed, this last point provides an alternative way of examining the relationship between the national and the Community courts. One can test who has ultimate power in a certain field by asking: who has the power to make mistakes that go unchallenged? In this context, that test would seem to indicate that the position of national courts remains more equal than it might appear at first glance. After all, if the House of Lords refuses (or fails) to apply Community law correctly, at the end of the day it is the House of Lords' view that will prevail in that particular case.[12] Again, the development of the *Francovich/ Brasserie du Pêcheur* case law might slowly serve to undermine that conclusion, for if national courts, too, can be subject to damages actions for a sufficiently serious breach of Community law[13] then ultimately, even in the particular case, the ECJ's view may yet prevail. However, at this stage this possibility remains no more than an untested one and the strict conditions for there being any liability in damages at all are likely to limit the extent to which damages claims may influence this relationship.

In conclusion, therefore, the relationship between the national and Community jurisdictions is undoubtedly a complex, finely balanced and shifting one, but it is also one which remains fundamentally co-operative in character, not hierarchical. This would seem to be thoroughly consistent with the complex notion of a constitutional order of States, a notion close to the heart of one of the authors.[14]

(2) The role of the Court of Justice

There was a wide measure of agreement at the conference that it should explicitly be recognised that the ECJ has the role of a *constitutional court*. This view went on to inform much of the debate concerning how scarce judicial resources

[10] E.g. Case C-106/89 *Marleasing SA* v. *La Comercial Internacional de Alimentacion SA* [1990] ECR 4135 and Case C-323/93 *R* v. *H.M. Treasury* ex parte *British Telecommunications plc* [1996] ECR I-1631.

[11] See *Brasserie* on its return to the German courts [1997] 1 CMLR 971.

[12] See, e.g. *Duke* v. *GEC Reliance* [1988] A.C. 618.

[13] See *Brasserie du Pêcheur* (*supra* n. 8) This matter is by no means decided as yet: see A-G Léger in Case C-5/94 *R* v. *Ministry of Agriculture, Fisheries and Food* ex parte *Hedley Lomas* [1996] ECR I-2553, para 114 (p. I-2582).

[14] See (1996) 21 ELRev 113, at p. 114.

should be used and how the workload of the ECJ ought to be limited. It should be given enough breathing space to fulfil the 'constitutional court' role, without losing jurisdiction over any areas essential to the performance of that function.

The difficulty of providing any precise definition for this 'constitutional' role for the ECJ lies in the very particular nature of the Community's constitution and development. Many of the areas in which the ECJ clearly has a strong vested interest would never be considered by any *national* constitutional court to be essential to the proper functioning of a constitutional court. Yet such areas as the uniform development of substantive Community law are clearly vital to the still maturing (and not yet mature) constitution of the Community. The closest phenomenon which one might be able to find in national court praxis might be the influence of some fundamental constitutional principles (such as freedom of expression and rights of personality and private life) on the development of substantive private law.[15] Even here, however, one would be forced to admit that the constitutional court is involved only because provisions of the constitution itself are at stake. By comparison, the Community's 'constitution' simply contains a number of elements which will never be present in any national constitutional settlement, due to the particular nature of the (developing) Community system.

Hence, it will be difficult to argue that any comparative study of national legal systems can assist us in delimiting the role of the ECJ in this context. Perhaps the key elements in the jurisdiction of a *Community* constitutional court are: disputes about the relationship between the EC and its Member States; disputes concerning the relationship between the European institutions themselves; and *novel* issues of Community law raised by references for a preliminary ruling. This latter element aims to cater for the fear that an over-traditional approach to the role of a constitutional court might discard at least some of the wheat with the chaff: the particular nature of the developing Community constitution requires greater attention to maintaining uniformity of interpretation with regard to novel and important issues, at least until a sound level of experience and jurisprudence has been established.

Naturally, there is a certain inescapable tension between any restructuring of the ECJ's role into that of a constitutional court and the widely-held belief that references for preliminary rulings should continue to flow from national courts to Luxembourg. This subject will be covered in detail below, in the context of more specific proposals for re-organising references under Article 234 EC. In the end, trade-offs will have to be made and compromises reached to achieve the

---

[15] See the involvement of the *Bundesverfassungsgericht* in certain areas of private law: Markesinis, *The German Law of Obligations*, Volume II: *The Law of Torts – A Comparative Introduction* (Oxford: Clarendon Press, 1997), especially pp. 352-416.

various aims sought by any judicial re-organisation, and these accommodations must be made in the context of the system as a whole. In this light, the situation with regard to *direct* actions brought before the Community courts will first be examined, before moving on to the thorny issue of the reform of the system of references for preliminary rulings under Article 234 EC.

(3) Direct actions

One means by which the overall burden on the ECJ could be reduced might be to give the CFI a further extended jurisdiction over direct actions. However, the Courts' paper states that 'the proposals for transferring jurisdiction ... are not aimed at reducing the volume of cases before the Court of Justice', although it is acknowledged that continuing growth in the volume of cases might force a review of this position.[16] As Professor Arnull has pointed out in his chapter,[17] the current proposed transfer excludes matters which could raise institutional questions, and he argues that these proposals have been influenced by the ECJ remaining wedded to the notion of the CFI as a court to deal with cases with a complex factual background, and not much more. Arnull's fear is clearly that an emasculated conception of the CFI's role may prevent the CFI from fulfilling its full potential in the future development of the Community's judicial architecture.[18] There always remains the appellate jurisdiction of the ECJ on points of law as the last word on such matters, and the CFI's record has not been unimpressive in the fields already within its jurisdiction. Since the Courts' paper itself recognises that there may be a need to return to this issue, and since one of the main thrusts of that paper is the need to secure the administration of justice in the face of an ever-increasing workload, one would have to suggest that this option needs and deserves some serious consideration.

Of course, if every case transferred to the CFI ends up at the ECJ's door anyway (on an appeal concerning a point of law) then such a transfer may have little practical impact, and there has been an 'ominous' (Arnull) growth in the proportion of appealed judgments in the last few years. Thus, a useful accompaniment to such a transfer of jurisdiction could be the institution of a leave procedure, whereby the ECJ would have to grant leave to appeal from a judgment of the CFI. The Courts' paper proposes such a procedure in trade mark and possibly staff cases,[19] and Professor Arnull contemplates that this could (in time) be extended to cover all appeals from the CFI.[20] A possible leave criterion

[16] See the Courts' Paper, p. 21.   [17] See p. 43, *supra.*   [18] *Ibid*, pp. 43-44.

[19] See the Courts' Paper, p. 16.

[20] See pp.43-44, *supra.* The Court of Justice and Court of First Instance contribution to the IGC has recently underlined the need for this approach, particularly focusing on the new trademark appeals. This paper can be found at http://www.curia.eu.int/en/txts/intergov/cig.pdf. Furthermore,

might be whether or not there is a point of law of general Community interest at stake in the instant case.

These ideas of jurisdictional transfer, combined with what is essentially a kind of filtering process (by means of leave to appeal), have recurred in the debate concerning the possible reform of the preliminary ruling procedure. It should be remembered both that under Article 234 EC some different features must be accommodated and that there is a particularly delicate inter-relationship between Article 230 and Article 234 EC. With these points in mind, it is to Article 234 EC that we now turn.

(4) Preliminary rulings: uniformity, easing the burden and the need for speed

One of the clearest concerns expressed at the conference related to the very delicate nature of the relationship between national courts and the ECJ within the Article 234 EC procedure, which the ECJ has taken great pains over the years to establish. The great fear is that certain reform proposals may have an unpredictable and irreversible impact upon this relationship, by placing too much emphasis on the need to deal with the ECJ's increasing workload (and delays) under Article 234 EC. This clearly underlines the need to consider the ideas which follow very carefully, placing them in their proper context and looking at all of the relevant angles, lest we rush into ill-considered recommendations.

(a) To whom should references be sent?

The issue of whether the CFI should be the major recipient of Article 234 EC references is closely bound up with the points discussed above. The ECJ is, slowly but surely, drowning in a sea of references, with a consequent increase in the already significant delays in providing a response for the referring national court. Furthermore, if the ECJ's true calling is that of a *sui generis* constitutional court, then it stands to reason that it should only be troubled with those references which fall within that constitutional remit.

Involving the CFI in the Article 234 process could be achieved in two ways. One could either retain the ECJ as the original destination, with a significant proportion of cases being passed down to the CFI, or else all references could in principle be sent to the CFI, subject to an internal procedure for deciding that certain cases need to be referred up to the ECJ (such as cases raising entirely novel points of EC law, where no guidance can be found in the ECJ's previous case law).

the recent Interim Report by the Conference of the Representatives of the Governments of theMember States of 31 March 2000 has discussed this option and shows a measure of support for the idea from some delegations, although this is by no means conclusive as yet (CONFER 4729/00, available on the Council's website).

How one should decide between these two routes is a difficult issue. It was argued by some at the conference that there is a certain logic in making the CFI the first port of call for Article 234 EC references. After all, it is often the case that direct actions by private individuals under Article 230 EC raise issues similar and even identical to those faced by the Community judicature in an Article 234 EC reference. Yet at present, different courts hear the case depending upon which route has been taken. In response, it must be pointed out that, at some stage in the procedure, under *either* provision, the facts pertinent to the dispute must be found. The current use of the CFI to do just that in Article 230 EC cases is fully consistent with the original perception of its role (dealing with disputes involving complex factual matters, etc). Ultimately, the ECJ will still have the chance to have the final say on *legal* matters whichever route is taken and this illustrates the co-operative analysis taken above: each court involved has a particular and essential role to play in the procedure.

One thing upon which most can agree is that, whichever option is chosen (i.e. national court to CFI, then reference up; or to the ECJ, then reference down), there should be *no appeal*, in the strict sense, in references for preliminary rulings. These rulings must be decided once and for all by whichever Community court they end up in; the possibility of appealing would create intolerable delays of the very kind which a restructuring of the Article 234 EC procedure would seek to remedy. The key is to devise a mechanism by which references for preliminary rulings can be distributed appropriately between the Community courts. Given the widely acknowledged need to reduce the burden on the ECJ (especially if it acquires an explicitly constitutional mandate), the best solution may be to direct all references to the CFI in the first instance, subject to an internal procedure for 'reference up' to the ECJ.

It should, however, be noted that this proposed solution to the 'destination' question under Article 234 EC has received some criticism. In the context of the delicate national court – ECJ relationship, it has been argued that the experience of co-operation built up over the years in this relationship might be damaged if the CFI were to get involved, implying that national courts are likely to view the CFI as somehow a less 'legitimate' repository of such authority than the ECJ.[21] Naturally, there is also always the problem of demarcation: how are we to define the types of case in which it should be for the ECJ alone to guide national courts? While acknowledging this inevitable difficulty, the reader is directed to section

---

[21] This may tie in with the discussion on the composition of the two courts (*infra*) and questions of legitimacy and representation. It should be noted that the Courts' Contribution to the IGC (see n. 20 *supra*) maintains this proposal to transfer some references to the CFI; however, the Interim Report of the Presidency to the Conference of the Representatives (see n. 20 *supra*) shows significant Member State resistance to this idea and emphasised the need for residual ECJ control in this area.

3(2) above,[22] where the constitutional role of the ECJ has been discussed. Furthermore, given the undoubted need to reduce the ECJ's burden in this area, thus increasing the speed with which references are answered, such a redirection of references should not summarily be dismissed. At the same time, other ways of addressing these concerns have also been put forward.

(b) Filtering mechanisms

One such option might be to operate, at the level of the Community courts, a filtering of Article 234 EC references, enabling the ECJ to take on only those cases that it deemed to be of sufficient importance to merit its intervention.[23] Were a reference to be rejected in this manner, the national court would then be expected to decide the EC law point in the case for itself. Such an approach has the two-fold aims of reducing the ECJ's burden while encouraging national courts to take more responsibility in EC law matters. The latter aim will be considered in more detail below. At this point, however, certain difficulties concerning the introduction and operation of a filtering mechanism should be discussed.

(i) The impact upon the co-operative relationship between national courts and the ECJ

Much of the hesitation evident at the conference concerning filtering proposals seemed to stem from the unpredictable impact that such a process might have upon this co-operative relationship between jurisdictions. The rejection of references made by national courts might discourage the future reference of issues which the ECJ would consider highly significant, which could in the long run jeopardise the uniformity of interpretation of EC law which the ECJ is so anxious to maintain.[24] While this is by no means certain, the fact that it cannot be ruled out completely as a possible consequence certainly gives one pause for thought.

(ii) The importance of the Article 230 EC – Article 234 EC inter-relationship

As Angela Ward has pointed out in her chapter,[25] a filtering mechanism could place yet more constraints on individuals seeking to challenge Community acts. The strict conditions for *locus standi* under Article 230 EC have made the likelihood of success in direct actions very small[26] and as a result, private parties do

---

[22] See section 3 (2), *supra*, (at p. 59).

[23] See the Courts' Paper, pp. 24-27.

[24] A long-standing concern of the ECJ, recently articulated in the Courts' Paper (p. 18).

[25] See *supra*, p. 39.

[26] See Case 25/62 *Plaumann & Co* v. *Commission* [1963] ECR 95 and subsequent developments.

rely to a great extent upon national courts when challenging Community acts.[27] Their hope is that the national court will make a reference for a preliminary ruling to the ECJ, especially since the ECJ has made it clear that national courts have no competence to declare EC acts null and void.[28] The introduction of a system of filtering references would diminish greatly the possibility of indirect judicial review via Article 234 EC and (if implemented) could risk upsetting the delicate balance between Articles 230 and 234 EC.[29] The frequency of references from national courts on such issues underlines that this fear for the maintenance of effective judicial protection is a very real one indeed.

(iii) *Which* criteria *should be used to conduct the filtering exercise?*

One way to overcome the fears that the relationship between national courts and the ECJ would be damaged by the introduction of a filtering process might be for the ECJ to publish criteria which it would apply in deciding which references would be filtered out and which would be accepted. This would provide greater guidance for the national courts and could even encourage them to operate more of a filter at national level on the cases referred (a point to which we will return below). On the other hand, this could lead to a duplication of efforts on both sides of the procedure and might still act as a deterrent to national courts making the kind of references that might not be filtered out. The difficulty is to frame these criteria with sufficient generality to allow the necessary flexibility for the ECJ in the filtering process, while providing a satisfactory level of certainty for the referring national court to assess its own position. These uncertainties seemed only to add to the unease expressed by many about an EC-level filtering procedure.[30]

(c) *Giving national courts a greater role*

The fears just discussed concerning any filtering process on an EC level have led many to suggest that a more fruitful approach to improving the operation of the Article 234 EC procedure would be to improve the contribution made by the national courts. In their own way, they too could act as a filter of the references which find their way to the ECJ, thus both improving the quality of the questions which do require an answer 'from on high' and limiting the volume of cases referred in the first place.

---

[27] Indeed, the ECJ has been known to advise them to follow this very route. See, e.g. Case C-290/94 P *Buralux SA* v. *Council* [1996] ECR I-615, paras. 35-36 of the judgment (pp. I-648-649).

[28] See the *ICC* and *Foto Frost* cases (n. 9) *supra*.

[29] See, *supra*, p. 39.

[30] And see p.66 , *infra*, on this question of the appropriate criteria to use in such a process.

(i) 'Best practice' in dealing with EC law matters raised in national court proceedings

One possible avenue of worthwhile comparative research in this area would be to study how different national courts approach the definition, discussion and decision of EC law matters. Sometimes, one gains the impression that, had a national court had more time or expertise at its disposal to consider an issue of EC law, a reference might have been found to be unnecessary.

One example of particular national devices for dealing with EC law points is the Dutch courts' ability to appoint a special 'assessor' to help them to define the issues at stake more accurately. As another, one might even add the Commission's belief in its vocation as a kind of *amicus curiae* in competition law cases before national courts, where the national judge is unsure of the Commission's position in a particular situation.[31] It should be noted, however, that the Commission's claims in this field have raised great fears in some quarters of excessive Commission influence and involvement in such cases, on both 'sides' of the one fact situation.

Properly organised, this approach could reduce the number of references made overall, as well as improving the clarity and focus of any references made. However, concerns were expressed by some at the conference that national courts might not be able to cope with such matters on their own: expertise and particularly resources may often be lacking, so this may not provide a complete solution. Nevertheless, purely as a matter of improving the operation of the system, encouraging such greater responsibility on the part of national courts cannot do any harm as part of an overall package of measures, and may even bring some significant (if at the outset perhaps somewhat uneven) benefits.

(ii) Criteria for when a reference is appropriate

One important factor in encouraging national courts to take more responsibility in making references under Article 234 EC is undoubtedly the provision of guidance for them on when a reference will be appropriate in any given case. The ECJ's attitude to this question seems to have developed over the years, as the Community legal system has grown and the bare bones of its procedures have been given flesh. Thus, in the early years the ECJ was willing to redraft poorly focused questions and provide answers, to encourage the national courts to refer questions of EC law so that awareness could be raised and EC law developed and given uniform application.[32] Once a significant body of case law had developed, the ECJ was willing to frame certain situations in which a reference

---

[31] [1993] OJ C 39/6.

[32] See Case 16/65 *Firma C. Schwarze* v. *Einfuhr – und Vorratsstelle für Getreide und Futtermittel* [1965] ECR 877 and Case 6/64 *Costa* v. *ENEL* (*supra*, n. 7).

would not be necessary[33] and, more recently, the Court of Justice has begun to reject references if their statements of the facts or the questions posed are inadequate.[34] More recently still, Advocate-General Jacobs in the Wiener case has suggested that a reference would generally not be appropriate:

'where there is an established body of case law which could readily be transposed to the facts of the instant case; or where the question turns on a narrow point considered in the light of a very specific set of facts and the ruling is unlikely to have any application beyond the instant case.'[35]

If a reference were still made in such a case, then he suggested that the ECJ should do no more than call the national court's attention to the previous body of law and leave it to the national court to decide the issue raised.[36]

These later developments are clear reactions to the steadily increasing burden upon the ECJ, which has become something of a victim of the success of its own policy of encouraging references in the early years. It was suggested at the conference that, in the light of this, some other relevant factors should clearly be set out by the ECJ to guide national courts in making references; matters such as resources, the Community interest and the translation burden on the Court could all be relevant to the decision of whether or not to refer a particular issue under Article 234 EC. Quite how one could operate the proposed resources and translation burden criteria without arousing suspicion and ill-feeling on the part of national courts and litigants alike is not immediately clear; the Community interest criterion may be more promising, although some would see this as merely a function of getting national courts to think more carefully about which cases they refer. Either way, the Court could be more pro-active in this regard, perhaps by issuing a more detailed follow up to its 'Information Note on References by National Courts for Preliminary Rulings'.[37] This ties in with the proposals in the Courts' paper concerning procedural reforms: perhaps some form of practice direction on the subject would be possible, to clarify the Courts' general approach. We will return to these procedural questions below.[38]

---

[33] Case 283/81 *Srl CILFIT and Lanificio di Gavardo SpA* v. *Ministry of Health* [1982] ECR 3415 and Case 104/79 *Pasquale Foglia* v. *Mariella Novello* [1980] ECR 745 and Case 244/80 *Foglia (No. 2)* [1981] ECR 3045.

[34] See, e.g., cases C-320, 321 and 322/90 *Telemarsicabruzzo SpA* v. *Cirostel, Ministero delle Poste e Telecommunicazioni and Ministerio delle Difesa* [1993] ECR I-393.

[35] Case C-338/95 *Wiener* v. *Hauptzollamt Emmerich* [1997] ECR I-6495, p. I-6502.

[36] *Ibid*, p. I-6503.

[37] See http://www.curia.eu.int/en/txts/txt8.pdf; also cf Guidance on References by National Courts for Preliminary Rulings [1997] 1 CMLR 78.

[38] See Section 5 of this chapter, *infra*.

(iii)   Improving the quality of references: getting national courts to propose their own answers?

One proposal, which surfaced rather frequently at the conference, aimed at increasing the participation of national courts in the reference process, was that they should provide their own suggested answer to the EC law point in issue when they refer the matter to the ECJ under Article 234 EC. It has been pointed out that in Germany, references by lower courts to the *Bundesverfassungsgericht* are accompanied by the lower court's own proposed answer to the question raised.[39] Here again, it would be valuable to conduct a more in-depth study of his practice (and indeed inquire into any similar practices in other systems) to discover exactly how (and how well) it operates before suggesting that it could/should be applied in the present context.

Some worries have been expressed that such a system might have unpredictable consequences for the delicate balance of the current system between the ECJ and national courts. Some national courts might be more comfortable operating such a system than others and many judges might feel compelled to give an excessively thorough[40] judgment on the EC law point raised, mindful that their proposed solution would then be subjected to scrutiny by the Community judicature. Furthermore, it is not unthinkable that such a proposed answer from the national court could be relied upon excessively as the basis of the proceedings before the ECJ, at least by the parties, which could hamper the effectiveness of the hearing at the European level. One could even go so far as to repeat the fear that such a system might act as a disincentive for national courts to refer some matters to the ECJ for which a reference really *is* necessary.

These concerns should not be taken lightly, but at the same time they should not be overstated. While the impact of this suggestion might at the outset be somewhat uneven, this was equally true of the impact of Article 234 EC itself. Now that a firm and solid bridgehead has been secured, it is submitted that such smaller side-winds are unlikely to cause any real structural damage. This idea, too, deserves serious consideration.

(iv)   National courts delivering a 'judgment nisi*'*

A sophisticated version of the approach canvassed above was suggested at the conference, in the form of a judgment *nisi*. The idea of this suggestion would seem to be as follows. First of all, the national court would hear the case and come to its own conclusion on the relevant point(s) of EC law. This decision

---

[39] See, e.g., Michalowski and Woods, *German Constitutional Law – the protection of civil liberties* (Aldershot: Ashgate/Dartmouth, 1999), pp. 40-41; and see the comments of Schermers, p. 34, *supra*.

[40] In efficiency terms.

would then be delivered as its judgment *nisi*, while in the same order a reference would be made to the ECJ under Article 234 EC. This reference would be accompanied by a certain time limit of, say, 'x' months: if the ECJ then failed to respond to the reference (by, for example, communicating its acceptance thereof to the referring national court) within those x months, then the judgment *nisi* would become absolute. This approach makes it a matter for the ECJ to decide whether or not it will take the reference within the time limit in question.

In its way, this is also a filtering system, but it aims to *preserve* co-operation between the ECJ and the national courts. The time limit would need to be set on a uniform, EC-wide basis at a level that gives the ECJ enough breathing space to assess the significance of the issue(s) raised. Furthermore, the judgment *nisi* idea also aims to speed up the whole procedure at the national end. Under the filtering ideas discussed above, if the reference were filtered out by the ECJ, the national court would *then* have to decide the case for itself, thus extending the period of uncertainty for the parties to the litigation still further. Under the judgment *nisi* approach, what is effectively a 'rejection' by the ECJ of the reference is the final act of the drama: the provisional judgment becomes final and the parties have an answer with which they can work straight away. Finally, subject to the setting of a number for the 'x' month period, the speed of the ECJ's response would also be much greater where it decides not to accept the reference sent.

This ingenious solution certainly has much to commend it, although it is no doubt subject to doubts similar to those raised in the preceding section, given its inevitable need of a power in the ECJ to reject some references. Its great merit is that it seeks to combine the various aims underlying all of these filter-type proposals: reducing the ECJ's burden, improving the quality of references, reducing the delays now experienced in the Article 234 EC procedure and increasing the awareness and involvement of national courts.

(d) Procedural and practical reforms in the Article 234 EC procedure

Alongside some of the more far-reaching reform proposals discussed above, the implementation of streamlining and improvement measures on both a procedural and a practical level is likely both to facilitate more radical proposals and to have its own valuable impact upon increasing the efficiency and effectiveness of the procedure concerning references for a preliminary ruling. Thus, an improvement in the quality of references received by the ECJ might pave the way for the introduction of stricter time limits on the oral procedure and even for the disposal of such references by reasoned order where appropriate. However, these proposals are best discussed below, in the more general reform context; nevertheless, their particular relevance to the case-load burden on the ECJ and their possible impact upon speed and efficiency in the Article 234 EC procedure should not be forgotten.

4. THE STRUCTURE OF THE COMMUNITY COURTS

It rapidly becomes clear from the foregoing discussion that any attempts to deal with the multifarious challenges facing the Community judicature in the coming years will need to address the complex and interconnected nature of the problems raised. Thus, the suggestion that responsibility for many Article 234 EC cases be passed on to the CFI will have important repercussions for the provision and use of judicial resources on the EC level, while the projected enlargement of the EU will itself have an impact upon the internal structure and organisation of the Courts, as well as upon the substantive legal results which flow from their decisions. Hence, to meet the challenges presented by an ever-increasing case load, lengthen their delays in rendering judgment and the question of enlargement, it is clear that a long, hard look needs to be taken at the very structure of the Community's courts. A well-informed and well-organised plan of reform may allow these challenges to be turned to the advantage of the system as a whole, to the benefit of its users and participants.

(1) 'One Member State, one judge'

One of the great fears of enlargement and its impact upon the judicial system of the EC has been the potential for an increase in the number of judges to dissipate the coherence of the substantive output of the courts' work. Either the full court may become too large and unwieldy truly to sit as one court, or the division of a larger court into a number of smaller chambers could risk the development of conflicting approaches to similar problems. In the Courts' paper itself, these concerns are reproduced,[41] the Courts commenting that, '[f]rom the standpoint of maintaining a consistent body of case-law, a limit on the number of judges offers certain advantages which should not be underestimated'.[42]

Nevertheless, if only as a matter of *legitimacy*, it is pretty much inescapable that the ECJ will continue to contain one judge from each Member State. Precisely the same thinking underlies the UK practice of ensuring that normally, if not invariably, there is one member of the ECJ from the jurisdiction of England and Wales and one from the Scottish jurisdiction. Everyone needs to feel that their jurisdiction is 'represented', to ensure that they feel that their legal system is taken into account. After all, how could the ECJ continue to claim,

---

[41] See pp. 19-21.   [42] *Ibid*, p.19.

with a straight face, that it is developing a jurisprudence of human rights and the general principles of law, which is inspired by the constitutional and legal traditions of the Member States,[43] if the key sources of knowledge of such traditions from some Member States were not even present?

Ultimately, therefore, the key issue is not whether or not each Member State in an enlarged European Union should continue to provide one judge for the ECJ, but rather how we can go on to make best use of the (say) 21 judges at our disposal in a new enlarged ECJ. Furthermore, as the Courts' paper notes, questions would 'inevitably arise as to the organisational measures needed to guarantee the consistency and uniformity of [the ECJ's] case-law'.[44] Naturally, the current system of chambers[45] would need to be re-aligned with such an increase in the number of judges: with a larger fund of judges from which to draw, the use of chambers could increase significantly the ECJ's capacity to handle the growing case-load. The discussions below on the use of the chamber system go into these issues in greater depth.

One of the problems of such an enlargement is the practical point that the court that it might make more sense to enlarge is in fact the CFI, especially if the cogency of some of the arguments of the previous section is accepted. In this area, there was no suggestion that there need necessarily be a rule of one judge from each Member State. Indeed, visions of the CFI taking more of the strain within the Community judicial system will almost certainly (in time) require a greater expansion of the CFI than merely one judge from each Member State would provide.[46]

If, in spite of the arguments in favour of maintaining the 'one Member State, one judge' practice, it is decided that restricting the overall size of the Court of Justice is the favoured approach, then a mechanism would need to be found to counter the inevitable perception that some Member States would be 'losing out' by not being 'represented' in the ECJ. Currently, Member States nominate a judge for the ECJ and a judge for the CFI, stating which judge is to sit in which court. Proposals have been made to introduce an independent body to take charge of judicial appointments.[47] The creation of such a body would hope to

---

[43] See case 11/70 *Internationale Handelsgesellschaft* v. *Einfür- und Vorratsstelle für Getreide und Futtermittel* [1970] ECR 1125 and Case 4/73 *Nold* v. *Commission* [1974] ECR 491.

[44] See the Courts' Paper, p. 20.

[45] See the discussion in section 4(ii)(b) of this chapter, *infra*.

[46] Of course, this could also be achieved by limiting the size of the ECJ and passing on the remaining judges to the CFI, thus enlarging it by the same number of judges as there are new EU Member States (although not necessarily with all of the judges from those new Member States).

[47] E.g. the arguments of Koopmans (in (1991) 11 Y.B.E.L. 15) and Dashwood (CELS and Dashwood (eds.), *Reviewing Maastricht Issues for the IGC 1996* (London: Sweet & Maxwell (for LBE), 1996), at p. 157).

make the appointment procedure more transparent and to depoliticise it; these aims would become even more important were there to be a system in which it could not be guaranteed that each Member State would have one judge in the ECJ. An interesting and innovative suggestion made during the course of the conference, and one which seemed to command a great deal of support, was that Member States should continue to nominate two judges to become part of the European judicature. However, the decision on which judge would sit in which court would then be up to that body of judges itself, according to some kind of order drawn up by the group. This might be a more palatable way to retain the same number of judges from each Member State, while isolating the Member States from the nomination between the two courts and while preserving the benefits of a smaller and more closely-knit Court of Justice. Although it seems unlikely, at least politically, that this restriction on ECJ numbers will gain much support, this approach might be the best option for allocation between the two courts in any event, as a means of bolstering (further) the perception of the independence of the European judiciary.

(2) Specialisation

As the fields encompassed by EC law have grown ever wider, the need for specialised knowledge and experience on the part of the European judiciary has grown too. The need for expertise in the intellectual property field, in particular, has become increasingly acute as the programme of harmonisation and the introduction of Community-level rights have progressed. Furthermore, a better-focused usage of scarce judicial resources, covering the fields where the largest number of problems is presented (both in terms of case-load and of technical legal knowledge), may serve to improve the overall efficiency and effectiveness of the system. On the other hand, the pitfalls of excessive reliance on smaller and more specialised judicial instances should not be under-estimated. There is a danger of divergent interpretations of similar points of general relevance by different instances, necessitating clarification at a later date and causing uncertainty in the interim period. One might also cite the dangers of over-specialisation, which could lead to an expensive and ever-less transparent proliferation of courts which might be responsible in a particular situation, leading to problems of demarcation and endless rounds of appeals and delays.

In spite of such prophecies of doom, there seemed to be a large measure of consensus at the conference that at least a limited degree of specialisation would be both necessary and beneficial. Two possible methods of specialisation were discussed.

(a) Specialised, separate tribunals

In their paper, the Courts themselves suggested that inter-institutional tribunals could be set up to deal with staff cases.[48] These tribunals would be composed of an independent lawyer and trusted assessors, and would be an instrument of conciliation; as a last resort, it would also be a court for ruling on such disputes. Any such decisions could be challenged before the Court of First Instance, and any appeal to the Court of Justice "would have to be subject to a very strict filtering procedure".[49] Such proposals aim at achieving a reorganisation of the handling of staff disputes, without denying access to the Community judicial system where appropriate. This also seems to be in line with the suggestion that the ECJ should be conceived of as a (*sui generis*) constitutional court, dealing only with such matters as staff cases in situations of particular importance for the development or uniformity of Community law.[50]

These suggestions met with general approval during the conference. It was also proposed that at some point in the future a similar approach might prove necessary for cases concerning the European patent, although any moves in this direction will probably need to wait for experience in this field to accumulate.

(b) Specialised chambers in the court(s)

Currently, the Community courts do divide themselves into chambers, which are then allocated individual cases.[51] One way in which an increase in the resources of the Courts might be put to good use could be to designate particular chambers to specialise in a particular field of Community law. This idea was mooted by the CFI itself in 1995, hoping to see an increase in the efficiency of its output by setting up chambers with particular specialisations without running the risks inherent in establishing independent specialist courts.[52]

[48] See the Courts' Paper, p. 17, and the Courts' Contribution to the IGC (n. 20 *supra*). The Interim Report of the Presidency to the Conference of the Representatives (n. 20 *supra*) gave strong support to this idea. On a more general level, both the Courts' Contribution and the Interim Report recognise the value of the creation of a legal basis in the EC Treaty for the future creation of similar judicial boards of appeal.

[49] *Ibid*, p. 17.   [50] See p. 59, *supra*.

[51] See the useful discussion of the composition of chambers and the assignment of cases among chambers in Plender (ed.), *European Courts Practice and Precedents* (London: Sweet & Maxwell, 1997), Ch. 5 (D'Sa and Duffy), pp. 177-187. At present, the ECJ is divided into six chambers; the First, Second and Fourth Chambers now have *three* judges attached to the, while the Fifth and Third has four. Of the two larger Chambers, the Fifth currently consists of six judges and the sixth has seven (see [1999] OJ C333/1, The Court of Justice's latest decision on the composition of its chambers), the Court of First Instance, there are five Chambers of three judges each, and any of these can sit as a five judge chamber where necessary (see [1995] OJ C274/11).

[52] See the Proceedings of the Court of Justice and the Court of First Instance of the European Communities, May 22-26 1995, No. 15/95, at p. 16) (see [1999] OJ C333/1, the Court of Justice's latest decision on the composition of its chambers).

The proposal discussed during the conference was that (within the CFI at least) these could be operated by *rotating* judges' membership of them over a period, thereby enabling them to acquire expertise in handling these types of case and allowing them to contribute to that area. This could help to increase the effectiveness and efficiency of decision-making in these technical fields and allow a rapid acquisition of the expertise necessary to develop the legal rules in question.

This idea of judge-rotation between specialised chambers is not a wholly novel one. It was pointed out at the conference that the Dutch *Hoge Raad* sits in chambers that are not fixed: judges move between chambers, staying for approximately two years. This time period is intended to allow them to gain expertise, while not isolating individual judges from the full court by ensuring the continuation of the rotation process. A comparative research project, which investigated the operation and success of this system, could provide invaluable insights for the shaping of a similar approach on a European level.

Indeed, in the new European Court of Human Rights at Strasbourg we may see the development of a similar system on another European level. The new court will consist of forty judges (one from each Member State) divided into four Sections, which will have a duration of three years.[53] These Sections are then divided into Chambers, which will actually decide the bulk of cases heard; each Chamber will be made up of seven judges[54] drawn from that Section, headed by the President of the Section. To process questions concerning the admissibility of applications, Committees of three judges[55] are drawn by rotation from the Sections (so far, nine Committees have been created) and they will have a life span of one year. Finally, the Grand Chamber[56] exists to hear cases ceded or referred to it by Chambers,[57] either because a serious question of the interpretation of the Convention is in issue, or because the Chamber's decision might challenge a previous decision of the Court. It has a special composition, not related to the Section-Chamber-Committee structure, which uses an elaborate selection mechanism in an attempt to ensure that there is a core of experienced judges in every case, as well as adequately to represent the many different judicial backgrounds covered by the Convention.[58] While the EC and ECHR systems are clearly dissimilar in many respects, the operation of the Section-Chamber-Committee structure will repay study by Community lawyers as it begins to come to grips with cases under the Convention. While there is no suggestion that the Sections will become specialised in the way suggested above for the EC system, the time periods for each rotation form a potentially relevant

---

[53] Rules of the Court (RoC), Rule 25(1).
[54] Article 27(1) ECHR.
[55] Article 28 ECHR.
[56] Created by Article 27(1) ECHR.
[57] Articles 30 and 43 ECHR.
[58] See Rules 24 and 27 RoC for details.

factor for study, as do the provisions for reference of certain cases from Chambers to the Grand Chamber. As the new structure of cases under the Convention develops, a close eye should be kept on its organisation, experiences and reactions to any difficulties.

One practical problem concerning the mechanics of any rotation system is the length of the judges' overall mandate *vis-à-vis* the length of the rotation process. Any single rotation needs to be of sufficient length to enable the acquisition of expertise, yet if this time period takes up too much of the judge's tenure then it may undermine the full court's overall cohesion. Again, a study of the position in other systems will help to formulate optimum time periods, but the highly politicised nature of the European Union and its workings may yet play a significant role in all of this. After all, any suggestion that a judge's overall tenure be increased to deal with this problem is likely to be met by complaints of the undemocratic nature of the powerful European judiciary. Indeed, criticisms of the current provisions in Community law concerning a judge's tenure seem largely to have been ignored over the years[59] and it is highly likely that intense politicking between governments on the issue has played its part in preventing any changes to the current system.

Another worry about any movement towards a system of specialised chambers is the potential for decisions in different chambers of the same court that end up conflicting with each other on matters of general importance. Such conflicts could increase uncertainty and threaten the uniformity of the interpretation and application of Community law.[60] A number of mechanisms could be used to counter this possibility. If one were to introduce specialised chambers only at CFI-level, then a rule could be introduced requiring any chamber that intended to depart from the previous decision of another chamber to contact that first chamber to ask if it still held that view. If this were not sufficient to avoid a conflict, then a rapid 'referral up' or appeal to the ECJ could settle the matter once and for all. This idea is partly modelled on the system used in Germany to counter potential conflicts between the various different Supreme Courts by using a Great Senate as the final arbiter, and also reflects to some extent the idea of the role of the Grand Chamber adopted in the ECHR context. It also seems to be wholly consistent with the 'constitutional' role envisaged for the ECJ in the foregoing discussion.

Furthermore, it was also suggested at the conference that this problem of potential conflicts between chambers leading to divergences in the case law provides strong support for the role of the Advocate-General. An independent

[59] See Brown and Kennedy, *The Court of Justice of the European Communities* (4th ed., London: Sweet & Maxwell, 1994), p. 48.

[60] See the discussion at p. 32, *supra*.

judicial officer who examines and presents the existing case law to the tribunal of last instance can provide a clear impetus to consistency in decisions taken, highlighting conflicts and suggesting how they might be resolved.

Finally, a similar reasoning process could be applied to conflicts between different chambers within the Court of Justice, leading to consultation between the two chambers potentially at odds. As a last resort, the case could be referred to the full court for decision in a manner similar to the procedure now followed when deciding whether or not to allocate a particular case to a chamber or the full ECJ or CFI.[61]

(c) The role of the Advocate-General

Indeed, one element in the jurisdictional and structural discussions upon which we have yet to touch is the role of the Advocate-General. In some ways, this role creates an extra language and translation burden for the Court of Justice, as a further opinion must be translated and published alongside that of the ECJ. However, as the preceding discussion has made clear, the office of the Advocate-General performs some very useful functions; moreover, recent experience suggests that the ECJ increasingly defers to the opinion of the Advocate-General, sometimes even expressly referring to the opinion in its judgments.

In the hurly-burly of many of the proposals discussed in this chapter, one should not lose sight of the fact that many of these ideas will have a significant impact upon the role of the Advocate-General. Thus, were one to make the recommendation that smaller, specialised chambers be introduced in the ECJ (as well as the CFI), this might conceivably entail the removal of the Advocate-General in such cases, to increase the efficiency savings made by such a procedure. Also, even proposals concerning accelerated procedures and the disposal of cases by reasoned orders[62] are implicitly about the Advocates-General: where they are applied, such proposals may truncate or eliminate the Advocate-General's role, unless serious thought is given to *how far* we want that role to be preserved.

This consideration of the role of the Advocate-General in the context of the changes to the *procedure* of the Courts moves us neatly on to a discussion of various proposed changes to the procedural environment, contained both in the Courts' own proposals for procedural reform and in the conference's discussion of how the procedure for *changing* various provisions relating to the European judicial system should be developed in the future.

---

[61] See Plender (ed.), *European Courts Practice and Precedents* (n. 57, *supra*), pp. 181-184.
[62] See the Courts' Paper, pp. 10-11 and 13 respectively.

5. PROCEDURAL MATTERS

As will have become apparent from the preceding sections, many different possible reforms of the European judicial system have been mooted which will require significant amendments to the current provisions governing the courts. Some of these changes could be made without any need for amendments to the founding Treaties, while others would require that such changes be made. There is thus great interest in the forthcoming IGC and its attitude towards judicial matters, not only because of its potential to achieve the one-off reforms necessary to the applicable provisions, but also because of the chance it presents to change the rules which govern how such matters could be changed in the future.[63]

(1) Proposals for procedural reform now on the table

The Courts' paper makes certain proposals[64] for the amendment of the Rules of Procedure, which can be achieved without the need to amend the Treaty. Once again, many of the concerns stem from the expansion in the breadth of the law that the European courts must interpret and apply. Thus, the paper envisages the possibility of questions arising before the ECJ that need urgent answers in fields such as the interpretation of the 'Brussels II' Convention and Title IV of the EC Treaty[65]. In the CFI, complex matters of competition law in the merger field may prejudice the prevailing commercial situation if a judgment is too long in the making, while applications by members of the public for access to Community documents may well be rendered meaningless if the CFI cannot rule on the case within a short period of time.[66] Without the ability, *ad hoc*, to leave out certain stages of the current procedure in cases of 'manifest urgency', the Courts fear that judgment may not be rendered speedily enough to be of any use in the case at hand, thus undermining public confidence in the European judicial system. Indeed, these elements may well be a significant influence upon the decision of the UK government concerning how far it wishes to be involved in (for example) the Justice and Home Affairs area of Schengen.

The suggestion that the oral procedure is also in need of reform was met with a certain degree of caution by many of the participants at the conference. The

[63] See p. 105, *infra*.

[64] Two of which were considered in some detail at the conference: the comments which follow are restricted to these areas. Certain amendments adopted by the Court in May 2000 (after receiving the approval of the Council) can be found in Part One, C *infra*, with a brief commentary.

[65] On the external aspects of freedom of movement for persons.

[66] See the *Carvel & Guardian Newspapers* v. *Council* saga (Case T-194/95, [1995] ECR II-2765).

Courts' paper emphasises that the oral hearing is a valuable part of the procedure, but that its use could be more effective if the parties could be persuaded not to use it simply to re-hash the same points made (at great length) in the written submissions.[67] Many at the conference stressed that this focus on improving the *quality* of the hearing should not be taken so far as to restrict the oral procedure unnecessarily. Thus, the ECJ's proposal that the parties should have to submit reasoned applications, setting out the points on which they wish to be heard,[68] was met with a degree of caution. Parties may be inclined to make out reasons why they should be heard on many points, if only to cover the possibility of missing out an element which is only obviously vital once the line of questioning taken by the Court has become clear. On the other hand, as experience in using such a system grew, these difficulties would no doubt become less pronounced.

(2) Changes to the way in which the Rules of Procedure can be amended

As noted above, one of the key difficulties of reform proposals such as those canvassed at the conference is finding the requisite political will on the part of the Member States to carry them through. This problem becomes particularly acute where these reforms must compete for attention with many more grandiose and eye-catching issues during the course of an IGC. The reform of the judicial system has never been viewed as a 'vote-winner' and indeed often tends to arouse more bad feeling among opponents of any change than some politicians are willing to risk.[69] One answer to this predicament could be to provide a legal provision in the Treaty under which any future reforms would not need to win any political 'beauty contests' at an IGC, but rather could be dealt with in the normal run of Community legislative business (or even by the Court of Justice itself).

Currently, any amendments to the Rules of Procedure of either the ECJ or the CFI require the unanimous approval of the Council.[70] Some such amendments have already been passed,[71] while others are now before the Council.[72]

---

[67] See the Courts' Paper, pp. 11-12; and see the Proposals for Amendments to the Rules of Procedure of the Court of Justice, 1 July 1999, which have now been passed by the Council (see the document published at http://www.curia.eu.int/en/txts/txt5a.pdf and see Part One C(1) of this volume, *infra*).

[68] *Ibid*, pp. 3-4 concerning Articles 44a and 104(4) of the Rules of Procedure.

[69] See the recent defeat in the House of Lords for the UK government's proposals to curb the right to trial by jury.

[70] Articles 245 and 225 EC respectively.

[71] A single judge can now hear cases in the CFI ((1999) OJ L135/92 of 29 May 1999), and the first such case has already been decided (Case T-180/98 *Cotrim v. Cedefop*, judgment of 28 October 1999: see the press release at http://www.curia.eu.int/cp/cp99/cp9986en.htm).

[72] The transfer of certain areas of jurisdiction from the ECJ to the CFI discussed in the Courts' Paper (at p. 19).

One very minor alteration to the current amendment procedure would be to remove the requirement that the Council act unanimously: achieving only a qualified majority in Council would prevent many political blockades of reforms, especially in the light of the possible future extended composition of the Council as a result of the projected enlargement of the EU. While this would still leave the Courts in a distinctly unempowered position *vis-à-vis* their own working practices, some participants at the conference were concerned about taking the more radical step of conferring a power on the Courts to alter their own Rules of Procedure. In his contribution,[73] Pekka Nurmi voiced concerns as to a possible wholesale transfer of the power of amendment of those Rules to the Court of Justice, in the absence of a clearer vision of which rules should be governed by provisions at which level (in the Treaty, the Statute or the Rules of Procedure).

At the same time, there was a wide measure of consensus among those at the conference that the Court should be given a relatively free hand in the practical management of its business. Given that it seems unlikely that the Member States will be willing to cede complete authority over such changes to the Court of Justice, one possible compromise would be to grant such a *general* power to the Court, subject to a set of provisions of a quasi-constitutional nature, which would be reserved to the Council to decide upon.[74] This would once again raise some thorny questions of demarcation, but would at least give the Court greater control over its own destiny in a wide(r) range of areas of procedural concern. However, ironing out the demarcation questions might well prove to be more politically troublesome than the IGC may be prepared to stomach.

In the light of all of this, one particularly attractive idea to emerge from the conference was the suggestion that all of these issues need not be decided and laid down in any Treaty amendment. Rather, the Member States could insert a power-conferring rule into the Treaty, which would provide that in future the Council would have the power to decide upon the attribution of the power to change the Courts' Rules of Procedure. Thus, a new sub-paragraph could be added to Articles 225 and 245 EC concerning the amendment of the Rules of

---

[73] See pp. 23-24, *supra*.

[74] In the Courts' Contribution to the IGC (n. 20 *supra*), this is essentially the proposal made: it should be for the Court itself to amend its Rules of Procedure, subject to possible reservations of particular areas for (unanimous) Council approval. However, in the Interim Report of the Presidency to the Conference of the Representatives the majority of delegations "expressed very considerable reservations about giving the Court of Justice and the Court of First Instance themselves the power to take independent decisions on any amendments to their Rules of Procedure that might be deemed appropriate". Nevertheless, there was strong support for making Council amendments subject to qualified majority voting, subject to certain areas (such as linguistic requirements) which would still require unanimous approval.

Procedure, providing that the Council may, by unanimous decision, decide how those rules may be amended in future: some areas could be left to the Court, others preserved for the Council.[75] This minimalist solution may be the best practical approach, as it would get the Member States to accept the *principle* of the need to decide how these rules can be altered, while leaving the finer details to be worked out at a later date. To the objection that these kinds of changes ought to involve national parliaments as well, one could envisage that the power-conferring provision be of the 'organic law' type, thus requiring ratification by the Member States before it could come into force.

As a final comment on this point, if the last of the above suggestions proves to be the way forward, then it may be useful to open the debate as to which sorts of provisions should be reserved to the Council alone to amend, and indeed which should require Treaty amendment. It is highly likely that the Courts would be concerned to preserve some of the fundamental features of the preliminary ruling procedure as matters of a constitutional character, so making these amenable only to amendment by changing the provisions of the Treaty. By contrast, the provisions concerning the remit of the Court of First Instance[76] might be placed entirely within the Council's competence. Matters on a more day-to-day management level could then be left to the Court to decide upon.

6. PRACTICALITIES OF THE JUDICIAL SYSTEM

The knock-on effects of the large increase in the case load of the European Courts on the practical, day-to-day management of the Courts' business follow logically on from the preceding discussion. Indeed, two of the questions most fundamental to any reform process can be said to fall under this heading: language and money.

(1) Languages and translation

The burdens imposed by the many languages with which the Courts must deal are clear for all to see. Continuing to publish all cases in all languages will only become more difficult as enlargement gathers pace, while the translation burden (both written and oral) already means that there are often significant delays

---

[75] The basic outline of this proposal received a favourable response in the Interim Report of the Presidency to the Conference of the Representatives (n. 20 *supra*), subject to some possible reorganisation of the contents of Articles 225 and 245 EC, the EC Statute of the Court of Justice and the Rules of Procedure to ensure that the appropriate changes could be made to particular rules without the need for recourse to Treaty amendments.

[76] E.g. opening up the possibility for the CFI to decide certain references for a preliminary ruling (see the discussion at pp. 62-64, *supra*).

before some cases are available in certain languages. As Schermers has argued in his chapter,[77] practicalities will ultimately demand a reduction to a smaller number of languages which are more commonly used throughout the European Union; nevertheless, this is likely to prove highly unattractive, both politically at a Member State government level and in practical terms for those who find that they do not speak any of these languages.

It is uncontroversial that legislation *must* continue to be published in all EU languages: how else can the claim to respect the rule of law and equality before the law be maintained? Again, Professor Schermers has made the interesting if somewhat controversial suggestion that one might require the Member States whose language is used as a working language to meet the costs of the translation of legislation, given the sizeable benefits they obtain by being able to work in their own language.[78] Once more, this may prove to be a non-starter on the political level at present, but the time may well come when such options will have to be given serious consideration.

However, a thornier issue is the resolution of these problems in the area of the Courts' work. The Courts' response in their paper to 'the crisis resulting from the lack of resources of its translation service'[79] is simply that it should be provided with the extra translation staff and resources that it needs. Naturally, this raises a funding problem and the allocation of large sums to the judicial budget has never been a popular political move likely to find a high profile at the IGC.[80]

Alternatively, the Courts may well have to accept that they can no longer expect to publish all of their judgments in every language. After all, nowadays staff cases are not published in full in all of the official languages and, as Professor Arnull points out,[81] in some sets of cases arising from the same basic fact situation only one 'representative' judgment is published in full, with abstracts of the other cases being made available in the languages other than the language of the case. If this practice were expanded to cover all but the most important cases then a significant reduction in the translation burden could be achieved. However, persuading any Member States to give up having cases reported in their own language as a matter of course will not be an easy task. Perhaps a stark choice should be presented to them: pay for the necessary resources to do the translation job properly, or reassess how much can be expected from the resources that we are prepared to fund.

---

[77] See p. 35, *supra*.   [78] See p. 35, *supra*.   [79] See the Courts' Paper, p. 9.

[80] Although early indications are that the Court's budget claims are unlikely to be rejected by the Council.

[81] See p. 49, *supra*.

The difficulty of this choice might explain the idea to involve the parties in the translation of various materials for the Courts so as to ease the translation burden as regards the documentation for a case. Thus, Member States could be required to supply translations of their interventions (in direct actions) or observations (in references for a preliminary ruling) in the language of the case, rather than simply contributing in their own language.[82] It was even mooted that the parties should have to provide translations of their documentation for the Courts, in a kind of 'privatisation' of the translation process. However, this latter suggestion may founder on the rocks of access to justice: only those wealthy enough to be able to afford to provide such translations would be able to bring cases before the European judiciary. Furthermore, it was argued at the conference that there is a risk that leaving translation to the parties to organise could lead to excessive diversity in the translation of similar or even identical material, causing inconsistency and even poor quality in translations in some cases.

There are no easy or clear-cut solutions here, and it is almost inevitable that these difficulties will only intensify as the volume of Community law and the number of Member States increases. Hard choices may have to be made soon; the trouble is finding space for such potentially divisive issues of detail in an IGC that may be unwilling to deal with them until they are really unavoidable.

(2) Resources and the budget

The consistent thread running through all reform proposals is, of course, finance. How are we to pay for any proposals that may require a greater supply of resources? In times of financial belt-tightening, the question of the budget is always a vexed one, as Member States seek to reduce their contributions wherever possible, while expecting a sizeable return on their 'investment' in the fields closest to their own hearts. Traditionally, the reform of the judicial system is not something that many states are prepared to fight long and difficult battles over, especially in the current climate.

The difficulty for the ECJ lies in its extremely weak position in the budgetary procedure. It has very little leverage *vis-à-vis* the other institutions: the Commission is an ever-present in the procedure, while the European Parliament and the Council are the ultimate decision-makers. While the EP and Council effectively fix their own budgets,[83] the ECJ must in the end take what it is given,

---

[82] As is possible at present under Article 29(3) of the Rules of Procedure: see Arnull, *supra*, p. 50.

[83] Subject to a certain amount of wrangling over whether certain expenditure is compulsory or not, a matter which has a decisive impact upon the Parliament's influence over the final adoption of the budget: see Hartley, *The Foundations of Community Law* (4th ed., Oxford: Clarendon Press, 1998), pp. 44-48.

having no greater input than the submission of its estimate of its own expenditure to the Commission at the outset. Thus, the adequacy of its funding is entirely dependent upon the cogency of its claims during the budgetary procedure and upon the attitude of the other institutions towards that claim.

Given how jealously the institutions currently involved in the budgetary procedure guard their powers over it, it is highly unlikely that the Court will ever gain any greater role than it has at present. Nevertheless, if the smooth functioning of the European judicial system is to be secured, then the Member States need to be sensitive to reasonable claims to greater resources made by the Court in the coming years, especially if the political goals of enlargement and an 'area of freedom, security and justice'[84] are to be attained.

---

[84] Article 2, fourth indent TEU.

B. THE WORKING PARTY REPORT

The Working Party Report*

OLE DUE

Former Judge and President of the Court of Justice
Chairman of the Working Party

The Working Party on the future of the European Communities' Court system was established by the Commission in May 1999. It was composed of people who had been members of one of the two courts or who otherwise had an intimate knowledge of those courts.

The Working Party was asked to consider the efficiency of existing legal remedies, the composition of the courts, the procedural rules and, where appropriate, the overall structure of the judiciary, including the relationship between Community courts and national courts. In fact, this last issue formed a natural point of departure for the discussions of the Working Party. The two courts had just published a working paper[1] in which they had examined the pros and cons of different ways to reorganise this relationship with a view to making the judicial system of the Communities more efficient. And, of course, this relationship is the foundation of the Community court system. The solutions to most of the other issues are dependent on the choice that is made concerning this Community – national court inter-relationship. So, the Working Party began with a thorough discussion of the present system of *preliminary references* and of the possible alternative solutions, taking the working paper of the two courts as a basis.

The most radical solution would certainly be to replace the dialogue and co-operation with the national courts with a hierarchical system, where the national court decides all issues of Community law and where parties may then bring appeal proceedings before the Community court. However, the Working Party soon rejected this solution as contrary to the present structure of the Union. A federal system should not be introduced by the back door.

---

* This is the text of a paper presented to a meeting of the Centre for European Legal Studies held at Sidney Sussex College, Cambridge on 9 May 2000.
[1] The Courts' Paper – see Part One C(2) of this volume, *infra.*

Another radical solution would be to devolve, or rather partly to renationalise the preliminary rulings jurisdiction. A specialised court could be set up in each Member State with the task of examining all preliminary questions, answering the greater part itself and referring only the most important questions to the Court of Justice. The greatest advantage of such a system would be that most questions could be treated exclusively in the language of the devolved court, without inviting observations from other Member States or from Community Institutions. On the other hand, the rulings of the devolved court would have no authority outside the Member State of that Court. Such a system could not ensure the uniform application of Community law throughout the Union. This disadvantage might be somewhat reduced if all questions were first submitted for assessment by the Court of Justice, which would then remit the less important issues to the devolved court. However, this would considerably reduce the administrative advantages of the devolution scheme. The same would be true if the devolved courts were organised as regional Community courts, while under all three systems a number of cases would have to be examined by no fewer than three courts in succession. So, in the eyes of the Working Party, the advantages of devolution would clearly be outweighed by its inconveniences.

Another idea that had been advanced, in particular by the German government, was the exclusion of national courts of first instance from the power to make references. This, however, would have a perverse effect at national level by encouraging litigants to pursue their cases to the higher court, simply to gain access to the Court of Justice. It might also discourage courts of first instance from applying Community law.

A solution, which, at least in principle, would preserve the dialogue between all national courts and the Court of Justice, would be to empower the Court of Justice to select those preliminary questions that it considered sufficiently important for the development of Community law. The other references would then be returned to the referring courts, if possible with references to earlier case law that could be helpful to the national court. This direct docket control would be simple, flexible, free of costs and ensure at least a minimum of uniformity. It might, however, in the long run endanger the good and confident relations between national courts and the Court of Justice.

Finally, therefore, the Working Party decided in favour of preserving free access for all national courts to a centralised Community court system. It therefore concentrated its attention on the relationship between the Court of Justice and the Court of First Instance. On this point, the Working Party found that the most important task for the development and proper application of Community law is the giving of preliminary rulings. Therefore, this task should essentially remain the responsibility of the supreme Community court. Nevertheless, the

Working Party has proposed the repeal of the last sentence of the first paragraph of Article 225 EC, which at present excludes the transfer of preliminary questions to the Court of First Instance. In the view of the Working Party, such a transfer is possible and even advisable in certain special and well-defined areas of law.

In fact, some of the preliminary cases concern areas that have only tenuous links to Community law in general. The Brussels Convention provides a good example. Article 65 EC promises a considerable extension of judicial co-opera-tion in civil matters. A growing number of preliminary references in this area may justify the creation of a specialised chamber in the Court of First instance and – in the long run – maybe even a new specialised court. The future develop-ment of direct actions concerning, for instance, intellectual property may also justify the creation of specialised chambers in the CFU. If so, there may be a case for a pooling of jurisdiction, including preliminary references within the same area.

However, preliminary questions are not well suited to two-tier proceedings. This is due both to the delays that this would cause and to the fat that the preliminary reference procedure is a dialogue between two courts, not litigation between two parties that may be given the right to appeal. On the other hand, the Court of Justice should maintain a certain control of the case law even in areas where preliminary ruling jurisdiction is transferred to the CFI. For this reason, the Working Party has proposed to confer on the Commission, in its capacity as guardian of the Treaty, the right to bring the issue before the Court of Justice as a point of general legal interest. Just like actions under Article 68(3) EC, such a case should only be intended to correct erroneous case law for the future and not to challenge the finality of legal decisions.

The proposed transfer to the CFI of preliminary ruling cases within certain special areas may slow, but certainly will not stop the steady increase in the number of preliminary references made to the Court of Justice. While the Working Party did not propose to confer on the Court of Justice the power to return questions to the referring court because of their lack of interest, it did, however, propose the encouragement of national courts to be bolder in applying Community law themselves, including the improvement of the capacity of national judges to do so.

As to the first of these ends, the Working Party has proposed the redrafting of Article 234 EC. It should state explicitly the principle that courts of the Member States have full authority to deal with questions of Community law that they encounter in the exercise of their national jurisdiction, subject only to their right or duty to refer questions to the Community courts. It has also been proposed that, before taking the decision to refer a question under Article 234 EC, national courts should take into account how important the question is to Community law and whether there is a reasonable doubt as to the answer to the question. As a consequence, it has been proposed to limit the obligation to refer, imposed on national courts of last instance, by the application of the same two criteria. This last part of the proposal of the Working Party has been challenged, especially by practising lawyers, yet it has been applauded by several national judges as a confirmation in law of what in fact is already the present situation.

Improving the capacity of national judges to apply Community law without systematically referring all problems of interpretation to the Court of Justice must, however, be the combined responsibility of the Member States and the Court of Justice itself. The Member States should provide better training to all of those involved in referring questions for preliminary rulings. They should also provide an efficient information system to cover the current state of Community law. The Working Party has recommended the setting up of national information centres with computer links both to the services of the Commission, to the research and Documentation Service of the Court of Justice and between each other. For its part, the Court of Justice should include in its Rules of Procedure the mandatory requirements that, according to its case law, render a reference inadmissible if they are not complied with. These rules should be supplemented by comprehensive recommendations on when and how to draft references for preliminary rulings. The national courts should also be encouraged, though in no way obliged, to include in their references reasoned grounds for the answer that they consider most appropriate.

As far as *direct actions* are concerned, the Working Party considered that the CFI should become the first judicial forum for actions brought by a Member State or a Community institution. This principle should apply to actions for annulment and for failure to act, even in relation to acts of a normative character. There are, however, certain actions in which a rapid judgment is essential to avoid serious difficulties for the proper functioning of the Communities. Such actions must be excluded from the benefit of two-tier proceedings. The Working Party has enumerated some examples, of which only one represents a significant workload for the Court of Justice, namely *infringement actions* against Member States.

These infringement actions do in fact impose a heavy administrative burden on the Court, particularly as regards translation, even in spite of the fact that most of these actions are not seriously contested by the Member State involved. The most helpful reform would be to empower the Commission to adopt the decision establishing the infringement – a system known from the Coal and Steel Community. At the very least, actions concerning failure to implement Directives in time would be well served by such a system. The power to impose a penalty payment for failure to comply with the decision of the Commission should remain with the Court of Justice. In the event that this proposal is not accepted, the Working Party has also proposed a swift and simplified procedure for dealing with infringement actions where the defence lodged with the Court of Justice by the Member State already demonstrates the lack of any serious objections.

The number of *appeals* against judgments by the CFI has risen considerably during recent times and now constitutes an important source of work for the Court of Justice. However, the failure rate of these appeals has remained very high (around 90%). This situation justifies the proposal made by the Working Party that a preliminary filtering procedure should be established. This procedure should be based on criteria concerning the general importance of the grounds of appeal, either for the development of Community law or for the protection of individual rights.

By far the most radical proposal in relation to direct actions, however, concerns what the Working Party has called '*special cases*'. This notion is used for areas where a great number of similar cases are brought before the Community courts, where the link to Community law in general is only indirect, or where the issues require highly specialised judges to deal with them. In the view of the Working Party, such cases should be brought before specialised judicial bodies of first instance. Appeals against the decisions of such bodies should be possible on points of law only and should be brought before the CFI as the court of last instance. Control by the Court of Justice should be restricted to points of general legal interest, submitted by the Commission in the same way as when preliminary ruling jurisdiction is conferred on the CFI.[2] Good examples of this type are cases concerning intellectual property rights, which will at the outset mainly be concerned with the registration of Community trade marks. At present, decisions of the Office for Harmonisation in the Internal Market are in fact subject to three-tier judicial control. Instead of the current system, the Boards of Appeal of OHIM should be given the status of an independent tribunal. In staff cases, a similar system should be introduced by setting up an 'Inter-institutional Complaints Tribunal'. However, the future development of Community law may create new categories of special cases that may need to be dealt with in the same way. If the number of special cases then threatens to create an imbalance in the jurisdiction of the CFI, then a special appeals court could be set up, which would remain under the ultimate control of the Court of Justice on points of general legal interest. Such a system could provide the flexible docket control so often championed in the legal literature.

[2] See p. 91, *supra*.

These different proposals will extend the jurisdiction and role of the CFI. It follows that the Council and the European Parliament must agree to assign additional staff and funds to this court. It is in fact much easier to increase the production capacity of the CFI than that of the Court of Justice. In general, the CFI takes its decisions in chambers. Some of these chambers could be specialised and the number of judges in the CFI could be augmented without having to be tied to the number of Member States. However, the extended role of the CFI should also have consequences for its designation and its place within the Treaties as a whole.

The *Rules of Procedure* of the Court of Justice were adopted at a time when the present case load could not have been foreseen. These rules served as a model for the rules of procedure for the CFI. Many of today's cases do not merit the full application of these rules, which are both complex and rigid. To make these rules more flexible, the two courts have at regular intervals submitted modifications to the Council for its approval. However, such approval requires a unanimous decision. The judicial traditions in the Member States vary considerably. For instance, some Member States favour a thorough written procedure, while others attach greater importance to the oral hearing. Although the modifications are already the result of extensive internal discussions within the courts, the debate starts all over again in the *ad hoc* group of the Council. After lengthy negotiations within this group, approval is often linked to restrictions or conditions that reduce considerably the effects of the modifications. The Working Party has therefore given its strong support to the Courts' wish, already indicated in the Courts' Paper of May 1999,[3] that the approval procedure should either be abolished or changed to allow for majority decisions.

The Working Party has also expressed its support for a number of modifications now submitted by the two courts and has proposed further changes. Many of these changes will confer the power on the courts to skip some stages of the procedure in certain cases. Since practically all of these stages involve *translations*, such alterations will also lighten the translation workload, which today accounts for one third of the total duration of the procedure. However, the proliferation of procedural languages in the wake of future enlargements will seriously aggravate this problem and the Working Party has thus also indicated some specific measures in this area.

As most translations into the working language are of procedural documents, lawyers and agents should be persuaded to avoid excessively lengthy documents. One way to reduce translation workload could be to empower the two courts to demand an abstract of such documents, which would then be the only version

---

[3] See Part One C(2) of this volume, *infra*, at p. 126.

translated into the working language and used to draft the Report for the Hearing. All Community institutions should be obliged to present their documents both in the language of the case and in the working language. The Member States should be invited to do likewise wherever this is feasible. The bulk of translations from the working language concerns the judgments and the opinions of the Advocate-General. It would indeed be helpful if judgments of minor importance were only published in the form of analytical summaries; the full text in the language of the procedure and possibly also in the working language could then be placed on the Internet.

The Working Party was also asked to consider the *composition of the courts*. However, it is likely that the Intergovernmental Conference will, on this point, only be interested in proposals having a direct link to the enlargement of the Union. Here, the Working Party took it for granted that each Member State will continue to have one judge on the bench of the Court of Justice. This must have consequences for the composition of the plenary session, if it is not to become – in the words of the Court of Justice – a 'deliberative assembly'. The Working Party envisaged a composition of no more than half the total number of judges plus one or two, so that the odd number would permit the creation of a majority. The nucleus should be the President and the presidents of the grand chambers. To this nucleus should then be added the rest of the grand chamber in which the *juge-rapporteur* sits and the necessary remainder should be made up of other judges in rotation. There should, however, be a fixed maximum number of judges, for instance thirteen.

To ensure the coherence of the case law of the other compositions, the President and the presidents of the grand chambers should, at frequent and regular meetings, review the draft judgments of those compositions and should have the power to refer cases to the plenary session. The proposal of the Working Party to limit the participation of the Advocates-General to cases of major importance is significant. This should permit not only a considerable reduction in the number of Advocates-General, but should also shorten the proceedings in cases of minor importance and lighten the translation burden on the courts. With regard to the extended role of the CFI, the ideas of the Working Party on its composition are much the same as those concerning the Court of Justice. However, the number of judges should depend upon workload and not upon the number of Member States; furthermore, a certain specialisation of chambers seems desirable.

What, then, are the chances of all of these proposals coming to fruition? The contributions of the different EU institutions to the IGC may provide us with some hints in this respect. The contribution of the Commission[4] is to a great

---

[4] See Part One C(4) of this volume, *infra*.

extent based upon the report of the Working Party. However, the Commission has often been more prudent in its language and has mentioned alternatives to some of the Working Party's proposals. In particular, the Commission has expressed serious doubts about the proposal to limit the obligation on national courts of last instance to submit preliminary questions under Article 234 EC. The Opinion of the Legal Committee of the European Parliament has also supported a great number of the proposals; in particular, it favours those that may be combined with proposals increasing the influence of the Parliament.

More interesting, of course, is the contribution of the two courts, which comprises five proposals to modify Treaty provisions to allow:

– the transfer of preliminary ruling jurisdiction in certain areas to the CFI;
– the creation of an inter-institutional complaints tribunal for staff cases;
– the setting up of other specialised judicial bodies of first instance;
– a filtering system for appeals; and
– a more efficient procedure for the modification of the Rules of Procedure.

Three of these proposals were already heralded in the Courts' Paper of May 1999, while the other two seem to have been inspired by the Report of the Working Party. In general, these proposals take the form of relatively broad authorisations from the Council, acting on proposals from the Court of Justice. However, the explanatory notes (which are not very specific) indicate a lower level of ambition than that of the similar proposals from the Working Party. They also seem to reflect a desire on the part of both courts to combine a reduction in their workload with the maintenance of complete control. This is not very promising.

On the other hand, there is clearly a growing understanding among the governments of the need for radical reforms of the judicial system of the Communities. This in itself is a new and important development. It is also encouraging that the two courts (in their contribution) underscore that their proposals only constitute a minimum of the measures necessary for them to adapt to the development of Community law and that the reflection on the future of the judicial system must continue, taking into account other important proposals presented *inter alia* in the Report of the Working Party.

C. DOCUMENTS

DOCUMENT 1

*Amendments to the Rules of
Procedure of the Court of Justice*

Introductory Note

The amendments to the ECJ's Rules of Procedure, which were approved by the Council in May 2000, demanded inclusion in this volume. We felt that the ECJ's explanation of the reasons behind its request also needed to be reproduced here for the sake of completeness. The Court's Explanatory Note follows this introduction, and is followed by the Amendments approved by the Council. As noted above,[1] the final version of the amendments deviates in some respects from the ECJ's originally proposed text. The details of these differences will be set out below – please refer to the text of the amendments for full details. The main themes present in the Council's changes are as follows:

(a) a desire to ensure that any extra information acquired by the courts concerning the case shall be communicated to all of the other parties involved in the proceedings (see Articles 54a and 104a Rules of Procedure of the ECJ);

(b) an increase in the scope of the powers of the President of the ECJ to determine or vary time limits (see Articles 44a, 104a, 109b(1) and 120 Rules of Procedure of the ECJ) and to restrict arguments in urgent cases to the essential points of law raised (Article 104a Rules of Procedure of the ECJ);

(c) a wish to specify with greater precision the incidents of the accelerated procedure in cases of urgency (Article 104a Rules of Procedure of the ECJ); and

(d) an inclination on the part of the Member States and the other EU institutions to preserve the possibility of *insisting* on the inclusion of an oral part of the proceedings in cases concerning requests for an interpretation under Article 68 EC (see Article 109a(3) Rules of Procedure of the ECJ) and in the settlement of disputes under Article 35 TEU) see Article 109b(3) Rules of Procedure of the ECJ).

In some ways, these additions are illustrative of the points made by Professor Due on the need for unanimous Council approval for amendments to the Rules

---

[1] See p. 84, *supra*.

of Procedure of the courts: provisions allowing the Member States to opt for an oral hearing are redolent of just the sort of re-opening of the bargaining process that he describes. However, the fuller explanation of the accelerated procedure in cases of real urgency is a welcome clarification, which can no doubt be explained in part by the Member States' likely great interest in the areas that may come to be covered by this procedure in the future (such as immigration and asylum issues). Finally, these amendments underline the role of the President of the ECJ in implementing and supervising the case load management strategies that will become ever more important as the Union develops in the future.

Details of the additions made

1. Article 44a, last sentence and Article 104(4): additional provision that the President of the ECJ may extend the one month time limit within which parties must make an application with reasons why they should be granted an oral hearing.

2. Article 54a, last sentence: additional provided that any information requested by the *juge-rapporteur* and/or the Advocate-General must be communicated to the other parties to the case.

3. Article 104a receives a greater specification of the accelerated procedure in cases of urgency:

   • Up to 15 days to lodge statements of case and written observations (for the President to determine the exact time limit);

   • President may request such statements to restrict themselves to the essential points of law raised by the questions referred;

   • Statements of case or written observations shall be notified to the parties and the other persons in question prior to the hearing.

4. Articles 109a(3) and 109b(3): extra provision stating that the procedure shall include an oral part where the Member State or EC institution so requests.

5. Article 109b does not set a time limit of one month from the date of service for the submission of written observations as proposed by the ECJ, but instead leaves it to the President to set the time limit in each case.

6. Article 120, last sentence: the ECJ's proposal here concerned applications made to be heard after the closure of the written procedure, where the party in question felt that that procedure had 'not enabled him fully to

defend his point of view'. The final text covers the more general category of applications submitting 'reasons to be heard' and also provides the possibility for the President to extend this one month period where he considers it appropriate to do so.

EXPLANATORY NOTE

On 10 May 1999 the Court of Justice sent the Council a document containing proposals and reflections on "The Future of the Judicial System of the European Union". After summarising the difficulties with which the Community Courts are already faced, that document identifies the consequences which developments in Community law will entail for the exercise of the judicial function in the Union. It lists a series of specific measures for dealing with them. Some of them consist in amendments to the Rules of Procedure which can be adopted immediately by the Council without waiting for Treaty amendment. At the Council of Ministers of Justice of 28 May last the President of the Court of Justice presented those proposals, which are set out as formal amendments below.

In addition, a number of proposals are made for amendment of the Rules of Procedure made necessary by the entry into force of the Treaty of Amsterdam.

-o-o-o-

The object of the first set of amendments is to introduce a greater degree of flexibility in the application of the Rules of Procedure in order to extend the ways in which the procedure can be adapted to the degree of complexity and urgency of the case. These amendments are necessary to enable the Court of Justice to cope not only with an ever-increasing number of cases but also with the intensification of its judicial tasks which will result from the new areas of jurisdiction provided for by the conventions adopted in the context of the third pillar of the European Union (Justice and Home Affairs) and by the Treaty of Amsterdam.

The purpose of these amendments is to introduce an accelerated procedure enabling urgent references for preliminary rulings to be dealt with swiftly; to provide a more rational management of the oral procedure; to allow the Court to issue practice directions relating to the conduct of proceedings and to allow the Judge-Rapporteur and the Advocate General to request information or documents from the parties. More particularly, as regards references for preliminary rulings, the proposals envisage the possibility of requesting clarification from the national court and the extension of the simplified procedure to enable the Court to rule by way of order on simple questions the answer to which seems to be obvious.

Accelerated procedure

It is proposed to introduce a new provision (Article 104a) to enable **references for a preliminary ruling** to be dealt with by an accelerated procedure. In a declaration adopted during the "Justice and Home Affairs" Council of 28 and 29 July 1998 concerning the Convention on Jurisdiction and the Recognition and Enforcement of Judgments in Matrimonial Matters, [1] the Council has already stressed the need for an examination of means by which the length of preliminary ruling proceedings can be reduced. Also, in a resolution of 7 December 1998 on the free movement of goods, [2] the Council invited the Court of Justice to reflect on the possibility of accelerating the examination of cases falling under Council Regulation (EC) No 2679/98 of 7 December 1998 on the functioning of the internal market in relation to the free movement of goods among Member States [3] and undertook to examine urgently and with an open mind any proposal to amend the Rules of Procedure of the Court.

According to the proposed provision, an accelerated procedure can be applied only exceptionally and where it is established that the case is of particular urgency as compared with all other references for a preliminary ruling. At present the Rules of Procedure (Article 55(2)) do no more than allow a case to be given priority and do not allow any derogation from the various stages of the procedure as determined by the existing provisions. It is not proposed to lay down rigid rules but to provide the Court, on a reference for a preliminary ruling, with the means to adapt the procedure to the circumstances of the individual case. It is proposed in particular to allow the Court to proceed immediately, on the basis of the national court's order for reference, to the oral part of the procedure.

It goes without saying that in the event of an accelerated procedure being applied in a given case priority would be given to that case also as regards work internal to the Court such as the translation of documents, the drafting of the preliminary report, the drafting of the Report for the Hearing or of the Judge-Rapporteur, the fixing of the hearing, the preparation of the Advocate General's Opinion and the deliberations of the bench hearing the case.

As regards **direct actions**, the Court considers that the introduction of an accelerated procedure should also be contemplated. However, the introduction of such a procedure before the Court of Justice should be coordinated with the introduction of a similar procedure before the Court of First Instance, and the Court of Justice may submit a proposal on this subject at a later stage.

Adjustments to the oral procedure

---

[1]   OJ C 221 of 16.7.1998, p. 18.

[2]   OJ L 337 of 12.12.1998, p. 10.

[3]   OJ C 337 of 12.12.1998, p. 8.

It is proposed to amend Articles 44a and 104(4) on dispensing with the hearing. The Court can only dispense with this part of the procedure with the express agreement of the parties in the case of direct actions and, in the case of preliminary references, where none of the parties to the main proceedings or other persons entitled to participate in the proceedings before the Court has asked to be heard. Experience shows, however, that the oral procedure, even if requested by a party or other interested person, can take the form of a ritual repetition, word for word, by the agents, advisers or lawyers of the arguments which they have already presented during the written procedure.

The object of the proposed amendments is not to deprive the parties or other interested persons of their right to an oral procedure but to make their approach to the matter more carefully considered. It is thus proposed to allow the Court to omit the hearing unless a party or other interested person submits a reasoned application setting out the points on which he wishes to be heard. It is further proposed, for organisational reasons, to prescribe a time-limit for the submission of such an application by a party or other interested person. The proposal sets this time-limit at one month from notification of the close of the written procedure in the case of direct actions and one month from service of statements of case or written observations lodged in the case of references for a preliminary ruling.

As regards appeals, Article 120 of the Rules of Procedure at present allows the Court to dispense with the hearing save where one of the parties objects on the ground that the written procedure did not enable him fully to defend his point of view. It is proposed to align the drafting of this provision on that proposed for Articles 44a and 104(4), to specify that the party must submit a reasoned application setting out the points on which it has not been able fully to defend its point of view during the written procedure and to introduce a time-limit for submission of such an application.

Practice directions

Article 32 of the Rules of Court of the European Court of Human Rights provides for the possibility of issuing practice directions regarding such matters as the organisation of hearings and the lodging of written observations or other documents. It is proposed to insert a similar provision in the Rules of Procedure of the Court of Justice as Article 125a. The Court of Justice has already drawn up a guide for the use of advisers and lawyers which is sent to every agent or lawyer acting in proceedings before the Court. Such a guide, however, is no more than an information document regarding practice and custom in proceedings before the Court. The possibility of issuing practice directions would enable the Court to indicate to agents, advisers and lawyers precisely how it wishes pleadings to be drawn up or hearings organised.

Requests for information or documents

Article 49 of the Rules of Court of the European Court of Human Rights allows the Judge-Rapporteur to request information or documents from the parties. In practice, the Court of Justice often makes such requests to the parties following examination of the preliminary report of the Judge-Rapporteur. A provision similar to that contained in the Rules of Procedure of the European Court of Human Rights would make it possible to simplify the procedure by authorising the Judge-Rapporteur and the Advocate General to take the initiative of making such a request to the parties. It is proposed to insert this new provision as Article 54a.

Requests to national courts for clarification

Such a possibility is available to the EFTA Court under Article 96(4) of its Rules of Procedure (OJ 1994 L 278, p. 1). It is proposed to insert a similar provision in the Rules of Procedure of the Court of Justice as Article 104(5), the present paragraph (5) of the article becoming paragraph (6).

The introduction of such a possibility for the Court of Justice meets a genuine need. It is not uncommon for a reference for a preliminary ruling to give an inadequate description of the factual and/or legal context of the reference or insufficient information concerning the relevance of the questions put to the Court. The possibility of clarifying the context of such references could avoid their being declared inadmissible in certain cases or avert delays in procedure owing to imperfections in the reference. Under the proposed provision, a request for clarification could be addressed to the national court at any stage of the procedure. Ideally, a request for clarification would be made as soon as possible after the preliminary reference has been lodged and the clarification obtained could, where appropriate, be communicated to the parties, and to the Member States and institutions participating in the proceedings, along with service of the reference itself.

Simplified procedure for simple questions referred for a preliminary ruling

It is proposed to amend Article 104(3) of the Rules of Procedure which deals with questions referred for a preliminary ruling which are manifestly identical to a question on which the Court has already ruled and which enables the Court to rule by way of order, by extending it to include questions in respect of which the answer can be clearly deduced from existing case-law and questions in respect of which the answer admits of no reasonable doubt. The number of preliminary references before the Court is continually increasing and the questions raised are often so straightforward as to allow of only one answer or may call for an answer which can be deduced directly from existing case-law. It should be noted that the simplified procedure under Article 104(3) provides that, before giving its decision, the Court is to inform the referring court or tribunal of its intention to rule by way of order and is to hear the parties, and the Member States and institutions participating in the preliminary reference proceedings.

-o-o-o-

Lastly, as regards the amendments required following the **entry into force of the Treaty of Amsterdam**, it is necessary in particular to lay down, through the insertion of new Articles 109a and 109b, the procedure applicable in cases brought before the Court under Article 68(3) of the EC Treaty (requests for a ruling on a question of interpretation of Title IV of the Treaty or of acts adopted on the basis of that Title) and under Article 35(7) of the Treaty on Union (settlement of disputes between Member States or between a Member State and the Commission regarding the interpretation or the application of acts adopted in the sphere of Title VI of the Treaty, or of conventions established in that sphere). The proposed procedures are based largely on that laid down in Articles 107 and 108 for requests for an opinion under Article 300 of the EC Treaty and, like the practice followed under that procedure, may comprise an oral part.

It is also necessary to lay down the procedure to be applied in the case of requests for a preliminary ruling under Article 35(1) of the Treaty on Union. This provision does not prescribe the procedure before the Court of Justice, and the provisions contained in particular in the EC Statute of the Court are not applicable to these requests for a preliminary ruling. It is proposed to include such requests under Article 103(3), which governs procedure in references for a preliminary ruling under Article 41 of the ECSC Treaty.

Finally, it is necessary to adapt the references to the provisions of the EC Treaty to the new numbering resulting from Article 12 of the Treaty of Amsterdam.

COURT OF JUSTICE

AMENDMENTS TO THE RULES OF PROCEDURE OF THE COURT OF JUSTICE
of 16 May 2000

THE COURT,

Having regard to the Treaty establishing the European Community, and in particular the third paragraph of Article 245 thereof,

Having regard to the Protocol on the Statute of the Court of Justice of the European Coal and Steel Community, and in particular Article 55 thereof,

Having regard to the Treaty establishing the European Atomic Energy Community, and in particular the third paragraph of Article 160 thereof,

Whereas:

(1)   In the light of experience, it is necessary to make certain amendments to the provisions of the Rules of Procedure with a view to improving the conduct of proceedings.

(2)   In the case of references for a preliminary ruling involving particular urgency, it is necessary to provide for accelerated procedures.

(3)   Following the entry into force of the Treaty of Amsterdam and of the amendments made by that Treaty to the Treaty on European Union and to the Treaty establishing the European Community, it is necessary to adapt the provisions of the Rules of Procedure,

With the unanimous approval of the Council given on 13 April 2000,

HAS ADOPTED THE FOLLOWING AMENDMENTS TO ITS RULES OF PROCEDURE:

Article 1

The Rules of Procedure of the Court of Justice of the European Communities adopted on 19 June 1991 (OJ L 176, 4.7.1991, p. 1, with corrigendum in OJ L 383, 29.12.1992, p. 117), as amended on 21 February 1995 (OJ L 44, 28.2.1995, p. 61) and 11 March 1997 (OJ L 103, 19.4.1997, p. 1, with corrigendum in OJ L 351, 23.12.1997, p. 72), shall be amended as follows:

1. In Article 1, after the words 'In these Rules:', the following shall be inserted:

    '— "Union Treaty" means the "Treaty on European Union"';

2. Article 44a shall be replaced by the following text:

    'Article 44a

    Without prejudice to any special provisions laid down in these Rules, the procedure before the Court shall also include an oral part. However, after the pleadings referred to in Article 40(1) and, as the case may be, in Article 41(1) have been lodged, the Court, acting on a report from the Judge-Rapporteur and after hearing the Advocate-General, and if none of the parties has submitted an application setting out the reasons for which he wishes to be heard, may decide otherwise. The application shall be submitted within a period of one month from notification to the party of the close of the written procedure. That period may be extended by the President.'

3. The title of Chapter 2 of Title II of these Rules 'Preparatory Inquiries' shall be replaced by the following: 'Preparatory Inquiries and other Preparatory Measures'.

4. After Article 54, the following text shall be inserted:

    'Section 4

    Article 54a

    The Judge-Rapporteur and the Advocate-General may request the parties to submit within a specified period all such information relating to the facts, and all such documents or other particulars, as they may consider relevant. The information and/or documents provided shall be communicated to the other parties.'

5. Article 103(3) shall be replaced by the following text:

    '3.   In cases provided for in Article 35(1) of the Union Treaty and in Article 41 of the ECSC Treaty, the text of the decision to refer the matter shall be served on the parties in the case, the Member States, the Commission and the Council.

    These parties, States and institutions may, within two months from the date of such service, lodge written statements of case or written observations.

    The provisions of paragraph 1 shall apply.'

6. Article 104(3) shall be replaced by the following text:

    '3.   Where a question referred to the Court for a preliminary ruling is identical to a question on which the Court has already ruled, where the answer to such a question may be clearly deduced from existing case-law or where the answer to the question admits of no reasonable doubt, the Court may, after informing the court or tribunal which referred the question to it, after hearing any observations submitted by the persons referred to in Article 20 of the EC Statute, Article 21 of the Euratom Statute and Article 103(3) of these Rules and after hearing the Advocate-General, give its decision by reasoned order in which, if appropriate, reference is made to its previous judgment or to the relevant case-law.'

7. Article 104(4) shall be replaced by the following text:

'4.   Without prejudice to paragraph 3 of this Article, the procedure before the Court in the case of a reference for a preliminary ruling shall also include an oral part. However, after the statements of case or written observations referred to in Article 20 of the EC Statute, Article 21 of the Euratom Statute and Article 103(3) of these Rules have been submitted, the Court, acting on a report from the Judge-Rapporteur, after informing the persons who under the aforementioned provisions are entitled to submit such statements or observations, may, after hearing the Advocate-General, decide otherwise, provided that none of those persons has submitted an application setting out the reasons for which he wishes to be heard. The application shall be submitted within a period of one month from service on the party or person of the written statements of case or written observations which have been lodged. That period may be extended by the President.'

8. In Article 104, the following text shall be inserted as paragraph 5, the present paragraph 5 becoming paragraph 6:

'5.   The Court may, after hearing the Advocate-General, request clarification from the national court.'

9. After Article 104, the following text shall be inserted:

'Article 104a

At the request of the national court, the President may exceptionally decide, on a proposal from the Judge-Rapporteur and after hearing the Advocate-General, to apply an accelerated procedure derogating from the provisions of these Rules to a reference for a preliminary ruling, where the circumstances referred to establish that a ruling on the question put to the Court is a matter of exceptional urgency.

In that event, the President may immediately fix the date for the hearing, which shall be notified to the parties in the main proceedings and to the other persons referred to in Article 20 of the EC Statute, Article 21 of the Euratom Statute and Article 103(3) of these Rules when the decision making the reference is served.

The parties and other interested persons referred to in the preceding paragraph may lodge statements of case or written observations within a period prescribed by the President, which shall not be less than 15 days. The President may request the parties and other interested persons to restrict the matters addressed in their statement of case

or written observations to the essential points of law raised by the question referred.

The statements of case or written observations, if any, shall be notified to the parties and to the other persons referred to above prior to the hearing.

The Court shall rule after hearing the Advocate-General.'

10. After Article 109, the following text shall be inserted:

'Chapter 12

REQUESTS FOR INTERPRETATION UNDER ARTICLE 68 OF THE EC TREATY

Article 109a

1.   A request for a ruling on a question of interpretation under Article 68(3) of the EC Treaty shall be served on the Commission and the Member States if the request is submitted by the Council, on the Council and the Member States if the request is submitted by the Commission and on the Council, the Commission and the other Member States if the request is submitted by a Member State.

The President shall prescribe a time limit within which the institutions and the Member States on which the request has been served are to submit their written observations.

2.   As soon as the request referred to in paragraph 1 has been submitted, the President shall designate the Judge-Rapporteur. The First Advocate-General shall thereupon assign the request to an Advocate-General.

3.   The Court shall, after the Advocate-General has delivered his opinion, give its decision on the request by way of judgment.

The procedure relating to the request shall include an oral part where a Member State or one of the institutions referred to in paragraph 1 so requests.

Chapter 13

SETTLEMENT OF THE DISPUTES REFERRED TO IN ARTICLE 35 OF THE UNION TREATY

Article 109b

1.   In the case of disputes between Member States as referred to in Article 35(7) of the Union Treaty, the matter shall be brought before the Court by an application by a party to the dispute. The application shall be served on the other Member States and on the Commission.

In the case of disputes between Member States and the Commission as referred to in Article 35(7) of the Union Treaty, the matter shall be brought before the Court by an application by a party to the dispute. The application shall be served on the other Member States, the Council and the Commission if it was made by a Member State. The application shall be served on the Member States and on the Council if it was made by the Commission.

The President shall prescribe a time limit within which the institutions and the Member States on which the application has been served are to submit their written observations.

2. As soon as the application referred to in paragraph 1 has been submitted, the President shall designate the Judge-Rapporteur. The First Advocate-General shall thereupon assign the application to an Advocate-General.

3. The Court shall, after the Advocate-General has delivered his opinion, give its ruling on the dispute by way of judgment.

The procedure relating to the application shall include an oral part where a Member State or one of the institutions referred to in paragraph 1 so requests.

4. The same procedure shall apply where an agreement concluded between the Member States confers jurisdiction on the Court to rule on a dispute between Member States or between Member States and an institution.'

11. Article 120 shall be replaced by the following text:

'Article 120

After the submission of pleadings as provided for in Article 115(1) and, if any, Article 117(1) and (2) of these Rules, the Court, acting on a report from the Judge-Rapporteur and after hearing the Advocate-General and the parties, may decide to dispense with the oral part of the procedure unless one of the parties submits an application setting out the reasons for which he wishes to be heard. The application shall be submitted within a period of one month from notification to the party of the close of the written procedure. That period may be extended by the President.'

12. The following text shall be inserted after Article 125:

'Article 125a

The Court may issue practice directions relating in particular to the preparation and conduct of the hearings before it and to the lodging of written statements of case or written observations.'

13. The references to articles of the EC Treaty shall be amended as follows:

— in Article 7(1) the number '167' shall be replaced by the number '223',

— in Article 9(1) the number '165' shall be replaced by the number '221',

— in Article 16(7) the number '184' shall be replaced by the number '241',

— in Article 38(6) the numbers '181' and '182' shall be replaced by the numbers '238' and '239',

— in Article 48(4) the numbers '187' and '192' shall be replaced by the numbers '244' and '256',

— in the second paragraph of Article 77 the numbers '173' and '175' shall be replaced by the numbers '230' and '232',

— in Article 83(1), first subparagraph, the number '185' shall be replaced by the number '242',

— in Article 83(1), second subparagraph, the number '186' shall be replaced by the number '243',

— in Article 89, first paragraph, the numbers '187' and '192' shall be replaced by the numbers '244' and '256',

— in Article 107(1) the number '228' shall be replaced by the number '300',

— in Article 125 the number '188' shall be replaced by the number '245'.

Article 2

These amendments to the Rules of Procedure, which are authentic in the languages referred to in Article 29(1) of these Rules, shall be published in the *Official Journal of the European Communities* and shall enter into force on the first day of the second month following their publication.

Done at Luxembourg, 16 May 2000.

Document 2

The Future of the Judicial System of
the European Union
(Proposals and Reflections)
('The Courts' Paper')

OUTLINE

Introduction

Chapter I   The problems facing the Community judicial system

1.   Current position
2.   Foreseeable developments
3.   Capacity of the institution
4.   Problems of translation

Chapter II   Proposed immediate amendments to the Rules of Procedure

1.   Procedure generally
2.   Preliminary reference procedure in particular
3.   Conclusions

Chapter III   Proposed measures involving amendment of the Treaties or Statutes

1.   Procedure for amendment of the Rules of Procedure
2.   Filtering of appeals
3.   Changes to the handling of staff cases

Chapter IV   Thoughts on possible changes to the judicial system

1.   The composition and organisation of the Court of Justice and the Court of First Instance
2.   Transfer to the Court of First Instance of jurisdiction to hear and determine direct actions
3.   Reform of the system of references for a preliminary ruling

INTRODUCTION

The Court of Justice and the Court of First Instance have already, very recently, had to alert the Council to a dangerous trend towards a structural imbalance between the volume of incoming cases and the capacity of the institution to dispose of them. [1]

It is particularly important for appropriate solutions to be found since recent institutional developments risk further worsening the current state of the Community system of justice.

The third stage of Economic and Monetary Union ("EMU") began on 1 January 1999. The Treaty of Amsterdam entered into force on 1 May 1999. The two Courts will therefore be faced with an intensification of their judicial tasks. In addition, the various Conventions which the Council has adopted under the third pillar of the European Union (Justice and Home Affairs) provide for an extension of the jurisdiction of the Court of Justice.

The prospect of enlargement of the European Union also forms part of the framework for this discussion, since an intergovernmental conference is to be convened "in order to carry out a comprehensive review of the provisions of the Treaties on the composition and functioning of the institutions" at least one year before membership of the Union grows to more than 20 States, in accordance with Article 2 of the **Protocol on the institutions with the prospect of enlargement of the European Union** annexed to the European Treaties by the Treaty of Amsterdam.

In that context, it seems essential to set out the ideas and proposals of the Court of Justice and the Court of First Instance on the problems that need to be resolved so that the courts of the European Union can continue, within the scope of their own jurisdiction, to ensure effective enforcement of the law in the Union.

---

[1] -   See the "Proposals submitted by the Court of Justice and the Court of First Instance with regard to the new intellectual property cases".

In this document the Court of Justice and the Court of First Instance have focused principally on a number of specific measures which can be realised immediately. They are, however, aware that an in-depth examination of the role and structure of the judicial component of the Union is needed to find solutions sufficiently wide-ranging to provide a lasting response to the difficulties which are to be expected, and that such an examination must be undertaken as a matter of urgency.

Having summarised the current difficulties encountered by the Community courts in the exercise of their jurisdiction, the <u>first chapter</u> of the document identifies the additional consequences which the developments mentioned above will have for the exercise of judicial power in the Union.

The <u>second chapter</u> reviews the measures which could be adopted immediately by means of simple amendments to the Rules of Procedure.

The <u>third chapter</u> sets out reforms which do not affect the Community judicial structure and could therefore be decided on rapidly, but which do require amendment of the institutional rules of the Treaties or the Statutes.

The <u>fourth and final chapter</u> contains reflections of a more general and more fundamental nature on the future of the judicial system. They do not embody specific proposals at this stage but are intended to clarify the issues on certain points which appear important for the decisions to be taken by the intergovernmental conference.

Chapter I

The problems facing the Community judicial system

1. *Current position*

At the present time, the number of cases brought before both Courts shows a continuous, steady increase (in 1998, 485 cases were commenced before the Court of Justice and 238 before the Court of First Instance). [2] That trend points to the growing importance of Community law in the everyday life of Community citizens and companies and in the work of the national courts. The number of references for a preliminary ruling thus increased by roughly 10% in 1998 compared with the previous year and by more than 85% compared with 1990. References for preliminary rulings now account for more than half of the new cases brought before the Court of Justice (264 references out of 485 cases).

Since the two Courts have no control over the number of cases brought before them, they are faced with a structural increase in the number of pending cases. The constant increase in the number of cases dealt with by the Court of Justice and the Court of First Instance (768 cases were disposed of in 1998) is evidence of the efforts made to cope with the situation.

Despite the steps taken to improve the efficiency of working methods and procedural practices, such an increase inevitably entails a lengthening of proceedings. This situation is particularly regrettable in the case of references for preliminary rulings. In order for the rights of individuals to be safeguarded and for cooperation between national courts and the Court of Justice under the preliminary reference procedure to function properly, replies to the questions asked must be given as quickly as possible. The system of preliminary references is a key factor in the proper functioning of the internal market.

---

[2] —   See the tables reproduced in Annex I.

2. *Foreseeable developments*

The commencement of the third stage of EMU and the entry into force of the Treaty of Amsterdam and certain Conventions established under the third pillar of the European Union are expected to result in a considerable increase in the near future, if not immediately, in the number of cases brought before the Court of Justice and the Court of First Instance.

Enlargement of the European Union will also eventually bring an increase in the number of cases brought before the two Courts, even though experience shows that a certain lapse of time generally occurs before any significant number of cases originating from or concerning a new Member State are brought before the Community courts.

(i) <u>As regards the Court of Justice</u>, an increase is to be expected, in particular, in the number of preliminary reference proceedings concerning:

- Title IV of the EC Treaty (visas, asylum, immigration and other policies related to free movement of persons);

- the legislation relating to the third stage of EMU, particularly on the introduction of the Euro;

- Title VI of the Treaty on European Union (police and judicial cooperation in criminal matters);

- the provisions of a number of Conventions concluded between Member States on the basis of the former Article K.3 of the Treaty on European Union (the new Article 31). [3]

As regards direct actions, the right conferred on the Court of Auditors and the European Central Bank to initiate proceedings, as well as the similar right of Member States under Title VI of the Treaty on European Union, will probably also lead to an increase in the number of cases brought before the Court.

---

[3] —   See Annex II.

The growth in proceedings commenced before the Court of First Instance will result in a corresponding increase in the number of appeals to the Court of Justice. At present, appeals are taken against 20% to 25% of the Court of First Instance's decisions. This percentage is rising.

The Court of Justice will also have to tackle sensitive new fields such as those just mentioned, relating to police and judicial cooperation in criminal matters, the external aspects of the free movement of persons and problems linked to the third stage of EMU. It will additionally have to concern itself with new areas in the field of private international law, and in particular interpret the Rome Convention of 19 June 1980 on the law applicable to contractual obligations and the Convention of 28 May 1998 on Jurisdiction and the Recognition and Enforcement of Judgments in Matrimonial Matters (the "Brussels II" Convention).

There will be a pressing need to deal with cases rapidly where preliminary rulings are sought on the interpretation of the "Brussels II" Convention and on the provisions of the EC Treaty relating to the external aspects of freedom of movement for persons (Title IV). In the first case (Brussels II), the urgency stems from the need for a prompt reply in the interests of the individuals concerned. In the second (Title IV), it is to be expected that at national level there will be a tendency to stay proceedings before lower courts, pending a ruling from the Court of Justice on questions referred by supreme courts. Such proceedings must, given their nature, be decided swiftly not only in the interests of those concerned but also in the public interest.

(ii) The Court of First Instance will have to contend with an increasing number of cases concerning:

-   trade marks and the protection of plant variety rights;

-   access of natural and legal persons to documents of Community institutions and bodies (Article 255 EC);

-   penalties imposed by the European Central Bank on undertakings (Article 34.3 of the Protocol on the Statute of the European System of Central Banks and of the European Central Bank);

- audits carried out by the Court of Auditors on natural and legal persons in receipt of Community funds (Article 248 EC);

- the legal remedies available to officials of the European Central Bank and of Europol;

- the fight against fraud.

Nor can the possibility be ruled out that the Court of First Instance will eventually hear proceedings relating to the Community patent which, under certain proposals, would be governed by rules similar to those relating to Community trade mark proceedings.

It will be essential for the Court of First Instance, like the Court of Justice, to dispose of certain cases rapidly. In particular, the "Proposals submitted by the Court of Justice and the Court of First Instance with regard to the new intellectual property cases", recently submitted to the Council, indicate that the success of the Community trade mark will depend in part on setting short procedural time-limits, which presupposes that the institution has the means to act expeditiously in that regard without sacrificing the rest of its work.

3. *Capacity of the institution*

It follows from the foregoing that immediate consideration must be given to the adoption of measures to deal with the numerous problems, both quantitative and qualitative, which arise from the impending changes in Community law.

The organisational and procedural framework must be revised to enable the Court of Justice and the Court of First Instance to shorten existing time-limits and deal with further increases in the number of cases brought. Failing that, the new areas of jurisdiction will inevitably result, for both Courts, in delays on a scale which cannot be reconciled with an acceptable level of judicial protection in the Union.

Furthermore, in the case of the Court of Justice, the extra case-load might well seriously jeopardise the proper accomplishment of its task as a court of last instance which, in addition, has a constitutional role. The Court would then no longer be able to concentrate on its main functions, which are to guarantee respect for the distribution of powers between the Community and its Member States and between the Community institutions, the uniformity and consistency of Community law and to contribute to the harmonious development of the law in the Union. Such a failure on the part of the Court would undermine the rule of law on which, as stated in Article 6(1) EU, the Union is founded.

It is, of course, necessary, whenever considering the resources which must be allocated to the institution, to take account of the opportunities offered by new technology. Such technology quite clearly cannot take the place of the structural reforms and resource allocation that will be necessary, but it may affect the apportionment of costs in ways which call for specific studies.

4. *Problems of translation*

The Court also considers it necessary to draw particular attention to the crisis resulting from the lack of resources for its translation service. That situation may cause the functioning of the institution to break down. Reference is made to the report dealing with this particular problem which the Court recently sent to the European Parliament and the Council.

Chapter II

Proposed immediate amendments to the Rules of Procedure

Without having to await the adoption of Treaty amendments, the Court of Justice and the Court of First Instance wish to set out a series of measures which the Council could adopt now. All of these are designed to introduce greater flexibility in the application of the Rules of Procedure, so as to enable the adaptation of procedures to the degree of complexity and urgency of each case.

The specific proposals are concerned with the procedure generally and in particular the procedure relating to questions submitted for a preliminary ruling.

They supplement the amendments which have recently been adopted by the Council (introduction of a single judge to hear a case in the Court of First Instance) or are currently before it (transfer of areas of jurisdiction from the Court of Justice to the Court of First Instance).

1. *Procedure generally*

(i) Recourse to accelerated procedures

The Court of Justice is sometimes faced with cases whose features would justify particularly speedy disposal. While such circumstances remain the exception, they could arise in more acute form in cases where a preliminary ruling is sought on the interpretation of the "Brussels II" Convention and the provisions of the EC Treaty relating to the external aspects of freedom of movement for persons (Title IV); on the validity and interpretation of decisions and framework decisions; and on the interpretation of conventions concerning police cooperation and cooperation in criminal matters which, in the future, could be adopted by the Council or concluded by the Member States under Article 34 EU.

At the moment, neither the Statute of the Court of Justice nor its Rules of Procedure allow for an accelerated procedure which would enable the Court to decide, on an *ad hoc* basis, to deal with certain cases under a separate procedure derogating from the general rules normally applicable.

The first sentence of Article 55(2) of the Rules of Procedure merely provides that the President may, in special circumstances, order that a case be given priority over others.   However, that power does not allow the Court to dispense with certain procedural steps.

It would therefore be desirable to include in the Rules of Procedure a provision under which an accelerated procedure could, subject to certain conditions, be applied to cases of manifest urgency. Under such a procedure, the Court would be empowered, in accordance with the particular features of each individual case, to omit or to accelerate certain stages of the procedure, without having to follow an inflexible rule to be applied automatically to any particular category of cases.

It is likewise desirable for specific procedures to be introduced enabling the Court of First Instance to rule rapidly on the substance of cases in which there is a degree of urgency.   Such procedures would reduce the written pleadings to the essential minimum and assign greater importance to the hearing, and should result in decisions being reached more swiftly.   They would meet the legitimate and pressing expectations which arise in areas as diverse as the merger of undertakings and public access to administrative documents.

(ii) Changes in the oral procedure

In proceedings before the Court of Justice, the hearing must not become a ritual where the parties concerned merely repeat word for word the arguments which they have already presented during the written procedure.

While the Court of Justice recognises the usefulness of the oral procedure and does not wish to deny the parties concerned their right to a hearing, it considers that more careful consideration should be given to its use. To that

end, it would be appropriate to provide, in Articles 44a and 104(4) of the
Rules of Procedure, that a hearing is to take place either if the Court so
decides of its own motion or if a reasoned application is made by one of those
parties or one of the persons referred to in Article 20 of the EC Statute of
the Court of Justice, setting out the points on which that party or person
wishes to be heard. The condition that the application must be reasoned will
require the party or the person concerned to identify the points to be raised
at the hearing and will therefore make the hearing more useful.

In proceedings before the Court of First Instance, which is called on to carry
out in-depth examinations of complex sets of facts, the value of hearings is
more fundamental and could even be reinforced under the accelerated procedures
referred to above.

(iii) Directions and information

In order to render the proceedings more efficient and better suited to the
circumstances of each individual case, the Court should be able, in addition,
to use two procedural instruments which are available to the European Court
of Human Rights. First, the Court should have the power to issue practice
directions, particularly in relation to issues such as the holding of hearings
and the filing of pleadings and other documents (see Rule 32 of the Rules of
Court of the European Court of Human Rights). Second, it should be open to
the Judge-Rapporteur, in consultation with the Advocate General, to request
the parties to submit, within a given time-limit, any factual information,
documents or other material which he considers relevant (see Rule 49).

2. *Preliminary reference procedure in particular*

(i) Requests for clarification

In many orders for reference, the national court does not set out the factual
and/or legal context in sufficient detail or fails to provide enough
information as to the relevance of the questions raised. The ambiguities with
which the Court is faced in such cases can have the effect of lengthening

proceedings. An appropriate solution would be to insert in the Rules of Procedure a provision comparable to Article 96(4) of the Rules of Procedure of the EFTA Court (OJ 1994 L 278, p. 1), under which the latter may ask the national court for clarification.

(ii) Simplified procedures

Where a question submitted for a preliminary ruling is manifestly identical to a question on which the Court has already ruled, Article 104(3) of the Rules of Procedure allows the Court to give its ruling by reasoned order, but only after the persons referred to in Article 20 of the Statute have submitted their observations.

That provision is concerned with exceptional cases only, whereas a number of preliminary reference proceedings are such as to warrant the application of a simplified procedure. It would therefore be desirable to extend the possibility of deciding by order questions which have been submitted for a preliminary ruling.

For that purpose, the Court proposes that Article 104 of the Rules of Procedure should be amended to allow it to give preliminary rulings by order on simple questions to which the answer is straightforward and on questions which, having regard to the existing case-law, do not raise any new issue. However, the simplified procedure would be applied only on condition that the persons referred to in Article 20 of the Statute of the Court are first consulted on the matter.

3. *Conclusions*

Adoption of the amendments to its Rules of Procedure proposed above would help to enable the Court to focus its attention on the really important cases and could also have a positive impact on the time required for judgments to be given.

The Court notes that the Council has already stressed the urgent need for an examination as soon as possible of ways of reducing the time required to decide orders for reference which are submitted to it. [4]

---

[4] — Declaration, annexed to the minutes of the Council, adopted during the Justice and Home Affairs Council on 28 and 29 May 1998 when drawing up the Convention on Jurisdiction and the Recognition and Enforcement of Judgments in Matrimonial Matters (OJ 1998 C 221, p. 18).

Chapter III

Proposed measures involving amendment of the Treaties or Statutes

In addition to improvements which can be achieved by amending the Rules of Procedure, several measures could be contemplated at once without awaiting the outcome of an overall discussion on the function and organisation of the system of justice in the Community.

The three proposals set out below involve conferring on the Court of Justice and the Court of First Instance the power to amend their Rules of Procedure themselves, introducing a system for filtering appeals and altering the way in which staff cases are handled.

1. *Amendment of the Rules of Procedure*

The foreseeable increase in the number of cases may necessitate more frequent modifications of the Rules of Procedure to enable the Court of Justice and the Court of First Instance to guarantee the proper conduct of proceedings before them.

Under Article 245 EC, any amendment to the Rules of Procedure of the Court of Justice requires the unanimous approval of the Council. The same applies in the case of the Rules of Procedure of the Court of First Instance, by virtue of Article 225 EC.

There is a risk, in an enlarged Union with a Council of 20 or more members, that maintenance of this requirement will paralyse the process of amending the Rules of Procedure.

For those reasons, both Courts wish Article 245 EC, the corresponding provisions in the ECSC and Euratom Treaties and Article 225 EC to be amended so as to empower them to adopt their own Rules of Procedure or, at the very least, so that the Rules require Council approval by a qualified majority only.

It should be borne in mind that, within the framework of the Council of Europe, the Member States have accorded the European Court of Human Rights, ever since it was set up in 1954, the power to adopt its own rules of procedure.

Provisions of such importance that they should continue to be a matter for the Council could be inserted in Title III ("Procedure") of the Statute of the Court of Justice.

2. *Filtering of appeals*

Where questions raised in an appeal before the Court of Justice have already been considered and decided by an independent tribunal whose function is to establish the facts and apply the law in a dispute before that dispute is submitted to the Court of First Instance, the introduction of a filtering procedure for appeals to the Court of Justice could be justified. That procedure would involve the lodging of an application, on which the Court of Justice would rule without *inter partes* proceedings, before an appeal could be made.

Such a filtering procedure would seem appropriate in any event in the present situation of Community trade mark proceedings. Without prejudice to its possible adoption in other instances, it would also appear suited to staff cases, should the decision be made to set up interinstitutional tribunals with competence in this area, as proposed in section 3 below.

In view of the upward trend in the percentage of decisions of the Court of First Instance which are appealed and the considerable increase in the number of decisions made by that Court, such a measure, even if of limited application, would constitute a useful innovation.

The possibility of introducing a filter for preliminary reference proceedings is examined separately in section 3 of Chapter IV below.

3. *Changes to the handling of staff cases*

It would be possible to alter the way in which staff cases are handled without denying access to the Community judicature.   Interinstitutional tribunals could be set up to deal with applications.   These could be composed of an independent lawyer and assessors enjoying the confidence of the administration and of the staff.   They would be entrusted with the task of conciliation and, where appropriate, of ruling on disputes.   Their decisions could be challenged in proceedings before the Court of First Instance.   Any appeal to the Court of Justice would have to be subject to a very strict filtering procedure.   It would also be appropriate, when carrying out such a reform of the means of redress available to staff, to examine the question of where the burden of costs should fall.

Chapter IV

Thoughts on possible changes to the judicial system

As constituted at present, the Court of Justice, to which a Court of First Instance has been attached, is required to ensure, pursuant to the powers conferred on it, that in the interpretation and application of the Treaties the law is observed (Article 220 EC). However, jurisdiction to give preliminary rulings continues to be reserved to the Court of Justice. In addition, the Court of Justice hears and determines actions against Member States for failure to fulfil their obligations and direct actions for annulment, particularly in so far as they concern disputes between institutions, actions for failure to act, actions brought by Member States challenging legislative measures of general application and appeals from judgments of the Court of First Instance.

Measures of an organisational and procedural nature may help the Court of Justice and the Court of First Instance to cope in the short term with the increase in the volume of cases caused by the developments mentioned in Chapter I. However, more fundamental measures must be considered. In a European Union possessing very extensive powers and covering a wider area, the volume of actions, appeals and references for preliminary rulings is bound to reach unprecedented levels, exceeding the capacity of the existing judicial structure.

All ideas on the future of the Community's judicial system must take into account three fundamental requirements:

- the need to secure the unity of Community law by means of a supreme court;
- the need to ensure that the judicial system is transparent, comprehensible and accessible to the public;
- the need to dispense justice without unacceptable delay.

The measures referred to below must be assessed in the light of those requirements. The following thoughts and ideas, which are intended at this stage to stimulate discussion, do not constitute proposals for reform in any strict sense.

1. *The composition and organisation of the Court of Justice and the Court of First Instance*

(i) *The Court of Justice*

Although the link between nationality and membership of the Court of Justice or of the Court of First Instance is not provided for in the Treaty, it has always been tacitly agreed that there should be one judge from each Member State. Moreover, whenever the European Union has in the past been composed of an even number of Member States, an additional judge has been appointed in order to avoid the need for a judge to withdraw on account of the risk of a tied vote.

Five or six new States may accede to the Union in the not-too-distant future, to be followed, at a later stage, by at least five more. If the principle of "one judge per Member State" were to be maintained, the number of judges at the Court of Justice would increase from 15 to 21, and subsequently to 25 or more.

The Intergovernmental Conference will clearly need to consider whether the existing relationship between the number of judges and the number of Member States should be maintained following any enlargement of the European Union.

From the standpoint of maintaining a consistent body of case-law, a limit on the number of judges offers certain advantages which should not be underestimated. As matters stand, all the judges are still able to work together closely in the hearings and deliberations of the full Court.

As the Court of Justice pointed out in its 1995 Report [5] concerning this issue, two distinct considerations must be weighed in the balance:

---

[5] – Report of the Court of Justice on certain aspects of the application of the Treaty on European Union, Luxembourg, May 1995, point 16.

"On the one hand, any significant increase in the number of judges might mean that the plenary session of the Court would cross the invisible boundary between a collegiate court and a deliberative assembly. Moreover, as the great majority of cases would be heard by Chambers, this increase could pose a threat to the consistency of the case-law.

On the other hand, the presence of members from all the national legal systems in the Court is undoubtedly conducive to harmonious development of Community case-law, taking into account concepts regarded as fundamental in the various Member States and thus enhancing the acceptability of the solutions arrived at. It may also be considered that the presence of a judge from each Member State enhances the legitimacy of the Court."

If the number of judges at the Court were greatly to exceed 15, questions would inevitably arise as to the organisational measures needed to guarantee the consistency and uniformity of its case-law.

The Court itself would need, at the appropriate time, to find practical and effective ways of eliminating the risk of inconsistency and lack of cohesion in its case-law. Consequently, it does not appear necessary or even desirable at the present time to seek to anticipate, by the adoption of inflexible measures, the changes in the organisation of the Court which might be needed if its composition were to be altered.

(ii) *The Court of First Instance*

An increase in the number of Members of the Court of First Instance would not create the same problems. Although the resulting increase in the number of Chambers would necessitate additional measures for the coordination of the case-law, the intervention of the Court of Justice as the court of last instance should make it possible to ensure its unity.

Consequently, adjusting the number of judges in line with the growing volume of cases would constitute an appropriate means of avoiding congestion in the first-instance Community court. It is in that context that the "Proposals submitted by the Court of Justice and the Court of First Instance concerning the new intellectual property proceedings" recommended that the number of judges of the Court of First Instance should be increased in order to handle the influx of cases concerning the Community trade mark.

As to the structure of the Court of First Instance, any need for particular specialisation can be catered for, where appropriate, by the existing power of that Court to decide on the allocation of judges to Chambers and on the criteria governing the assignment of cases to those Chambers; however, the growth of litigation in certain areas, and in particular the possible attribution of jurisdiction in the field of patents, may necessitate a review of the situation in the future.

Lastly, the current administrative and budgetary structure may prove incapable of meeting the requirements of the two Courts, and may need to be adapted accordingly.

2. *Transfer to the Court of First Instance of jurisdiction to hear and determine direct actions*

As regards direct actions brought by Member States and the institutions, there are no grounds at present for proposing the transfer of any heads of jurisdiction over and above those whose transfer has already been proposed by the Court of Justice. However, the possibility cannot be ruled out that it may become necessary, if the volume of cases continues to grow, to review the basis on which jurisdiction is allocated between the two Community courts and to transfer further heads of jurisdiction to the Court of First Instance. Moreover, this could be done without amending the Treaty, pursuant to Article 225 EC.

It should be noted that the proposals for transferring jurisdiction which have recently been submitted to the Council are not aimed at reducing the volume of cases before the Court of Justice; they have been prompted solely by a concern to ensure the proper administration of justice.

3. *Reform of the system of references for a preliminary ruling*

The constant growth in the number of references for preliminary rulings emanating from courts and tribunals of the Member States carries with it a serious risk that the Court of Justice will be overwhelmed by its case-load. If current trends continue without any reform of the machinery for dealing with cases, not only will proceedings become more protracted, to the detriment of the proper working of the preliminary ruling system, but the Court of Justice will also be obliged to conduct its deliberations with such dispatch that it will no longer be able to apply to cases the thorough consideration necessary for it to give a useful reply to the questions referred.

It is highly likely that the impact of its decisions will diminish as their number increases and as they deal more frequently with questions of secondary importance or of interest only in the context of the case concerned.

This would seriously undermine those functions have become most characteristic of its role within the Community legal order, namely to guarantee respect for the distribution of powers between the Community and its Member States and between the Community institutions, the uniformity and consistency of Community law and to contribute to the harmonious development of the law within the Union.

If the Court of Justice is to continue to fulfil those essential tasks, it will be necessary to reform the preliminary ruling system in such a way as to curtail the number of cases to be dealt with each year.

Various kinds of measures could be contemplated to reduce the number of references for preliminary rulings which the Court of Justice is called upon to determine.

(i) Limitation of the national courts empowered to make references to the Court of Justice

The two existing options would be (a) to reserve the power to make references to supreme courts alone or (b) to exclude only courts of first instance.

In its 1995 Report, referred to above, the Court of Justice stated that *"to limit access to the Court would have the effect of jeopardising the uniform application and interpretation of Community law throughout the Union, and could deprive individuals of effective judicial protection and undermine the unity of the case-law"*.

Although the specific nature of the rules contained in Title IV of the EC Treaty (visas, asylum, immigration and other policies related to free movement of persons) and of the Conventions adopted by the Council under the third pillar (justice and home affairs) justified derogations in the Treaty of Amsterdam from the principle that all courts and tribunals are to have the power to make references to the Court of Justice, that solution cannot be directly transposed to the rules concerning the internal market and to joint policies and actions.

In its Report, the Court of Justice stated: *"The preliminary ruling system is the veritable cornerstone of the operation of the internal market, since it plays a fundamental role in ensuring that the law established by the Treaties retains its Community character with a view to guaranteeing that that law has the same effect in all circumstances in all the Member States of the European Union. Any weakening, even if only potential, of the uniform application and interpretation of Community law throughout the Union would be liable to give rise to distortions of competition and discrimination between economic operators, thus jeopardising equality of opportunity as between those operators and consequently the proper functioning of the internal market.*

One of the Court's essential tasks is to ensure just such a uniform interpretation, and it discharges that duty by answering the questions put to it by the national courts and tribunals."

For those reasons, it seems necessary for all national courts and tribunals to retain the right to refer questions to the Court of Justice. Although national courts and tribunals against whose decisions an appeal may lie under domestic law should be encouraged to apply Community law themselves, and not to resort too hastily to the solution afforded by a reference to the Court of Justice, the fact remains that the uniform application of Community law frequently depends on the answer to a question of interpretation raised before a national court not having to await the outcome of appeal proceedings but being given by the Court of Justice at the outset, so that the case-law can become established at an early stage in the Member States of the Union.

To deprive certain courts and tribunals of the right to refer questions to the Court of Justice would also be undesirable from the point of view of procedural economy. It would result in proceedings being brought before supreme courts in the Member States solely in order to enable the parties to seek a referral to the Court of Justice.

(ii) The introduction of a filtering system would enable the Court of Justice to decide which of the questions referred needed to be answered by it on account of, for example, their novelty, complexity or importance.

Such a mechanism, designed to weed out at a preliminary stage cases of lesser importance from the point of view of the uniformity and development of Community law, is radically different in nature from the procedure enabling the Court of Justice to rule by way of an order on certain questions referred for a preliminary ruling.

To confer on the Court of Justice the power to assess the expediency of examining questions referred to it for a preliminary ruling, and thus to reduce the number of answers to be given, would undoubtedly have a number of advantages.

The introduction of such a filtering system would prompt national courts and tribunals to exercise selectivity in choosing which questions to refer, and would thus encourage them to exercise yet more fully their functions as Community courts of general jurisdiction.

Moreover, the existence of a filtering mechanism would enable the Court of Justice to concentrate wholly upon questions which are fundamental from the point of view of the uniformity and development of Community law. Lastly, the ensuing reduction in the number of cases would help to reduce the translation work-load, by removing the need to translate observations lodged in written proceedings.

The effectiveness of such a power of selection would depend on its scope and on the conditions governing its exercise. In order effectively to stem the inflow of references for preliminary rulings, there would be a need for selection criteria capable of being applied in a flexible and prudent manner.

However, the introduction of a filtering mechanism in this area would involve drawbacks which should not be underestimated. Even if such a mechanism were applicable only to courts and tribunals which may, but are not bound to, refer questions to the Court of Justice, this might distort the "judicial cooperation" which has become established in the Community and which "requires the national court and the Court of Justice, both keeping within their respective jurisdiction, (...) to make direct and complementary contributions to the working out of a decision" (judgment in Case 16/65 *Schwarze* v *Einfuhr- und Vorratsstelle Getreide* [1965] ECR 877).

That cooperation is founded, in principle, on the assumption that the Court of Justice will answer any question referred by a national court or tribunal which fulfils the conditions of admissibility. If that assumption can no longer be made, national courts and tribunals might well refrain from referring questions to the Court of Justice, in order to avoid the risk of their references being rejected for lack of interest. Such a development would jeopardise the machinery for ensuring that Community law is interpreted uniformly throughout the Member States.

In order to mitigate the drawbacks of a filtering mechanism, a system could be set up whereby the national court would be requested to include in its decision a proposed reply to the question referred. That would lessen the adverse effect of the filtering mechanism on the cooperation between the national court and the Court of Justice, while the proposed reply could at the same time serve as the basis for deciding which questions need to be answered by the Court of Justice and which can be answered in the terms indicated.

A more radical variant of the system would be to alter the preliminary ruling procedure so that national courts which are not bound to refer questions to the Court of Justice would be required, before making any reference, first to give judgment in cases raising questions concerning the interpretation of Community law. It would then be open to any party to the proceedings to request the national court to forward its judgment to the Court of Justice and to make a reference for a ruling on those points of Community law in respect of which that party contests the validity of the judgment given. This would give the Court of Justice the opportunity of assessing, at the filtering stage, whether it needed to give its own ruling on the interpretation of Community law arrived at in the contested judgment.

Such a procedure, resembling an appeal in cassation, would facilitate the task of the Court of Justice. It would enable the Court to give its ruling on the reference in full knowledge of the national context, both factual and legal, in which the points of Community law raised in the case in question fall to be interpreted.

However, such a procedure would involve a fundamental change in the way in which the preliminary ruling system currently operates. Judicial cooperation between the national courts and the Court of Justice would be transformed into a hierarchical system, in which it would be for the parties to an action to decide whether to require the national court to make a reference to the Court of Justice, and in which the national court would be bound, depending on the circumstances, to revise its earlier judgment so as to bring it into line with a ruling given by the Court of Justice. From the point of view of national procedural law, this aspect of the system would doubtless raise problems which could not easily be resolved.

Lastly, a party who was not satisfied with a judgment given by a national court might well be more eager to seek a ruling from the Court of Justice - if only in order to defer enforcement of the judgment — than the referring court itself.

Thus, a system of filtering references for preliminary rulings - even one more flexible than that just envisaged - would not be easy to reconcile with the principle of mutual cooperation between the national courts and the Court of Justice which is a feature of the preliminary ruling procedure and which, by ensuring uniformity and consistency in the interpretation of Community law, has made such a major contribution to the proper working of the internal market. Nevertheless, a mechanism giving the Court of Justice the power to assess the appropriateness of a reference would constitute a possible solution to the problem of an excessive case-load. From that point of view, there is much to be said for a more thorough examination of such a mechanism and of the ways of implementing it.

(iii) Conferral on the Court of First Instance of jurisdiction in preliminary ruling proceedings

The difficulties attending a transfer to the Court of First Instance of jurisdiction in proceedings for a preliminary ruling have been indicated by the Court of Justice in its 1995 Report, referred to above. Despite those difficulties, the idea of such a transfer should not be rejected out of hand.

Conferral on the Court of First Instance of jurisdiction in this area would have the effect of transferring to it part of the work-load, even though it will itself have to contend with an influx of direct actions far exceeding the limits of its current capacity. Such a transfer would need to be accompanied by a corresponding increase in the number of judges.

It would also be necessary to ensure, by means of machinery for referrals and/or appeals in cases involving points of general legal interest, that the most important questions always come before the Court of Justice in the end.

Similar reasoning could apply to the idea of transferring jurisdiction in preliminary ruling proceedings to specialised courts, should such courts be set up in the future.

(iv) <u>The creation or designation, in each Member State, of decentralised judicial bodies responsible for dealing with references for preliminary rulings from courts within their area of territorial jurisdiction</u>

Such bodies, specialising in Community law, would be closer than the Court of Justice to the national legal system in which the questions referred were to be answered. Furthermore, they would operate in the language or languages of the State concerned, thereby affording the national courts and tribunals the widest possible access to the preliminary ruling procedure by avoiding the congestion resulting from the need for translation.

Those courts could have the status either of a Community or of a national body. Whatever the status chosen, the important factor would be to maintain the benefit gained from a substantial reduction in the translation burden borne by the Court of Justice.

A system of that kind, which would entail a very significant change from the existing mechanism, would undeniably involve major drawbacks as regards the maintenance of uniformity in the interpretation and application of Community law.

Any reorganisation of the preliminary ruling procedure on a national or regional basis, regardless of whether jurisdiction is conferred on national or on Community courts, involves a serious risk of shattering the unity of Community law, which constitutes one of the cornerstones of the Union and which will become still more vital and vulnerable as a result of enlargement of the Union. Jurisdiction to determine the final and binding interpretation of a Community rule, as well as the validity of that rule, should therefore be vested in a single court covering the whole of the Union.

However, certain measures may be envisaged which would reduce the risks inherent in a decentralised system. First, the national judicial bodies to be set up should have the power to refer to the Court of Justice any question of interpretation which raises legal issues of general relevance to the unity or development of Community law. Furthermore, provision would need to be made for the possibility of appealing to the Court of Justice "on a point of general legal interest", in accordance with detailed procedures to be laid

down, against preliminary rulings given by those bodies. This would, in
effect, create a decentralised filtering system in this area which would
nevertheless remain subject to review by the Court of Justice.

Certain problems could arise, however, as a result of the links between those
courts and the various national legal systems, which diverge considerably from
one another, at any rate if they are accorded the status of national courts.
In order to ensure that their decisions are sufficiently authoritative in the
national legal order, they would need to be established at the highest level
of the judicial hierarchy of the Member States. Consequently, the Member
States would have to decide to which of their supreme courts such a judicial
body should be attached; alternatively, if that proved impossible to decide,
it would be necessary to establish a forum common to the highest courts of the
State concerned.

Subject to that, the Court of Justice considers that, whilst the difficulties
connected with the implementation of a system for the decentralisation of the
preliminary ruling procedure should not be underestimated, in-depth
consideration should nevertheless be given to a system of that kind and to its
various detailed aspects.

* * *

Implementation of fundamental reforms of the judicial system, such as the
introduction of a filtering mechanism or the creation of new judicial bodies,
is not necessarily essential prior to the next round of enlargement. However,
in so far as the Member States are able to agree on certain lines of approach
with a sufficient degree of precision, they could profitably insert in the
Treaty provisions enabling the institutions of the Union progressively to
adopt the requisite measures as and when they are needed.

Annex I

Court of Justice

Cases completed - 1.1.90 to 31.12.98

	90	91	92	93	94	95	96	97	98
References for a preliminary ruling	162	131	157	196	163	162	205	301	246
Direct actions	124	142	171	583	100	96	113	116	136
Appeals		11	13	11	20	20	26	34	36
Special proceedings	6	4	3	2	9	9	4	5	2
Total	302*	288	344	792	292	287	348	456	420

* including 10 staff cases.

Cases brought - 1.1.90 to 31.12.98

	90	91	92	93	94	95	96	97	98
References for a preliminary ruling	141	186	162	204	203	251	256	239	264
Direct actions	221	140	251	265	125	109	132	169	147
Appeals	16	14	25	17	13	48	28	35	70
Special proceedings	6	3	2	4	10	7	7	2	4
Total	384	343	440	490	351	415	423	445	485

Cases pending 1990 to 1998

	90	91	92	93	94	95	96	97	98
References for a preliminary ruling	209	264	269	277	317	406	457	395	413
Direct actions	355	353	433	115	140	153	172	225	236
Appeals	16	19	31	37	30	58	60	61	95
Special proceedings	3	2	1	3	4	2	5	2	4
Total	583	638	734	432	491	619	694	683	748

Duration of proceedings 1990 to 1998*

	90	91	92	93	94	95	96	97	98
References for a preliminary ruling	17.4	18.2	18.8	20.4	18.0	20.5	20.8	21.4	21.4
Direct actions	25.5	24.2	25.8	22.9	20.8	17.1	19.6	19.7	21.0
Appeals		15.4	17.5	19.2	21.2	18.5	14.0	17.4	20.3

* average duration, expressed in months and tenths of months.

Court of First Instance

Cases brought - 1.1.90 to 31.12.98

	90	91	92	93	94	95	96	97	98
Staff cases	43	81	79	83	81	79	98	155	79
Other cases	12	12	36	506	316	165	122	469	136
Special proceedings	4	2	8	7	12	9	9	20	23
Total	59	95	123	596	409	253	229	644	238

Cases completed - 1.1.90 to 31.12.98

	90	91	92	93	94	95	96	97	98
Staff cases	71	48	76	79	78	64	79	81	120
Other cases	9	19	41	20	358	186	98	92	199
Special proceedings	2	-	8	7	6	15	9	13	29
Total	82	67	125	106	442	265	186	186	348

Cases pending - 1.1.90 to 31.12.98

	90	91	92	93	94	95	96	97	98
Staff cases	63	96	99	103	106	121	140	214	173
Other cases	80	73	68	554	512	491	515	892	830
Special proceedings	2	4	4	4	10	4	4	11	5
Total	145	173	171	661	628	616	659	1117	1008

ANNEX II

1. Council Act of 23 July 1996 drawing up the Protocol on the interpretation, by way of preliminary rulings, by the Court of Justice of the Convention on the establishment of a European Police Office (OJ 1996 C 299, p. 1).

2. Council Act of 27 September 1996 drawing up a Protocol to the Convention on the protection of the European Communities' financial interests, Art. 8 (OJ 1996 C 313, p. 1).

3. Council Act of 29 November 1996 drawing up the Protocol on the interpretation, by way of preliminary rulings, by the Court of Justice of the Convention on the protection of the European Communities' financial interests (OJ 1997 C 151, p. 1).

4. Council Act of 26 July 1995 drawing up the Convention on the use of information technology for customs purposes, Art. 27 (OJ 1995 C 316, p. 33).

5. Council Act of 29 November 1996 drawing up the Protocol on the interpretation, by way of preliminary rulings, by the Court of Justice of the Convention on the use of information technology for customs purposes (OJ 1997 C 151, p. 15).

6. Council Act of 26 May 1997 drawing up the Protocol on the interpretation, by the Court of Justice, of the Convention on the service in the Member States of the European Union of judicial and extrajudicial documents in civil or commercial matters, of the same date (Art. 17 of the Convention, signed on the same date) (OJ 1997 C 261, p. 17).

7. Council Act of 19 June 1997 drawing up the Second Protocol of the Convention on the protection of the European Communities' financial interests, Arts 13, 14 and 15 (OJ 1997 C 221, p. 11).

8. Council Act of 18 December 1997 drawing up the Convention on mutual assistance and cooperation between customs administrations, Art. 26 (OJ 1998 C 24, p. 1).

9. Council Act of 26 May 1997 drawing up the Convention on the fight against corruption involving officials of the European Communities or officials of Member States of the European Union, Art. 12 (OJ 1997 C 195, p. 1).

10. Council Act of 28 May 1998 drawing up the Protocol on the interpretation by the Court of Justice of the Convention on Jurisdiction and the Recognition and Enforcement of Judgments in Matrimonial Matters (Art. 45 of the Convention, signed on the same date' (OJ 1998 C 221, p. 19).

11. Council Act of 17 June 1998 drawing up the Convention on Driving Disqualifications. Art. 14 (OJ 1998 C 216, p. 1).

Document 3

*The Report by the Working Party on the Future
of the European Communities' Court System
('The Wise Persons' Report
or 'The Due Report')*

January 2000

CONTENTS

REPORT OF THE WORKING PARTY

By decision dated 20 April and 4 May 1999, the European Commission set up a Working Party on the Future of the European Court of Justice, with the following remit:

> "It shall be the task of the Group of Wise Men to review the various possible courses which may be taken in order to maintain the quality and consistency of case law in the years to come, bearing in mind the number and present duration of proceedings and foreseeable developments, in particular in the light of new jurisdiction conferred upon the Court by the Amsterdam Treaty and the forthcoming enlargement.

> To this end, it shall consider the efficiency of existing legal remedies, the composition of the Courts, the procedural rules and, where appropriate, the overall structure of the judiciary, including the relationship between Community courts and national courts".

The Working Party adopted this report on 18 and 19 January 2000; it sets out to answer these questions.

I.   Number and duration of proceedings in cases before the Community courts

A.   The pattern until the end of 1998

A close look at the Community judicial statistics throws three phenomena into sharp relief, all of them familiar enough and all of them evidence of a serious crisis in the current court system in the Communities.

They are:

–   the steady rise in the number of cases brought before the two Community courts;

–   the inadequate number of cases terminated in relation to the number of new cases brought;

–   the lengthening time taken by proceedings.

1.   The expansion of Community litigation to some extent mirrors the trend observed in all the Member States in the second half of the 20th Century, the origins of which lie both in the growing complexity of social relationships and in the rising economic and cultural standards of people at large, who are now better placed to defend their rights. But it has to be acknowledged that the expansion in the number of actions brought in the Community courts is a quite exceptional phenomenon, flowing from two additional factors: the gradual extension of the areas in which Community law applies and the regular enlargement of the Community.

The result was that in 1998, 723 new actions were brought in the Community courts taken together (Court of Justice and Court of First Instance ("the CFI")), as against only 279 in 1980 (when the Court of Justice was the only Community court); this represents a 159% increase in 19 years.

One of the reasons for the decision to establish the CFI in 1989 was to help solve the problem arising in these terms, and it is therefore worth looking at the trend in the number of cases commenced since then in each of the two courts individually.

(a)   The aggregate number of new cases brought in the Court of Justice rose from 384 in 1990 to 485 in 1998, a 26% rise in nine years, which is actually rather slower than in the preceding decade.

But this overall slowdown conceals two contrary motions:

–   the effect of the establishment of the CFI and the gradual extension of its jurisdiction has been a sharp drop in the number of direct actions in the Court of Justice, from 222 in 1990 to 147 in 1998 – a third in nine years;

–   meanwhile, the number of references for preliminary rulings maintained a steady growth rate, far higher than the rate for the aggregate number of new actions in the Court of Justice, which registered 264 requests for preliminary rulings in 1998, up from 141 in 1990 – 87% in nine years.

In addition there is the constant rise in the number of appeals against judgments of the CFI (70 in 1998, accounting for 14.5% of new cases in the Court of Justice that year and 31.3 % of the appealable CFI judgments).

(b)   There is little to be learned from the gross annual figures for new cases in the CFI. In recent years the figures have been somewhat distorted both by transfers from the Court of Justice under decisions extending the CFI's jurisdiction and by the introduction of a number of what might be termed group actions (milk quotas and customs agents, to name but two).

If, however, we take as our point of reference a situation that might be regarded as "normal", without such distorting factors, the result, as expected, is a sharp rise in the number of new CFI cases, which doubled in seven years, from 116 in 1992 to 238 in 1998. There is nothing surprising about this, as we are looking at a court whose rising power has been organised only gradually.

2.   The second conclusion to be drawn from the Community's judicial statistics is the well-nigh permanent inadequacy of the number of cases terminated in relation to the number of new cases brought.

The annual deficit is clear in the statistics both of the Court of Justice and of the CFI.

- In the Court of Justice it can be seen that between 1990 and 1998 the number of cases terminated[1] exceeded the number of new cases only in 1997. And for the full nine-year period the number of cases terminated was 3 085, as against 3 778 commenced, a cumulative deficit of 693 cases.

- The corresponding figures for the CFI are less meaningful: transfers from the Court of Justice in some years, and the influx of "group actions" in others, generated distortions which it was not possible to overcome immediately.

It is true that from 1992 to 1998 the Court of First Instance terminated a total of 1 652 cases while 2 485 new cases were commenced – an aggregate deficit of 833 cases, but it must be remembered that in 1993 and 1994, 465 cases were transferred from the Court of Justice to the CFI when the CFI's jurisdiction was extended.

It is interesting that in 1998 the number of cases terminated (excluding "group actions") – 279 – exceeded the number of new cases (including "group actions") – 238. There are grounds for hoping that this is the first sign of an increase in the CFI's productive capacity, which was reinforced by the last round of enlargement.

---

[1] Gross figures, including group actions, as for the number of new cases.

3.   The result to be expected of the phenomenon described at point 2 is, of course, a rise in the back-log of cases, with a parallel rise in the time taken for cases to come to judgment.

(a)   The seriousness of the situation in the Court of Justice must be underscored.

The number of cases outstanding on 31 December each year admittedly rose only moderately between 1990 and 1998 – from 583 to 748. But the figures give only a superficial impression, as they do not take account of the major volume of cases transferred from the Court of Justice to the CFI in that period. The back-log of cases outstanding at the Court of Justice fell from 736 at the end of 1992 to 433 at the end of 1993 as a result of that year's transfers. But the order book then expanded inexorably to reach 748 at the end of 1998 – 72% in just five years.

The consequence of this situation is that, despite a substantial rise in the number of cases terminated by the Court (from 302 in 1990 to 420 in 1998), the duration of proceedings lengthened markedly.

°   The transfers of jurisdiction to hear direct actions to the CFI alleviated the burden on the Court of Justice. The average time taken for this type of action to come to judgment – 24.9 months in 1990 – was down to 21 months in 1998. But the rising trend has resumed since 1996, probably under the impact of the sharp increase in the number of infringement proceedings. And it has become clear that the establishment of the CFI has not even provided the means of reverting to the average duration of proceedings in 1983 – 18 months – even though many of these actions were uncontested infringement proceedings which come to judgment relatively quickly.

°   In reality, the situation is especially preoccupying where preliminary rulings are concerned. The trend towards longer procedural delays has been uninterrupted: 12.6 months in 1983, 17.4 in 1990 and 21.4 in 1998. As these cases have to be fitted into proceedings in the national courts, it is essential that the 1983 situation, when preliminary rulings were generally given within the year, be restored. Preserving a genuine dialogue between the Court of Justice and the national courts depends on this.

°   One last point concerns the time taken for an appeal against a judgment of the CFI to come to judgment itself – 20.3 months in 1998. This, of course is added on to the time taken by the CFI to give its original judgment.

b)   The situation at the CFI has not yet stabilised.

The gradual extension of its jurisdiction and the transfers from the Court of Justice have inevitably lengthened its order book, from 171 cases in 1992 to 1,007 cases at the end of 1998. Its order book is considerably larger than that of the Court of Justice, but it does not have the same capacity to hear and determine cases (348 cases terminated in 1998, as against 420 in the Court of Justice). This situation obviously needs remedying. It is true that a large number of cases, notably in competition matters, are highly complex and call for meticulous, time-consuming examination. On the other hand the CFI often has to deal with group actions, where cases can be joined.

In any event, the current average time taken to examine a case coming to judgment before the CFI is far too long – 29.3 months in 1997, 32.2 months in 1998.

It is clear from the foregoing survey that since the end of 1998 the Community court system has not been able to face the constant growth of litigation and can no longer hear and determine the cases brought before it within an acceptable period of time.

B.   Future prospects

There is no doubt that in the absence of reform several decisions already taken or in preparation would seriously aggravate the already worrying situation described above.

- Among the measures already taken, the effects of which will be felt in the near future, the first to be mentioned is the entry into operation of the Community Trade-Mark Regulation, which has already prompted a mass of cases now pending at the Alicante Office.

   These cases will inevitably have a very rapid impact on the operation of the CFI and, subsequently, the Court of Justice.

Then, there are the new powers conferred on the Court of Justice by the Amsterdam Treaty, either under the new Title IV of the EC Treaty regarding visas, asylum, immigration, and judicial cooperation in civil matters with a trans-frontier impact, or under Title VI of the Union Treaty, regarding police and judicial cooperation in criminal matters.

It is not yet possible to measure the true impact of these new provisions on the Courts' workload, but what is certain is that much of the litigation will involve group actions in several Member States; whatever precautions may have been taken in the Treaties to alleviate the burden facing the Community courts, an aggravation of the present situation must inevitably be expected.

But this probably not where the real problem lies. The biggest challenge to the Community court system will flow from the enlargement of the Union envisaged for the coming years.

- The number of Member States will in all likelihood virtually double: the volume of litigation that will result from this will expand correspondingly in the more or less long term.

- There is also the burning question as to how the Court of Justice can operate satisfactorily with a much greater number of members.

- Lastly, it is important to be aware of the aggravation of the language problems that the Community courts will have to tackle. Eleven procedural languages are currently in use. All procedural documents received from parties to actions have to be translated from all these languages into the single working language, and all judgments drafted in the working language have to be translated into all of them. The cost of this process in terms of both money and time already represents a crushing burden. How can this be made tolerable if the number of languages also doubles?

For all these reasons, it is clear that the current structures of the Community court system can now longer face up to the inexorable evolution of the Union.

The European Council has repeatedly insisted on the need to adapt the Council and the Commission to the demands of an enlarged Union. The Working Party takes the liberty of suggesting that the same need arises – and urgently – as regards the Community court system.

II.   The Working Party's proposals

In drawing up the following proposals, the Working Party has highlighted three objectives, which seem to it to be fundamental. These are:

- to ensure that Community law is applied as uniformly as possible throughout the territory of the Union;

- to increase the effectiveness of the decisions of the Community courts by shortening proceedings;

- to maintain the protection conferred by the Courts on the citizens of the Union, Member States and Community institutions.

The Working Party stresses that its proposals are long-term ones and are intended to show what the system of Community courts could be like some fifteen years hence. The measures recommended do not need to be implemented as one: those who decide will have to take account of the changes that will occur in the years ahead. It is important, however, that the reforms are not simply ad hoc measures based on the needs of the moment, but should fit in with a plan which has been agreed within the Community institutions.

The Working Party's proposals for reform are divided into five categories, as follows:

A.   Preliminary rulings
B.   Direct actions
C.   Categories of special cases
D.   Procedural reforms
E.   Membership of the Community Courts

A.   **Preliminary rulings**

This is undoubtedly the most important issue currently confronting the Community Courts.

Through the direct dialogue which it has made possible between each national court and the Court of Justice, as the supreme judicial body in the Community, through the authority and certainty of the answers it thereby gives to the questions raised and through the simplicity of its operation, the current system of preliminary rulings has proved to be the most effective means of securing the uniform application of Community law throughout the Union, thereby forming the keystone of the Community's legal order.

The Working Party considers that the system's undeniable success is related to its current distinctive features and that consequently it should basically still be the Court of Justice which gives preliminary rulings, at least while the development of the Union so permits.

It is particularly desirable that the countries joining after the next enlargements should be able to benefit, as have the older Member States, from this exceptional instrument of integration into the Community legal order.

In the meantime, however, ways still have to be found of ensuring that the Court is not swamped by the tide of requests for preliminary rulings, whose number, as we have seen, is continually increasing.

1.   The Working Party immediately rejected two proposals put forward as medium-term solutions.

a)   The first of these involved making courts of final instance the only courts entitled to refer questions.

At 31 December 1998, about three-quarters of the preliminary questions referred to the Court *ab initio* came from courts other than national courts of final instance. It is clear, therefore, that to deny access to the Court of Justice for the national courts which have hitherto referred the great majority of preliminary questions would make excessive inroads into the cooperation and dialogue which must be maintained between national courts and Community Courts.

Furthermore, such a reform could have a perverse effect at national level by encouraging litigants, or at least the richer ones, to pursue their cases right through to the very highest courts in order to gain access to the Court of Justice by referring a question for a preliminary ruling. The aim is definitely not to create congestion in national courts of final instance.

For similar reasons, the less radical solution of excluding only references from national courts of first instance was also rejected.

b)   As to the second proposal, the Working Party considered that national courts could not be left to settle all questions of Community law by themselves, with the parties being entitled merely to bring the national judgment before the Court of Justice in a sort of longstop appeal claiming breach of Community law.

The Working Party felt that national courts and tribunals should be able to deal with issues of Community law arising in the exercise of their national jurisdiction, by being entitled or obliged to submit questions to the Court of Justice without having to pass through a hierarchy of national courts. Such a proposal would debase the entire system of cooperation established by the Treaties between national courts and the Court of Justice - a system that has proved its worth. Its implementation, indeed, would constitute a significant reform, which would imply that a radical change to the Union's structure had been decided in advance.

2.   The Working Party considers, on the contrary, that other ways should be sought of reducing the Court's workload due to preliminary questions, including the following:

a)   It is necessary, first of all, to encourage national courts to be bolder in applying Community law themselves. It is therefore proposed that three crucial amendments be made to Article 234 (ex Article 177) of the EC Treaty:

-    the first consists in stating explicitly a fundamental principle which is only implicit in the current text of Article 234 and which, consequently, is sometimes lost sight of by certain national courts: this is the principle that the courts of the Member States have full authority to deal with questions of Community law which they encounter in the exercise of their national jurisdiction, subject only to their right or their duty to refer questions to the Court of Justice for a preliminary ruling;

-    the second amendment proposed consists in informing courts other than those of final instance - which have only the option of consulting the Court of Justice - that they must endeavour not to refer questions systematically. When assessing the advisability of referring a question to the Court, such courts shouldconsider both the importance of the question in terms of Community law and whether there is reasonable doubt about the answer. In other words, they should be dissuaded from referring matters to the Court of Justice where Community law clearly states what the answer should be or where the point raised has no real significance for Community law.

The notion of "reasonable doubt" has already been clarified in *Cilfit* (Case 283/81 [1982] ECR 3415), and it will be for the Court of Justice to determine whether or not it needs to be made more flexible. As for the notion of "significance for Community law", this complies with the old maxim *de minimis non curat praetor*, and it is also for the Court of Justice, when requested by national courts, to determine the precise scope which it thinks should be given to it;

- the third amendment concerns the obligation imposed on courts of final instance by the Treaty to consult the Court of Justice when a question of Community law is raised before them. In practice, it has not always been possible to follow such a rigid obligation.

To be consistent with the above remarks on the ordinary courts, there should therefore be an obligation on courts of final instance to consult the Court of Justice only on questions which "are sufficiently important for Community law" and about whose solution there is still "reasonable doubt" after examination by the lower courts.

The Working Party wishes to emphasise that the flexibility which it is proposing to give this obligation does not present a new threat to the uniform application of Community law. There would still be two ways of remedying any breach by a court of final instance, at least where such a breach resulted in a decision which conflicted with Community law:

°   the first is for any other court in the same or another Member State to consult the Court of Justice on the point of Community law in question;

°   the second is for the Commission to bring an action for failure to fulfil its obligations against the Member State whose court has shown ignorance of Community law.

If, despite everything, the Member States felt that such flexibility increased the risk that some national courts of final instance would give incorrect judgments on important questions of Community law, the Working Party sees no reason why the Commission, in its capacity as guardian of the Treaties, should not ask the Court of Justice, without stipulating a time limit, to decide such questions. The resulting decisions of the Court of Justice would simply be intended to restore the uniform application of Community law for the future and, like the appeals in the interest of the law discussed in part C below, could not have any effect on judgments of national courts having the force of "*res judicata*".

- The three amendments to Article 234 of the EC Treaty proposed above lead the Working Party to propose a fourth, which has a different purpose. This is that the rule established in *Foto-Frost* (Case 314/85 [1987] ECR 4199), whereby any national court must consult the Court of Justice when it proposes not to apply a Community act on grounds of invalidity, should be incorporated in the Treaty. The fear is that an amendment of Article 234 which made no reference to this rule could be interpreted as obstructing the application of that Article. This is obviously not desirable, nor is it the Working Party's intention.

An amended version of Article 234 as proposed is given in the Annex.

b)   Secondly: irrelevant, premature or poorly-prepared references and those which concern only the specific application of Community law and not its interpretation should be kept to a minimum. The Court of Justice issued an information note to this effect on 9 December 1996. The Working Party proposes that mandatory provisions, failure to comply with which would render references inadmissible, should be incorporated in the Rules of Procedure. The Court could supplement these with pure recommendations, including for instance a "standard model" for the formulation of references.

c)   Two new rules should be included in the Court's Rules of Procedure:

-    the option should be created of replying to the national court by reasoned order at any stage in the procedure, where the reply is obvious. Examples where this would apply are where preliminary questions can be settled by simply referring to the existing case law or where there can be no reasonable doubt as to the interpretation;

-    secondly, national courts should be encouraged, though in no way obliged, through provisions inserted in the Rules of Procedure, to include in the preliminary questions reasoned grounds for the answers that the national court considers most appropriate. If in such a case the Court of Justice concurs with the national court, it could reply, specifying its reasoning by reference to the reasons given by the national court.

d)   Categories of special cases would be dealt with under special rules so as to shift preliminary questions concerning such cases from the Court of Justice to the Court of First Instance (cf. part C below). Such measures, however, should be exceptional.

e)   Lastly, the Working Party does not conceal that the essential purpose of the proposed reforms is that national courts themselves should be better placed to give informed decisions on a growing number of questions of Community law which they meet in the exercise of their national jurisdiction. It considers that this result can be obtained only through resolute, persistent action by the Member States.

Such action should have two aims:

o   first, there is an urgent need to give better training in Community law to all those involved in referring questions for preliminary rulings, be they judges or lawyers. The training should be complete and not just - as is too often the case at the moment - confined to a description of the Community institutions, without a detailed study of the case law;

o   secondly, powerful information systems should be made available to practitioners, providing them with easy access to the latest information on Community legislation and case law.

Accordingly, the Working Party recommends that the Member States set up national information centres on Community law, with computer links to the Commission's departments and to the Court of Justice's Research and Documentation Service. Run by experienced specialists in Community law, these would give invaluable aid to national judges and lawyers, enabling them gradually to settle, under proper conditions, an increasing number of difficulties themselves, which for lack of adequate information they currently refer to the Court of Justice.

3.   If these recommendations are not implemented, or not implemented satisfactorily, by the Member States, or if for any other reason the number of preliminary questions submitted to the Court becomes an impossible burden, are there any more

radical solutions which, despite everything, could resolve the problem in an acceptable way?

The Working Party considered this question, and examined three improvements which have already been studied by commentators and the Court itself. These are:

-    the Member States might set up devolved judicial bodies specialising in preliminary rulings;

-    the Court might select certain questions from among those referred to it; and

-    extended jurisdiction could be conferred on the Court of First Instance to give preliminary rulings.

The Working Party found that there were advantages, but also grave drawbacks, to each of these solutions.

a)   Setting up new, devolved courts at national level would have the twofold advantage of relieving the Court of Justice of examining those preliminary questions which are not specially significant for Community law and of reducing the administrative costs and time lags currently caused by the translation of the documents for the proceedings.

On the other hand, a devolved system would have serious disadvantages. A reference for a preliminary ruling is a dialogue between the national court hearing the principal action, which is the only court fully familiar with the case, and the Community court, which is alone capable of securing a uniform interpretation of Community law.

To interpose another national court between them would jeopardise the uniform application of Community law, even if that court were obliged to refer specially significant questions to the Court of Justice. What would happen is that the same problem would be considered by three courts in succession, thus prolonging the proceedings. The outcome would be similar, moreover, if all questions were first submitted for assessment by the Court of Justice, which would then remit the less important ones to the devolved court. Such a system could of course provide a degree of uniformity, but it would lose most of the advantages of devolution.

The administration of devolved courts would entail high costs for Member States and could distort the national court structure.

b)   The possibility was also discussed of giving the Court of Justice itself the power to select those preliminary questions which it considered were sufficiently important for Community law; the others would be remitted to the referring courts, possibly with observations that could help national judiciaries.   This would be similar to what the Supreme Court does in the United States.   It is simple and effective and would save money.   However, the Working Party believes that such an arrangement cannot be transposed at present to a system of courts which is radically different from that of the United States: unlike the American system, the Community courtsand national courts are not ranked in a hierarchical relationship   to each other - the system is based entirely on cooperation and dialogue between national courts and the Court of Justice.   It is this cooperation and dialogue which would be upset by such a crude form of selection as that just described.

c)   Lastly, conferring extensive preliminary ruling jurisdiction on the CFI would have the fundamental advantage of not affecting the uniform application of Community law, and the Working Party favours the limited allocation to the CFI of preliminary questions concerning certain special categories (cf. part C below). It therefore proposes that the last sentence of paragraph 1 of Article 225 (ex Article 168a) of the EC Treaty be repealed.

But, for the moment, it would be impossible to apply this approach widely and to transfer to the CFI many preliminary questions, let alone all of them. For one thing, as was pointed out above, the Working Party considers that giving preliminary rulings is the most important task for the development and proper application of Community law and that it would be only right and proper to leave the supreme Community court with responsibility for doing so. The special character of preliminary rulings would also rule out - for reasons of time and given the non-adversarial nature of the procedure - any appeal to the Court of Justice from the CFI's rulings. For another, it must be recognised that a large-scale transfer of preliminary questions to the CFI would simply shift the problem and might seriously disrupt the operation of that court.

In short, the Working Party is sticking to the measures recommended above: their implementation requires that Member States acknowledge their responsibilities. If, later on, these measures were to prove inadequate, it would be up to the competent Community institutions to re-examine the problem in the light of new data emerging.

B.   Direct actions

1.   The fundamental choice to leave to the Court of Justice the essential jurisdiction for preliminary rulings requires that, in order to avoid overburdening it with a caseload that it would be impossible for it to rule on within reasonable time limits, the powers of the Court of First Instance to deal with direct actions be very markedly increased.

In this respect, the Working Group considers that the principle must be established that the Court of First Instance should become the first judicial forum for direct actions. This must apply not only to actions for compensation but also to proceedings for judicial review of the legality of all Community acts, including the lawfulness of legislative measures. All actions for annulment or for a declaration of failure to act would thus in principle fall within the jurisdiction of the Court of First Instance, even where the applicant was a Member State or a Community institution. The two levels of judicial authority in fact constitute an additional guarantee which must benefit the Member States and the Community institutions as much as individuals. It should also be noted that such a development is consonant with the provisions of Article 225 (ex 168a) (1) and (2) of the EC Treaty and may be implemented without amending the Treaty.

2.   However, the Working Party is perfectly aware that the principle that has just been expressed must not have an unbounded scope: there must be a number of exceptions, whose scope, however, must be as limited as possible. It is clear that certain direct actions must be dealt with by the Court of Justice, ruling at first and last instance.

The question therefore arises as to the guiding principle which must govern the choice of direct actions for which the Court will have exclusive competence.

a)   A widely contemplated option would be to attribute to the Court of Justice all the actions of a "constitutional" or "quasi-constitutional" nature only. The Working Party does not automatically dismiss the possibility of using such a criterion, but after careful scrutiny it considers it impossible to use it with the treaties in their current form, because of its imprecision. For one thing, it must be noted that the Treaties make no distinction between those of their provisions which are fundamental in character, and could be regarded as constitutional, and the other provisions. In the second place, the Treaties make no distinction among normative Community acts, between those which are "legislative" and those which are merely "executive" measures. At most it can be said that measures issued by the Commission alone are "executive" measures, but one only has to read a number of Council regulations or directives to establish that they are not the only ones.

Of course, if the efforts made to concentrate the treaties on their fundamental provisions and to define those normative Community acts which were of a legislative type were successful, the question could be re-examined.

b)   In the current circumstances, the Working Party recommends that a more pragmatic guiding principle than this be followed, viz. that of the <u>urgency and importance</u> of settling certain direct actions which are incompatible with the time involved in the two levels of judicial authority.

It is true that all applicants may give good reasons why the judgment of their action is "urgent" and "important". This concept, which should be used to determine the competence of the Court as a first and last instance, should therefore be assessed much more strictly and used to select only those actions for which a rapid judgment is essential to avoid serious problems in the proper functioning of the Community institutions.

3. To give just one example, it would be possible according to this guiding principle to maintain the Court's direct powers for the following cases:

a) actions for failure to fulfil obligations under Articles 226 to 228 (ex 169 to 171) of the EC Treaty. The Working Party nonetheless considers that the current procedure for examining these actions should be thoroughly reviewed.

The number of these actions is constantly on the increase, and in 1998 they accounted for 80% of the direct actions brought before the Court of Justice (118 actions for failure to fulfil obligations out of 147 direct actions). Those cases impose a heavy administrative burden on the Court, particularly regarding translation, despite the fact that a good many of them are not seriously disputed by the Member States involved.

It would appear that, for the Court of Justice, the most helpful reform would be to make the Commission responsible, as is provided for in Article 88 of the ECSC Treaty, for adopting decisions in cases of failure to fulfil obligations, leaving Member States who really disagree with those decisions to bring actions for annulment before the Court of Justice. If a

Member State failed to challenge the Commission's decision before the expiry of the time limit for appeals, or if such an appeal were rejected, the decision finding a failure to fulfil the obligation would become final. On the other hand, it is clear that the Court of Justice would retain its powers under Article 228(2) (ex Article 171) of the EC Treaty to impose a penalty payment on any Member State which has not complied with a decision recording its failure to fulfil its obligations which had become final.

If this proposal were not accepted, the Working Party considers that a very swift and simplified procedure would have to be introduced enabling the Court of Justice to deal with actions for failure to fulfil an obligation in cases where it is clear that the Member State's defence is not well founded: as soon as the Member State's defence was lodged, the President of the Court would be empowered to adopt a decision interrupting the inquiry and judgment could be delivered quickly, without the need for an Advocate-General's opinion.

b)   actions deemed comparable to proceedings for failure to fulfil obligations, provided for in Article 88 (ex 93) (2) and (3), the second paragraph of Article 298 (ex 225), or Article 237(d) (ex 180, amended) of the EC Treaty;

c)   actions for annulment of decisions taken by the Council in the case of an excessive public deficit, pursuant to Article 104 (ex 104c) (11) and (12) of the EC Treaty;

d) actions for annulment of the authorisation granted by the Council to certain Member States which are proposing to introduce closer cooperation between themselves, pursuant to Article 11(2) of the EC Treaty;

e) actions for annulment of a Council decision intended to suspend certain rights of the Member States, pursuant to Article 309(2) and (3) of the EC Treaty;

f) actions for annulment of the acts adopting the Community budget;

g) referrals to the Court to decide, pursuant to Article 35(7) of the EU Treaty on disputes between Member States or between Member States and the Commission in the field of police and judicial cooperation in criminal matters;

h) requests for opinions presented by the Council, the Commission or a Member State pursuant to Article 300 (ex 228) (6) of the EC Treaty.

An instrument of secondary legislation, adopted under enabling provisions of the Treaty, would be required to draw up, in line with these criteria, the restrictive list of the categories of direct actions retained within the jurisdiction of the Court of Justice as the instance of first and last resort.

4.   Stepping up the powers of the Court of First Instance to deal with direct actions should be supplemented by the introduction of a more efficient system than that currently in place for <u>filtering appeals against judgments by the CFI</u>.

a)   Currently, pursuant to Article 225(1) of the EC Treaty, appeals to the Court of Justice must be "on points of law only". In spite of this requirement, the rate of appeal is never below 20%, and sometimes even exceeds 30%, while during the last three years the failure rate for this kind of appeal has remained very high (from 75% to 93%).

It would therefore seem reasonable to add to the current filtering criterion a second criterion, requiring the appeal to have major importance either for the development of Community law or for the protection of individual rights.

b)   The recommended procedure would be as follows:

- a written request for authorisation to appeal against a CFI ruling would be presented to the Court of Justice within the time limit for appeal. This request should give grounds and aim to establish the importance of the case in the light of the new criteria.

- the request would be examined by a chamber of three judges appointed each year by the Court of Justice. The procedure would be swift and in writing, the other parties to the first instance proceedings being called on to put forward their arguments.

- the chamber would issue a reasoned opinion, without an Opinoin from by an Advocate-General.

- the decision giving or withholding authorisation to appeal would be taken by the President of the Court of Justice, in the light of the Chamber's opinion. His decision would be briefly reasoned and not open to appeal. A decision by the President granting the right to appeal could be limited to examining only the grounds recognised by him as meeting the filtering criteria.

- the time limit for appealing before the Court of Justice would start from the notification of the authorisation decision taken by the President of the Court.

C.   Categories of special cases

There is a present need, which will emerge even more clearly in future, for certain categories of special cases to be dealt with according to special rules, because either they are brought in large numbers, or their link to Community law is only indirect, or they require highly specialised judges to deal with them, or because any other general-interest consideration requires it.

Such special cases exist in most national legal orders, and the Community legal order will also have to use this system to unblock the Community courts enjoying general jurisdiction - the Court of Justice and the Court of First Instance.

The competent Community authorities will have the task of undertaking the required reforms when the need is felt. However, the Working Party considers it possible ven at this stage to point out, without making any claims to exhaustiveness, possible fields of application for these special cases.

1.   **Staff cases** currently certainly fall into this category.

The Working Party recommends that an "interinstitutional complaints tribunal" be set up as quickly as possible to deal with those cases as a judicial body of first instance, which would be given the status of a genuine independent tribunal in terms of the criteria set out in Article 6(1) of the European Convention on Human Rights.

This tribunal would be composed of three independent members: a legally qualified president, an associate judge proposed by the Community institutions, and another associate judge proposed by the representatives of the staff. Members would be appointed by the President of the Court of Justice. Before giving its decision, the tribunal would encourage the parties to reach a settlement.

An appeal against the tribunal's decisions could be made only on a point of law; it would be to the Court of First Instance, functioning as a court of final appeal here. The exceptional rules concerning costs in staff cases should be repealed.

An appeal to the Court of Justice would lie only on a point of general legal interest, at the request of the Commission acting in the exercise of its function as guardian of the Treaty.

Appeals on points of general legal interest in these special cases are intended only to correct erroneous case law for the future, not to challenge final legal decisions.

2.   **Intellectual property** cases also call for special treatment.

a)   At present the most pressing problems arise in cases involving the Community trade mark. Disputes over the registration of marks must be distinguished from disputes over infringement.

   –   Cases involving the registration of marks concern the lawfulness of individual decisions adopted by the Office for Harmonisation in the Internal Market (OHIM), a Community agency based in Alicante. At present there are three grades of appeal against those decisions, to the OHIM Board of Appeal, the Court of First Instance and the Court of Justice on appeal against the judgment of the Court of First Instance.

   The Working Party proposes that appeals against OHIM decisions should lie only to the OHIM Boards of Appeal, which should be given, if they do not already have it, the status of independent tribunal, with, perhaps, an appeal to the CFI on questions of law. The position would thus be the same as in staff cases; the Court of Justice would no longer have jurisdiction in these cases except as appeals on a point of general legal interest, at the request of the Commission.

–   On the other hand, infringement cases come within the jurisdiction of the national courts under the current rules. Under those rules, the national courts can refer a question to the Court of Justice for a preliminary ruling on the interpretation of provisions concerning the Community trade mark.

The Working Party considers that in these circumstances there should be a pooling of jurisdiction; such preliminary questions should be assigned on an exceptional basis to the Court of First Instance, which already has jurisdiction over cases involving the registration of marks.

b)   The Working Party suggests that similar arrangements should be made for designs, the protection of plant varieties, and patents.

c)   The Working Party does not rule out the possibility that, if intellectual property cases became so numerous in future as to disrupt the proper working of the Court of First Instance, this jurisdiction might instead be assigned to one or more specialist Community courts. However, the Court of Justice would remain the court of final instance, through appeals on a point of general legal interest.

3.   **Judicial cooperation in civil matters** (Article 65 – ex Article 73m – of the EC Treaty) gives rise to very specific issues of private international law which, by their nature, differ from those normally encountered in Community law.

Hitherto the Brussels I Convention has been the only relevant instrument in this area and it has generated few preliminary questions. The regulations which are to supersede the Convention of Rome and the Brussels II Convention by virtue of Article 65 of the EC Treaty may well change this situation profoundly.

If this proves to be so, the Working Party considers that preliminary questions concerning judicial cooperation should be withdrawn from the Court of Justice and assigned to a Community court with members drawn from specialist private international lawyers. An appeal to the Court of Justice on a point of general legal interest, at the request of the Commission, would be retained.

4.   Title VI of the Union Treaty on **cooperation in the fields of police and home affairs** and Title IV of the EC Treaty on **visas, asylum and immigration** have conferred jurisdiction on the Court of Justice in further areas whose quantitative importance cannot be assessed at present.

Those provisions of the Treaty have yet to be implemented, but if this generates a very large number of cases in future, at least part of those powers would have to be assigned either to the Court of First Instance or to one or more specialised courts, on terms that would require further reflection.

5.   **Competition cases**

There is currently a similar uncertainty as to the evolution of competition law as envisaged by the White Paper on modernisation of the rules implementing

Articles 85 and 86 of the EC Treaty, published by the Commission on 12 May 1999 in OJ C 132.

These proposals are aimed at abolishing the current centralised system, whereby exemption of restrictive practices that meet the conditions provided for in Article 81(3) of the EC Treaty (ex Article 85(3)) is granted by the Commission, and replacing it with a directly applicable legal exception system, without a prior decision by the Commission.

It is therefore now for the national courts to rule on the application of Article 81(3), on the occasion of cases which are submitted to them.

This reform could have a dual impact on the work of the Community courts:

○   first, by increasing the number of questions referred to the Court of Justice for a preliminary ruling to interpret the competition rules under the new system;

○   secondly, by increasing the number of direct actions brought before the CFI, in that the Commission will be able to focus on the most serious infringements of the competition rules and will thus adopt a greater number of prohibition decisions, which may be appealed against.

The Working Party does not challenge the usefulness of such a reform. It merely observes that if it resulted in a significant increase in the number of cases brought before the Court of Justice and the Court of First Instance, the question should be examined whether Community competition disputes should not, in future, also be categorised as "special cases" with all the consequences referred to above, in particular the pooling of jurisdiction in this area in favour of the Court of First Instance, enabling it to rule on preliminary questions in this area.

* * *

The reforms suggested in parts B and C above assume that the Council and Parliament would agree to assign additional staff and funds to the Court of First Instance to enable it to discharge its extra duties much more quickly than it can at present. Unlike the Court of Justice, which rules on many major cases in plenary session, the Court of First Instance generally makes its decisions in chambers of three or five members. It is therefore possible to increase the production capacity of the Court of First Instance much more easily than that of the Court of Justice, by increasing the number of judges, even beyond the number of Member States. However, this is of course subject, as we shall see below, to measures being taken to ensure the coherence of the decisions it takes in its various configurations.

* * *

Following these first three series of proposals, a medium-term possibility for the structure of the Community court system is beginning to emerge.

1.   The jurisdiction and role of the CFI would be substantially extended:

   a)   it would still be the first forum for direct actions under the general law, subject to the exceptions considered above;

   b)   but it would become the final court for direct actions in litigation on matters recognised as "special";

   c)   lastly, jurisdiction might also be conferred on it to give preliminary rulings at the request of national courts recognised as specialising in certain areas of this "special" litigation (such as trade mark infringement cases).

   As has been seen, if direct actions in special areas came to constitute an excessive workload for the CFI and jeopardised its smooth operation, they might be transferred in whole or in part to specialised Community courts. Careful thought would have to be given to the membership of such courts on a case-by-case basis; there would, for instance, have to be not only specialised judges but also generalists with an eye for compliance with the general principles underlying the building of the Community.

It follows from the foregoing that the position of the CFI within the Community court system would undergo radical change. Its name would have to be changed. Article 7 and the institutional provisions of the Treaty would need amending to take account of the new court structure.

2. The Court of Justice, as the Union's Supreme Court, would have three main functions:

a) The first would still be to answer requests for preliminary rulings from national courts, subject to point 1(c) above;

b) The second would be to give the first and final judgment on certain direct actions, few in number but acknowledged to be so urgent and important in the interests of Community law as to be incompatible with the maintenance of a two-tier jurisdiction;

c) The third would be to act as supreme "governor" of the Community court system.

   Two distinct procedures would be available:

   - Regarding direct actions under the ordinary law, the Court would review judgments of the CFI on appeal, coming to it via a strengthened filter mechanism;

   - Regarding direct actions in special areas of litigation and preliminary rulings given by the CFI, the Court would review decisions given by the CFI or specialised Community courts by means of an "appeal in the interest of the law", presented, without conditions as to time-limits by the Commission in its capacity as guardian of the Treaties as defined in Article 211 (formerly Article 155) of the EC Treaty.

D.   Procedural reforms

In addition to the foregoing proposals concerning the general architecture of the Community court system, reform of the internal procedures of the two courts might at first sight seem somewhat secondary. But in reality it would be wrong to underestimate the impact of certain measures capable of improving the way they operate and their productive capacity.

In their working paper of May 1999 the Court of Justice and the CFI presented a series of proposals for improvements to the procedure for handling cases brought before them. This report will not go over the ground again, but asks that some of these proposals be put into effect without delay.

All that will be given here are the following additional remarks to complement the points made at 2 (b) and (c) of part A above.

1.   In general terms the Working Party notes that the respective Rules of Procedure of the Court of Justice and of the CFI diverge in a number of respects. But the proposed changes in the jurisdiction of the CFI would warrant a review of the two sets of Rules of Procedure so as to attain the highest possible degree of unification.

It is immediately apparent that there are four points on which the rules can easily be aligned.

a)   First of all, simplification of the written procedure.

Article 117(1) of the Court of Justice's Rules of Procedure provides that an appeal against a judgment of the CFI may be supplemented, where the President allows it on application made by a party, by a reply and a rejoinder. It is thus for the President to decide whether these supplementary pleadings are necessary to enable the party concerned to put forward its point of view or provide a basis for the decision on the appeal.

- For one thing, the application for authorisation to present reply or rejoinder must give reasons so that the President can assess its usefulness.

- For another, this same system for controlling the extension of written procedures should be extended to appeals presented in the CFI where it acts as the final court in matters within the purview of "special" litigation.

b)   Then there is the question of certain measures organising the written and oral procedures.

Article 64 of the CFI's Rules of Procedure empowers that court to decide on measures of organisation of procedure to ensure that the written and oral stages proceed efficiently and to facilitate the taking of evidence, to determine the points on which the parties need to amplify their arguments, to clarify the scope of the submissions, grounds and arguments and even to facilitate an amicable settlement.

Provisions such as these have already proved their effectiveness; they should be written into the Rules of Procedure of the Court of Justice as well.

c)   Regarding the possibility of improving the oral procedure, the Court has proposed that provision be made in Articles 44a and 104(4) of its Rules of Procedure for a public hearing to be held either if the Court so decides of its own motion or upon reasoned request from one of the parties or persons interested to whom Article 20 of its Statute applies, specifying the points on which such party or person wishes to be heard.

There is no comparable provision in the CFI's Rules of Procedure. Given the additional jurisdiction which it is proposed be conferred on it, there are no reasonable grounds for the continued existence of this divergence between the two sets of Rules of Procedure. The CFI's Rules should be aligned on those of the Court of Justice, amended as specified above.

d)   Regarding the possibility of an Order, stating reasons, to dismiss an action which is "manifestly inadmissible", the possibility is available in the CFI under Article 111 of the Rules of Procedure.

In the Court of Justice, however, the possibility is available only as regards appeals against CFI judgments (Article 119 of the Court of Justice's Rules of Procedure).

As there is no justification for such a divergence, the Rules of Procedure of the Court of Justice should be aligned on those of the CFI as regards all direct action remaining within the Court of Justice's jurisdiction.

2. The two sets of Rules of Procedure should also be amended on three further points to reduce the length of proceedings.

a) By Article 42(2) of the Rules of Procedure of the Court of Justice and Article 48(2) of the Rules of Procedure of the CFI, "No new plea in law may be introduced in the course of proceedings unless it is based on matters of law or of fact which come to light in the course of the procedure."

The purpose of these provisions is to oblige applicants to set forth all the grounds and arguments which they are planning to plead as soon as the action is commenced, so as to shorten the time taken by the procedure, but the effect is often contrary to the objective pursued.

Applicants seeking urgent measures of interim relief, acting under pressure of time, tend to include in their application precautionary arguments that do not actually correspond to any of their grounds in point of fact but which they think might turn out helpful to them after the case has been considered on the merits in depth.

The effect of this way of proceeding is to overload the pleadings with matters that are devoid of substance but which the Judge-Rapporteur and the Advocate-General must nevertheless examine and which must be answered in the judgment.

It would therefore seem desirable to tone down the requirement of the Rules of Procedure and leave the applicant with the option of submitting new material up to the reply stage. The other party would still have the opportunity of answering these new points in his rejoinder. Precautionary arguments, and the resultant pointless excess workload on the courts, would then become unnecessary.

b)   The additional time allowed for distance, ranging from two days to a month, should also be abolished. It is quite unnecessary in these days of fax and e-mail.

This means that the Court of Justice and the CFI would have to agree, in the Rules of Procedure, to allow parties to use these modern techniques, subject to a few precautions to secure the authenticity of documents transmitted.

c)   The Working Party observed that the practical effect of the current provisions of the Rules of Procedure relating to interventions is to lengthen proceedings considerably. Without going into detail, it believes that the two courts should put proposals to the Council for reform here.

3.　The Working Party attaches importance to the adoption of certain measures relating to the sound organisation of work at the Community courts that would not call for amendments to the legislative instruments.

　　a)　The aim here is to focus the work of the Judges-Rapporteurs and the Advocates-General in a tighter time-frame. They could start preparing their preliminary draft judgments and provisional conclusions on the basis of the pleadings even before the oral procedure begins, and would later simply have to amend them in the light of what they hear at the public hearing. Conclusions could be distributed and the deliberation could begin soon after the hearing, which would be only right and proper. This would have two advantages: the procedure would be shorter and the Judges' workload would be lightened, as they could deliberate without having to refresh their memories of the main points of the case several weeks or months after the hearing.

　　b)　In the same spirit, there is much to be said for developing a practice whereby the Judge-Rapporteur, before the hearing of a complex case, would brief the Court in its relevant composition on the points which in his view are not adequately clarified and on which he wishes questions to be put to the parties. After this discussion, the Judge-Rapporteur would inform the parties of the points to be examined in greater detail at the hearing.

4. Problems regarding translation

Translation is involved at most stages of the procedure under the current Rules of Procedure. On average, this accounts for a third of the duration of the procedure.

A good number of the reforms proposed above and of those presented by the two Courts in their reflection paper seek to make the rules more flexible, and in particular to remove some of the stages. These reforms would also help to lighten the translation workload.

Notwithstanding these reforms, translation needs will continue to weigh heavily on the two courts and make it impossible to cut the duration of proceedings as far as might be wished, especially in complex cases. Proliferation of procedural languages in the wake of future enlargements will seriously aggravate the problem, unless, of course, the Member States can come to an agreement on ways of limiting it.

To lighten the burden significantly (in the long run it will become unbearable), the Working Party would like to draw attention to the following possibilities:

a) Most translations into the working language are of procedural documents. Lawyers and agents must be persuaded of the need to avoid excessively long documents, for example by means of practice directions (instructions) which the Court should be able to issue if action is taken on its proposal for a new Article 125a of the Rules of Procedure. To support these directions or recommendations it might be worth amending the two sets of Rules of Procedure so as to empower the two courts to demand an abstract of an excessively long document, this version alone being taken as a basis for drafting the report for the hearing and translated into the working language. Another possibility would be to amplify the rules governing the costs which a party may be ordered to reimburse (Article 72(a) of the Court of Justice's

Rules of Procedure and Article 90(a) of the CFI's Rules) to include expressly the costs of translation of excessively long procedural documents.

Lastly, the Community institutions, which are by definition multilingual, should be under an obligation to present their documents in the procedural language plus the working language. It would be helpful if the Member States also agreed to make a similar effort wherever feasible.

b)   The bulk of the <u>translations from the working language</u> concern publication of the courts' judgments and Opinions of the Advocates-General. It is essential that the case decisions be published in all official languages, as they are a major source of law, but the principle is not the same for repetitive cases or cases of minor importance; here an analytical summary could be published in all languages. The full text of such judgments and conclusions could be published on the Internet in the procedural language alone (with possibly the working language for judgments and the Advocate-General's own language for the Opinion).

E.   **Membership of the Community courts**

1.   Court of Justice

   a)   Number of Judges

Although a decision may be taken at some future date that there are to be fewer Judges than Member States, the Working Party assumes that the present rule will remain in force.

It has always been acknowledged that each national legal order should be represented by a Judge at the Court, to ensure that each national legal tradition makes its contribution to Community law and that the national courts abide more closely by the Court's case-law. For these reasons the Working Party finds it acceptable that no change should be made to the present rule and that in future the number of Judges should remain the same as the number of Member States.

   b)   Plenary session

Further enlargements of the Union will mean an end to the present rule whereby the Court sits, in principle, with all its Judges present. If the quality of the Court's rulings is to be maintained, there must necessarily be a strict limit on the number of Judges attending plenary sessions.

In the light of enlargement forecasts, the Working Party considers that the limit should be set at half the number of Judges, plus one or two, so that the odd number results in a majority. Plenary sessions would comprise, in addition to the President of the Court and the Presidents of the five-judge Chambers (see below), and the five-judge Chamber in which the rapporteur sits. It would be for the President of the Court to ensure that, where circumstances so require, the representative of the legal order most directly concerned was included in the plenary session.

No matter how many Member States there may eventually be, the Working Party takes the view that the total number of Judges in a plenary session should never exceed a fixed maximum, e.g. thirteen.

c)   Status of the Presidents of the five-judge Chambers[2]

The Presidents of the five-judge Chambers must be given a greater role if the proper consistency of the Court's case-law is to be maintained as the number of Judges and sessions rises sharply.

The Working Party therefore proposes:

–   that the terms of office of the Presidents of the five-judge Chambers should be three years, as for the President of the Court;

---

[2]   The Chambers which consist of seven Judges of whom five vote are apparently those with the largest number of Members. If membership of the Chambers were to be altered at some future date, the following proposals would clearly apply to the Presidents of the Chambers with the widest membership.

– that the President and the Presidents of the five-judge Chambers should constitute the permanent core of the plenary session;

– that these same Presidents should verify, at frequent and regular meetings, the consistency of the draft judgments prepared by the various sessions of the Court and should decide whether certain cases should be referred to the plenary session, where necessary;

– that the Presidents of the five-judge Chambers should be elected by the Judges of the Court.

d)   Membership of the chambers

The membership of the Court's Chambers is determined each year by a meeting of all the Judges of the Court, on a proposal from the President. Membership must be such as to ensure balanced representation of the main legal systems to which the various Member States of the Union belong.

e)   Advocates-General

At the present stage in the development of Community law, it no longer seems necessary that each case should be the subject of an Advocate-General's conclusions.

Advocates-General need to give their opinions on important cases, e.g. those where new points of law have to be interpreted, where changes to the Court's case-law may be required or where, given the complexity of the case, it has to be verified that no submissions have been overlooked. It would be for the President of the Court, at the request of the rapporteur and after consultation with the First Advocate-General, to identify the cases which required the intervention of an Advocate-General.

This reform should make it possible to reduce the number of Advocates-General in line with the number of important cases and would substantially lighten the Court's administrative workload, particularly the translation workload.

2.   Court of First Instance

a)   The above proposals concerning the Presidents of the five-judge Chambers should also be implemented in respect of the Presidents of "extended" Chambers at the CFI.

b)   Plenary sessions could consist of the Judges of the Chamber to which the case has been assigned and the Presidents of all the other Chambers. This would not require any amendment to the Treaty but merely an amendment to Council Decision 88/591/ECSC, EEC, Euratom of 24 October 1988 establishing a Court of First Instance of the European Communities[3].

c)   It would be preferable if the Chambers became specialised to some extent, where a sufficient number of cases have to be tried in the same subject area and where the nature of such cases is quite distinct from

---

[3]   OJ L 319, 25.11.1988, p. 1.

that of the other cases coming before the Court. In the near future this will apply to cases relating to Community trademarks and possibly to other categories of dispute in the course of time. Specialisation of this kind does not mean that the Judges themselves must become specialised: the Members of the specialised Chambers must remain full Members of the Court of First Instance, having received the same training and having been appointed on the same terms as their colleagues. Moreover, the assignment of a Judge to a specialised Chamber should not normally be on a permanent basis.

d)   The single-judge system was introduced by Council Decision 1999/291/EC, ECSC, Euratom of 26 April 1999.[4]   In the light of experience with this system, consideration should be given to extending the jurisdiction of the single judge to other fields where the case-law is well established.

e)   The system whereby Advocates-General are chosen at intervals from among the Judges has not proved satisfactory and must therefore be abandoned. Now that the Court of First Instance has wider jurisdiction, it should have a limited number of permanent Advocates-General whose activities would be subject to the same rules as those outlined above for the Advocates-General at the Court of Justice.

3.   Court of Justice and Court of First Instance

---

[4]   OJ L 114, 1.5.1999, p. 52.

a)   Members' term of office

The Working Party would suggest that, to ensure the smooth working of both courts, the term of office of their Members should be increased to twelve years as from the date of actual appointment and that this term should not be renewable.

b)   The Working Party would also suggest that the appointment of all Members of the Court of Justice and the CFI should be scrutinised on the basis of a comprehensive file submitted by each Member State. To assist the Member States in their deliberations, an advisory committee consisting of highly-qualified independent lawyers should be set up to verify the legal competence of candidates.

* * *
*

It is clear from the foregoing that the adaptation of the Community courts to meet new challenges will call for several reforms over a long period of time. The Working Party would strongly recommend that new provisions be incorporated in the Treaties so that both the structural reforms and the procedural changes required by the development of the Union can be brought about more rapidly than has been possible in the past.

* * *
*

The Working Party adopted the bulk of its proposals by consensus. On certain points, however, members of the Working Party expressed divergent opinions but refrained from making separate proposals.

Adopted on 19 January 2000 by the Working Party consisting of:

Mr Ole DUE, Chairman of the Working Party,
former Judge and President of the Court of Justice of the European Communities,

Mr Yves GALMOT, Rapporteur,
former Judge of the Court of Justice of the European Communities,

Mr José Luis DA CRUZ VILAÇA,
former Advocate-General at the Court of Justice and President of the Court of First Instance of the European Communities,

Mr Ulrich EVERLING,
former Judge of the Court of Justice of the European Communities,

Mr Aurelio PAPPALARDO,
Lawyer,

Ms Rosario SILVA DE LAPUERTA,
Public Prosecutor (Spain),

Lord SLYNN of HADLEY,
former Advocate-General and Judge of the Court of Justice of the European Communities.

ANNEX

Proposed new wording for Article 234 of the EC Treaty

1. Subject to the provisions of this Article, the courts of the Member States shall rule on the questions of Community law which they encounter in the exercise of their national jurisdiction.

2. The Court of Justice shall have jurisdiction to give preliminary rulings concerning:

   (a) the interpretation of this Treaty;

   (b) the validity and interpretation of acts of institutions of the Community;

   (c) the interpretation of the statutes of bodies established by an act of the Council, where those statutes so provide.

3. Where such a question is raised before any national court or tribunal, that court or tribunal may, if it considers that a decision on the question is necessary to enable it to give judgment, request the Court of Justice to give a ruling thereon. When determining whether to consult the Court of Justice, the national court or tribunal shall in particular take account of how important the question is to Community law and whether or not there is reasonable doubt as to the answer to that question.

4. Where any such question is raised in a case pending before a national court or tribunal against whose decisions there is no judicial remedy under national law, that court or tribunal shall bring the matter before the Court of Justice, provided that the question is of sufficient importance to Community law and that there is reasonable doubt as to the answer to that question.

5.   A national court or tribunal shall consult the Court of Justice where it proposes not to apply an act of Community law on the grounds that the latter is invalid.

Document 4

Reform of the Community courts
(Additional Commission Contribution to the
Intergovernmental Conference on
institutional reform)

Additional Commission contribution to the
Intergovernmental Conference on institutional reform

Reform of the Community courts

Introduction

The Commission considers that one of the foundations of the European Union is and remains the fact that it is a Community based on the rule of law. Litigants – the citizens of Europe – must be in a position to count on a court system that guarantees the fair, coherent and effective application of Community law.

In its Opinion to the Intergovernmental Conference of 26 January 2000 *'Adapting the institutions to make a success of enlargement'*, the Commission announced that it would be preparing a specific contribution on the reform of the judicial system.

In order to prepare the ground for this reform, in May 1999 the Commission set up a working party consisting of former Members of the Court and the Court of First Instance and high-level experts with first-hand experience of the Community judiciary, whose job it was to find solutions that could be introduced at once and in the longer term. The Working Party's report was presented to the President of the Commission on 4 February last. The Commission draws on it for many of its proposals in this document.

I. The need for ambitious reform

The Court of Justice is an essential institution of the Union: its function is to 'ensure that in the interpretation and application of [the] Treaty the law is observed' (Article 220 of the EC Treaty). The Single European Act attached a Court of First Instance to the Court of Justice.

In an enlarged Union it will be necessary to safeguard the effectiveness of the Community's judicial system and the consistency of its case-law, factors which are essential if Community law is to be applied uniformly in an increasingly diverse Europe. Enlargement will entail an increase in the volume of litigation, not only in quantitative terms but also in qualitative terms as the courts of the new Member States will have to become familiar with Community law. Account will have to be taken of a variety of parameters, including the need to ensure effective judicial protection while at the same time maintaining the consistency of the case-law and compliance with it throughout the Union.

The statistics show that the Court and the CFI are having increasing difficulty in fulfilling their role in the fifteen-member Community.

This is essentially the result of the constant increase in the number of cases brought before the Community Courts (87% increase in requests for preliminary rulings in nine years[1], doubling of the number of cases before the CFI in seven years[2]) and is reflected in the undue delays before judgment is given[3] and the appreciable increase in the number of cases still to come to judgment.[4]

Only ten years after the CFI was set up, it has to be admitted that the present structures are no longer suitable and a thorough overhaul is necessary, otherwise there is a danger that the Community will no longer be truly based on the rule of law.

The time taken for cases to come to judgment in the Court of Justice and the Court of First Instance, according to statistics from the Courts themselves, reveals that the institution has reached the limits of its capacity. After enlargement, it will certainly not be in a position to cope with its expanding workload in a reasonable time-frame. The situation is preoccupying in a Community based on the rule of law, only ten years after the CFI was established and in the run-up to enlargement.

The Commission proposes that, first of all, **the structure of the judiciary should be redefined**, given that even now neither the Court nor the CFI can perform their roles satisfactorily. The composition and operation of the Court and the CFI should then be addressed in the light of the workload of the two courts. The Commission believes that the number of Judges should be determined first and foremost by the caseload.

II.   Clarification and redistribution of the Courts' jurisdiction as part of a flexible design

The Commission believes that the present congestion in the Court of Justice and the Court of First Instance could be significantly reduced by adopting three sets of measures:

- clarification of the roles of the Court of Justice and national courts, so as to give the latter more scope in the handling of the preliminary ruling procedure;

- redistribution of powers between the Court of Justice and the Court of First Instance with regard to direct actions so as to limit the role of the Court of Justice, in its capacity as the Union's supreme judicial body, to questions which are regarded as fundamental to the Community legal order, and to give the Court of First Instance general jurisdiction in this field;

- reduction of the Court's and the CFI's volume of certain categories of special case.

---

[1]   141 requests for preliminary rulings in 1990, 264 in 1998.
[2]   116 cases in 1992, 238 in 1998.
[3]   21 months on average for the Court, 30 months on average for the CFI.
[4]   Court: 433 cases pending at end-1993, 748 cases pending at end-1998;
CFI: 171 cases pending at end-1992, 1007 cases pending at end-1998.

a.   Preliminary rulings

(i)   Jurisdiction of the Court of Justice

The preliminary ruling procedure is undoubtedly the keystone of the Community's legal order. Forty years' experience have shown that it is the most effective means of securing the uniform application of Community law throughout the Union and that it is an exceptional factor for integration owing to the simple, direct dialogue which it establishes with national courts. The Commission considers that this regulating function, which is essential to the Community legal order, must therefore in principle be the exclusive responsibility of the Court of Justice.

The Working Party shares this opinion. But it proposes that the last sentence of Article 225(1) of the EC Treaty be deleted to give the CFI exceptional jurisdiction to give preliminary rulings in very specialised areas of Community law.[5] The Working Party considers that special categories of case, including preliminary questions in such areas, should be entrusted as a whole to the CFI and that the Court of Justice, as the supreme court of the Union, should become involved where appropriate only in appeals on points of law lodged by the Commission.[6]

This proposal will have to be examined in connection with any specific changes to jurisdiction that will have to be provided for in certain categories of special case, such as intellectual property proceedings.

(ii)   Clarification of the roles of the Court of Justice and the national courts

To preserve the effectiveness of the preliminary ruling procedure, it is essential that the Court of Justice should be able to concentrate on genuinely new questions and give its judgments considerably sooner. To this end, the Commission believes it is necessary to amend Article 234 (ex Article 177) of the Treaty in order to clarify the distribution of jurisdiction between the Court of Justice and national courts.

1.   The first amendment proposed seeks to give national courts greater responsibility as courts of ordinary law in Community matters. At present, this function is not expressly laid down in the Treaty. It can only be inferred from reading Articles 234 and 240 together. It is therefore essential to correct this omission by spelling out the introductory provision in Article 234, clearly stating that it is for the national courts in the first place to apply Community law to the cases before them and that they may consult the Court of Justice when faced with a specific problem of interpretation.

2.   In similar vein, it could be worthwhile amending the second paragraph of Article 234, so as to invite national courts other than those of final instance to specify why they have doubts as to the meaning of the rule of Community law applicable in the case before them and why they feel the need to put a question to the Court of Justice. This provision could be accompanied by the requisite corollary changes to the Rules of Procedure.

---

[5]   E.g. intellectual property (trade marks, patents and industrial designs, etc.).
[6]   As provided by, for instance, Article 68(3) of the Treaty.

3.   As part of this clarification exercise, it is necessary, lastly, to insert in Article 234 the rule established in case-law whereby, in cases of doubt as to the validity of a Community act, whereby all national courts must consult the Court of Justice since the latter has the monopoly of the review of Community legality.

The Commission does not feel it would be right to give flexibility to the obligation on courts of final instance to refer preliminary questions, currently laid down in the third paragraph of Article 234, requiring them to consult the Court of Justice only if the question were sufficiently important for Community law and if, after examination by the lower courts, there were still reasonable doubts as to the reply. The Commission considers that the advantages of such flexibility as far as the Court's workload is concerned are very slight[7] and that there are real dangers for the uniform application of Community law, especially with enlargement on the horizon. It therefore thinks it is essential to stick with the current wording of the third paragraph of Article 234. Naturally, the flexibility introduced by case-law[8] would continue to apply.

The Commission further wonders whether it might be worth harmonising the procedure for preliminary rulings in matters of free movement of persons (Title IV) with the ordinary procedure.

See the Annex for the draft new wording of Article 234.

b.   Direct actions: a new division of jurisdiction between the Court of Justice and the Court of First Instance

The Court of Justice currently rules on direct actions brought by the Member States and the institutions, while the Court of First Instance decides on actions brought by natural and legal persons. The Court of Justice has already pointed out the areas of overlap and unwieldy procedures that this division generates and has asked that direct actions in certain fields be dealt with exclusively by the Court of First Instance.

The Commission's opinion is that this approach should be extended to all direct actions in order to **give the Court of First Instance general jurisdiction in this area and to retain for the Court of Justice only those questions that are essential for the proper working of the Community and which, as such, require it to intervene in its capacity as the Union's supreme court.** These would be actions against Member States for failure to fulfil their obligations, interinstitutional actions, actions filed against legislative instruments of general scope or applying to certain fields such as fundamental rights and Article 309 of the Treaty, closer cooperation, EMU, the budget, Title IV of the EC Treaty and Title IV of the Treaty on European Union.[9]

The transfer of a large proportion of the direct actions to the Court of First Instance will significantly relieve the workload of the Court of Justice only if it is accompanied by a change to the current system of appeals against rulings of the Court of First Instance. The Commission's view is that appeals should in future be subject to **an initial filtering**

---

[7]   Since three quarters of preliminary questions are referred by the lower courts.

[8]   *Cilfit* [1982] ECR 3415.

[9]   Requests for opinions under Article 300 (ex 228) of the EC Treaty and requests for settlements of disputes under Article 35 of the TEU would also be kept within the exclusive powers of the Court of Justice.

procedure by the Court of Justice, in accordance with modalities to be specified in the Protocol to the Court's Statute.

The change in the division of jurisdiction regarding direct actions between the Court of Justice and the Court of First Instance can be implemented under Article 225(2) of the Treaty, though the wording should be changed. The raison d'être of this provision, which authorises the Council to determine the actions for which the Court of First Instance has jurisdiction *at the request of the Court of Justice*, after consulting the Commission and Parliament, lay in the fact that it was decided at that time to "attach" a Court of First Instance to the Court of Justice[10] and allow the latter, when applicable, to delegate some of its powers to the former. The intention now is to redesign the judicial system in its entirety, by dividing jurisdiction in such a way as to make the Court of Justice the genuine supreme court of the Union and to give the Court of First Instance, which would acquire autonomous status, general powers as an ordinary court. Consequently, the instrument of secondary legislation to govern the new division of jurisdiction should be adopted via an ordinary legislative procedure, after consulting the Court of Justice and the European Parliament.

The Commission considers that thought should be given, lastly, as suggested by the Working Party's report, to reforming the procedure for failure to fulfil obligations, notably in cases of failure to transpose directives. The Working Party's suggestion proceeds from the observation that the bulk of the actions brought in the Court of Justice under Article 226 of the Treaty relate to such matters, and are rarely seriously contested by the Member States. It might be possible, taking Article 88 of the ECSC Treaty as a model, to have such failures recorded by a Commission Decision, against which an action for annulment could then be brought in the Court of Justice.

The question deserves thorough consideration in the light of all the factors at play, and in particular the fact that:

- such a high level of cases of failure to fulfil obligations which are not really contested, after *pre*-litigation proceedings, illustrates the difficulties of ensuring that Community law is respected even in simple cases;

- the administrative burden (dossier management, translations etc.) which such actions generate for the Court of Justice is disproportionate, in spite of all the procedural simplifications which may well be put in place to allow rapid settlement of this type of case;

- the Community courts, which will have to face the inevitable growth in litigation after the next enlargement, will have to concentrate on real disputes. A start could be made by relieving it, for example, of failures to transpose directives within the specified time limits.[11]

c.   Categories of special cases

---

[10]   As stated in Article 225(1).

[11]   NB: in 1998 actions for failure to fulfil obligations accounted for 80% of the direct actions brought before the Court of Justice (118 actions for failure to fulfil obligations out of a total of 147 direct actions).

(i)   The extension of the application of Community law to highly specialised areas such as trade marks, designs and models, the protection of plant varieties and, in the near future, patents prompts the Working Party to conclude that in view of the large number of cases that these matters seem to generate,[12] they should not be heard by the CFI but by autonomous specialised tribunals. The CFI is already under severe pressure and would not be able to contend with a triple increase in its workload resulting from the extension of its jurisdiction to cover all direct actions as proposed above, enlargement and the influx of a mass of specialised cases.

In order to offer the CFI immediate relief, the Working Party proposes that it be relieved of cases relating to trade marks and of the other specific category of cases, namely those relating to staff of the Community institutions.

- For *trade marks*, this would mean merging the Boards of Appeal of the Alicante Office into a single body which would be given court status and would hear in first instance actions brought against decisions of the of the Alicante Office.

- On matters relating to *Community staff*, it is suggested that the proposal made both by Parliament and by the Court of Justice be taken up and an "Interinstitutional Appeals Tribunal" be established whose role would be to seek reconciliation between the parties before giving a decision and which would also have the status of an independent tribunal.[13]

Decisions given by these tribunals might be appealable, on points of law only, at the discretion of the parties to the action.

(ii)   The Commission believes that a solution should be found to the whole range of special litigation, as the volume of it will become a crushing burden on the Community courts.

A number of solutions can be envisaged:

(1)   An increase in the number of judges at the CFI.

Article 225(2) of the Treaty empowers the Council to determine the composition of the CFI and hence to increase the number of judges beyond that of the number of Member States. The Commission feels that it should be seen whether such a decision might not suffice to contain the CFI's workload, to begin with at least for trade mark cases.[14]

(2)   A second solution might consist, given the special nature of these categories of litigation, of relieving the CFI of its jurisdiction at first instance in favour of autonomous specialised tribunals, as suggested by the Working Party.

---

[12]   In the area of trade marks the number of cases which could be brought before the CFI is estimated at 400 a year.

[13]   This would mean deleting Article 236 (formerly 179) of the Treaty and amending the relevant provisions of the Staff Regulations.

[14]   A request along these lines from the Court is currently before the Council.

If it is decided to set up such tribunals, appeals against their decisions should be confined to points of law and would first have to be filtered as mentioned above.

The Working Party suggests that the CFI[15] should hear such appeals for the following reasons:

- given its present jurisdiction, the CFI would be in a position to deal with the decisions given by these new tribunals;

- the new division of jurisdiction between the Court of Justice and the Court of First Instance is intended to relieve the Court of the need to hear a large number of specialised actions. The volume of litigation relating to intellectual property suggests that the number of cases will continue to be high despite the filtering procedure;

- the Court of Justice would act as governor of Community case-law in a more appropriate manner by hearing appeals in the interest of the law presented, without conditions as to time limits, by the Commission in its capacity as guardian of the common interest.

The Commission is more inclined to feel that the Court should in principle retain jurisdiction to hear appeals for the time being. It suggests, however, that a provision be inserted in the Treaty which will make it possible, when this becomes necessary, to transfer all litigation in these categories to autonomous specialised tribunals, which would then give judgment both in first instance and in cassation.

(3)   It should be noted that if this last solution is adopted the Court of Justice will retain its jurisdiction to give preliminary rulings in litigation concerning alleged patent infringements in the national courts.

Regarding intellectual property rights under Community law, particularly with the prospect of the Community patent, consideration should be given to establishing a specialised tribunal with jurisdiction in cases concerning patent validity and infringements, in order to secure legal certainty regarding unitary documents having effect throughout the Community and to relieving the Court of Justice and the CFI of all this highly specialised litigation.

(iii)   If jurisdiction to hear appeals is conferred on an autonomous specialised tribunal, the Commission believes there should still be the possibility of an appeal in the interests of the law to the Court of Justice.

III.   Membership, operation and procedures of the Community courts

a.   Membership and operation

If the above guidelines were followed, the Court of Justice would henceforth exercise its jurisdiction not only as a court of first and final instance for certain direct actions but

---

[15]   Which would then change its name.

would also govern the case-law by its rulings on preliminary questions and on appeals or actions in the interests of the law.[16] The Court of First Instance, which would acquire autonomous status, would have its jurisdiction extended to cover all direct actions.

The number of Judges at the Court of First Instance will have to be decided in the light of its new areas of jurisdiction and so as to ensure its effectiveness. The number of Judges should not depend on the number of Member States.

In the case of the Court of Justice, the Working Party acknowledged that the various legal orders had to be represented and that the Community courts had to work effectively. It has attempted to balance the equation by proposing that the present rule whereby there is one Judge per Member State should be maintained, subject to a strict limit on the number of Members in the plenary session (a maximum of 13 Judges) and the necessary imposition of a hierarchy led by the President of the Court, assisted by the Presidents of the Chambers.[17]

An alternative way of ensuring the effectiveness and consistency of case-law would be to limit the number of Judges at the Court of Justice to 13. An increase in the Members of the Court would entail an increase in its Chambers or other formations. Such a development could jeopardise the proper performance of the Court's tasks, however.

Other alternatives could be envisaged. The Conference should conduct a general examination of this issue. In any case it will be important to ensure that the Court's judgements win the degree of acceptability which is needed for the maintenance of the Court's authority. Lastly, account should be taken of the changes which the Conference decides to make to the structure of the Community institutions as a whole.

The Commission supports the Working Party's proposal that the number of Advocates-General at the Court should be reduced. Consideration should also be given to the Working Party's suggestions on such matters as Members' term of office and the way in which Members are appointed by the Council.

Regarding the appointment of Members of the Court of Justice and the CFI, the Commission feels it would be desirable to examine the possibility for a system to be established at the Council to secure the proper degree of legal excellence, possibly going so far as to have them selected from lists of several names put forward by the Member States.

The Commission proposes that appointments be made by qualified majority vote.

b.   The Rules of Procedure of the two Community courts

The Commission takes the view that the Rules of Procedure of both the Court of Justice and the CFI should be drawn up in the same way as codes/laws of procedure are adopted in the Member States. It suggests that the said Rules of Procedure should be adopted by the Council acting by a qualified majority, in response to an initiative from the

---

[16]   See footnote 9.

[17]   A similar arrangement could be devised for the CFI to ensure that its case-law remains consistent.

Commission (having consulted the Court of Justice) and from the Court of Justice (having consulted the Commission).

The second paragraph of Article 245 should be deleted and a clear distinction should be made between those provisions which are to be kept in the Statute of the Court of Justice and those which are to remain in the Rules of Procedure.

*   *   *

By way of conclusion, the Commission proposes that the Conference:

- clarify the role of the Court of Justice and the national courts in order to give the latter more extensive responsibilities in the handling of preliminary rulings;

- redistribute jurisdiction between the Court of Justice and the Court of First Instance in relation to direct actions, so as to confine the role of the Court of Justice to questions considered essential to the Community legal order as the Union's supreme court, and give the CFI general jurisdiction in this respect;

- adjust the roles of the Court of Justice and the CFI in respect of certain special categories of cases;

- provide that Judges will be appointed by the Council, acting by a qualified majority, with a system for verifying nominees' legal abilities;

- consider the question of reforming the procedures for failure to discharge obligations;

- determine the membership of the Court of Justice and the CFI in the light of their caseload.

ANNEX

Current text of EC Treaty	Proposed new wording
Article 234	**Article 234**
The Court of Justice shall have jurisdiction to give preliminary rulings concerning:	1. Subject to the provisions of this Article, the courts and tribunals of the Member States shall rule on the questions of Community law which they encounter in exercise of their national jurisdiction.
(a) the interpretation of this Treaty;	2. The Court of Justice shall have jurisdiction to give preliminary rulings concerning:
(b) the validity and interpretation of acts of the institutions of the Community and of the ECB;	(a) the interpretation of this Treaty;
(c) the interpretation of the statutes of bodies established by an act of the Council, where those statutes so provide.	(b) the validity and interpretation of acts of the institutions of the Community and of the ECB;
Where such a question is raised before any court or tribunal of a Member State, that court or tribunal may, if it considers that a decision on the question is necessary to enable it to give judgment, request the Court of Justice to give a ruling thereon.	(c) the interpretation of the statutes of bodies established by an act of the Council, where those statutes so provide.
Where any such question is raised in a case pending before a court or tribunal of a Member State against whose decisions there is no judicial remedy under national law, that court or tribunal shall bring the matter before the Court of Justice.	3. Where such a question is raised before any national court or tribunal, that court or tribunal may, if it considers that a decision on the question is necessary to enable it to give a judgement, request the Court of Justice to give a ruling thereon. In that event, it shall specify why the validity or interpretation of the rule of Community law raises difficulties in the case before it.
	4. Where any such question is raised in a case pending before a national court or tribunal against whose decisions there is no judicial remedy under national law, that court or tribunal shall bring the matter before the Court of Justice.
	5. A national court or tribunal must consult the Court of Justice where it proposes not to apply an act of Community law on the grounds that the latter is invalid.

Part Two: The Outcome at Nice

PROFESSOR ALAN DASHWOOD

Sidney Sussex College, Cambridge

ANGUS JOHNSTON

Trinity Hall, Cambridge

A. *The Outcome at Nice: An Overview*

1. INTRODUCTION

The Tampere European Council declared its determination:

'. . . to develop the Union as an area of freedom, security and justice [and to] place and maintain this objective at the very top of the political agenda.'[1]

That is a highly laudable aim, and one to which the European Council did indeed show great commitment. However, no emphasis was given to the role of the Court of Justice in such an area. The only mention of the Court in the Tampere Conclusions was in the context of the body established to elaborate a draft EU Charter of Fundamental Rights: it was to nominate two members to act as observers of the work of that body.

The Presidency Conclusions at Helsinki were equally unspecific as to the priority to be accorded to Treaty amendments affecting the Court of Justice, by what is there described as 'the Intergovernmental Conference on institutional reform'. The matters specifically mentioned as ones to be examined by the IGC were: 'the size and composition of the Commission, the weighting of votes in the Council and the possible extension of qualified majority voting in the Council, as well as other necessary amendments to the Treaties arising as regards the European institutions in connection with the above issues and in implementing the Treaty of Amsterdam'.[2] It was further noted that the incoming (Portuguese) Presidency 'may propose additional issues to be taken on the agenda of the Conference'.[3]

The silence of the Helsinki Conclusions as to the reform of the Union's judicial architecture might have been thought to confirm the generally downbeat view of those attending the conference in July 1999, that the IGC was unlikely to deal with much more than the so-called 'Amsterdam leftovers'. The tight timetable set for the IGC (to complete its work by December 2000, so that the necessary amendments can be agreed at the Nice European Council)[4] also

---

[1] Presidency Conclusions, Tampere European Council, 19 October 1999, paras. 2 and 3 of the introductory section: see the summary at http://ue.eu.int/en/Info/eurocouncil/index.htm.

[2] Presidency Conclusions, Helsinki European Council, 10 and 11 December 1999, para. 16.

[3] *Ibid.*   [4] *Ibid*, para. 15.

seemed to militate in favour of a short agenda, with controversial items kept to a minimum. On the other hand, the Governments of several of the Member States were known to be willing to 'do something' for the Courts. Moreover, the Courts have a doughty ally in the Commission. In its additional contribution to the IGC, which was formulated in the light of the Report presented in January 2000 by the Working Party of 'Wise Persons',[5] the Commission acknowledged the need for ambitious reform.[6] Furthermore, the Interim Report of the Presidency to the Conference of the Representatives of the Governments of the Member States suggested that the delegations to the IGC were well aware of the urgent need for significant reform of the Community judicial system.[7] The Courts themselves have been keen to keep these issues in the spotlight and published a Contribution to the IGC of their own, highlighting the various Treaty amendments that they consider to be necessary.[8] There were reasonable grounds, therefore, for hoping that some at least of the very real problems identified in the Courts' Paper, and confirmed by the Wise Persons, would be addressed by the IGC.

In the light of this complex background, the actual outcome of the negotiations for the European judicial system is largely unsurprising. Certain areas proved uncontroversial and contained issues on which it was easy to reach political consensus, while other problems have remained highly contentious. The changes are, for the most part, not momentous, but they do indicate a willingness on the part of Member States to address serious judicial reform issues, both now and in the future. The summary that follows is modelled on the structure used above in summing up the issues for debate.[9]

2. TEXTUAL REORGANISATION

There has been an extensive reorganisation of the provisions of primary law texts on the Community Courts. The Protocols on the Statute of the Court of Justice, annexed to the EC Treaty and the Euratom Treaty, are to be repealed and replaced by a uniform Statute annexed both to those Treaties and to the

---

[5] Also known as the 'Due Report' – see Parts Two and Four (3), *infra*.

[6] See Part Four (4) of this volume, *infra*.

[7] See n. 20 on p. 61, *supra*. 'The Group's first and principal unanimous conclusion is that, with the enlargement of the Union in prospect, and given the gradual extension of Community competence, it is essential to embark on a reform of the Community's judicial system. This is a matter of urgency, since the growing number of cases could in the medium term undermine one of the fundamental pillars of the European venture' (Interim Report, p. 1).

[8] See n. 20 on p. 61, *supra*.

[9] See *Synthesis of the Debate*, in Part One of this volume, from p. 55, *supra*.

TEU. Council Decision 88/591/ECSC, EEC, Euratom of 24 October 1988 establishing a Court of First Instance of the European Communities, as amended, is to be repealed. Provisions relating to the composition, organisation and jurisdiction of the CFI are now juxtaposed with those relating to the ECJ, either in the Treaties themselves or in the Statute. Transitional arrangements will apply to the ECSC Treaty until its expiry in 2002.

3. JURISDICTIONAL STRUCTURE

Many controversial proposals for dealing with the challenges facing the Courts were canvassed above under this heading. However, the IGC's response has been very restrained: it focuses on enabling difficult decisions to be taken at a later date by means of Community legislation, rather than relying upon repeated Treaty amendments.

(1) *Direct actions*

Perhaps the most significant immediate impact of the reforms will be felt in the sphere of direct actions before the Community Courts. The Member States have decided to provide a Treaty basis for the establishment of 'judicial panels to hear and determine at first instance certain classes of action or proceeding brought in specific areas'.[10] The details concerning this development will be discussed below under Court Structure; for now, it should be noted that under Article 225(2) EC the CFI will be competent to hear appeals from such panels on points of law only, unless the Decision establishing the panel also allows the factual determinations of the panel to be challenged.

This clear recognition of the jurisdiction of the CFI in a Treaty article is given more general expression in Article 225 EC, where the full extent of its current jurisdiction is recorded.[11] Previously, this information had been contained only in the various decisions that had established and then increased the CFI's role. However, this list of fields has not been extended to include the possibility for actions under Articles 226 and 227 EC to be brought before the CFI, which is underlined by a proposed amendment to the Statute of the Court of Justice (which Article 225(1) expressly permits to lay down exceptions to these basic fields of CFI competence). This amendment emphasises that any action brought

[10] Article 225a EC.

[11] These fields are listed in Article 225(1) EC as the 'actions or proceedings referred to in Articles 230, 232, 235, 236 and 238' of the EC Treaty, covering actions for annulment, actions for failure to act, damages claims under Article 288 EC, staff cases and cases concerning arbitration clauses in contracts respectively. Excepted from this are those cases assigned to a judicial panel and those reserved in the Statute for the ECJ.

by an EC institution, the ECB or a Member State will fall within the jurisdiction of the ECJ, even in those fields stated by Article 225 EC to fall within the CFI's competence. Thus, it seems that the IGC has set its face against any such extension, although it should be noted that the definition of such exceptions in the Statute will allow amendments to be made by the Council by unanimous vote. Furthermore, a statement by the Conference 'calls on the Court of Justice and the Commission to give overall consideration as soon as possible to the division of competence between the Court of Justice and the Court of First Instance, in particular in the area of direct actions, and to submit suitable proposals for examination by the competent bodies as soon as the revised Treaty enters into force'. Perhaps, then, in the medium term, we may expect some progress in this area, although given the clear message sent by the IGC concerning such an extension of CFI competence and the Member States' apparent inability to reach agreement on this issue, this may prove difficult to achieve.

There has been no attempt by the IGC to address the many calls for a relaxation of the standing criteria for private parties under Article 230 EC. In some ways this is quite logical, given the clear focus in the majority of the reflection documents concerning the Courts on the need to equip it with the means to bear its workload more effectively: increased access to those courts by direct actions could well have absorbed and indeed engulfed any of the improvements that might have been made. Furthermore, the definition of such criteria would have been a highly technical and potentially difficult issue, with which the IGC may not have been able to deal satisfactorily given the time pressures on its agenda. Nevertheless, a European Union that professes to attach the highest value to establishing an area of 'freedom, security and justice' will undoubtedly need to pay greater attention to such fundamental issues of access to justice in the future, especially as the power of European law to influence the daily lives of individuals continues to increase.

There is, however, one significant change to Article 230 EC. The European Parliament has been made a 'privileged applicant', on the same footing as the Member States, the Council and the Commission. The Parliament's right of *légitimation active* is thus no longer restricted to the protection of its own prerogatives.

Finally under this heading, there is a new provision (Article 229a EC) enabling the Council to adopt provisions 'to confer jurisdiction, to the extent that it shall determine, on the Court of Justice in disputes relating to the application of acts adopted on the basis of this Treaty which create Community industrial property rights'. For that purpose, the Council is to act by the so-called 'organic law' procedure: the Council must act unanimously on a proposal from the Commission and after consulting the European Parliament; it must then recommend the provisions to the Member States 'for adoption in accordance with their respective constitutional requirements'.[12] Quite apart from its potential significance in the specific area of judicial competence allocation, it should be stressed that this provision is also revolutionary in general institutional terms.

(2) *Preliminary rulings*

No amendments to Article 234 EC have been adopted by the IGC, so those who feel strongly that the only sensible way to deal with the flood of cases from national courts is to send the appropriate signals by means of new wording in the Treaty will be disappointed. However, an enabling provision of much potential significance has been included in the new provisions on the CFI. Article 225(3) EC provides that '[t]he Court of First Instance shall have jurisdiction to hear and determine questions referred for a preliminary ruling under Article 234, in specific areas laid down by the Statute'. Presumably, this provision is also covered by the statement made by the conference quoted above, calling for proposals from the Commission and the Court on the appropriate division of jurisdiction between the CFI and the ECJ, so it seems highly likely that movement on removing at least some types of case from the immediate remit of the ECJ can be expected after the ratification of the amended version of the Treaty. The question for debate will then become: in which 'specific areas' should the Statute allow the CFI to make preliminary rulings? The current obvious candidate would appear to be cases in national courts concerning EC-level intellectual property rights, such as the Community Trade Mark and the Community Design Right and a possible future Community Patent. However, there has been little discussion of other possible areas of limited scope that might be suitable for transfer; it may prove more difficult to build this jurisdiction up step by step in the way employed when the CFI's direct actions jurisdiction was developed.

However, this apparently substantial gain in flexibility for the European Courts in allocating their workload may be tempered by the possibility provided for by Article 225(3): '[w]hen the Court of First Instance considers that the case requires a decision of principle likely to affect the unity or consistency of Community law, it may refer the case to the Court of Justice for a ruling'. Furthermore, under Article 225(3) decisions actually taken by the CFI on a reference from a national court may 'exceptionally' be reviewed by the ECJ: it will be for the First Advocate General to determine (within one month of the delivery of the CFI's judgment) whether or not there is a serious risk of the uniformity or consistency of Community law being affected: if he does find such

---

[12] This confers competence to give the CFI jurisdiction in *inter partes* disputes re EC IP rights.

a risk, then he may propose that the ECJ should review the decision of the CFI. The ECJ must decide within one month of its receipt of that proposal whether or not it will review the decision. The Conference has expressed its view that, in such exceptional cases, the ECJ should 'decide by an emergency procedure'.[13] It is not yet clear whether this refers to existing emergency procedures, or whether the Court, Commission and Council will need to devise a special emergency procedure for this particular purpose.

The extent to which such a procedure could threaten the possible gains of granting this jurisdiction to the CFI will depend upon how regularly it appears necessary to use it. The Working Party report came out strongly in favour of such references under Article 234 EC only being heard once, subject to the possibility of an appeal by the Commission 'in the interests of the law', which would not have affected the course of the case in the national court at all.[14] The risk of causing unacceptable delays to national actions must be avoided, but even if this can be achieved, there is still the danger that such a procedure could undermine the authority of preliminary rulings made by the CFI, having a detrimental effect on the respect paid to them by national judges. The IGC showed that it was aware of these issues by adopting a Declaration on 'the essential provisions of the review procedure', which are to be defined in the Statute. Those provisions should, in particular, specify: the role of the parties in any proceedings before the ECJ, any impact of this review on the enforcement of the CFI's decision in the case and the effect that the ECJ's review might have on the dispute between the parties to the case. It is a pity that the IGC did not see its way clear to resolving these matters at Nice.

Overall, therefore, there is much to support in the changes made to the framework covering the jurisdictional structure of the Courts. While the IGC itself has not dealt in any real detail with the issues of exactly which areas may be moved, it has at least put in place a system for analysing these issues once the amended Treaty is ratified and enters into force. However, some of the new provisions contain worrying indications about the possible course of such future developments, which could undo some of the good work. Especial vigilance and wide discussion will be necessary to ensure that these dangers are avoided when the relevant parties begin to assess the possibilities in this area.

---

[13] Declaration 15 to The Final Act of the Conference on Article 225(3) EC.

[14] A similar debate arises regarding the possibility of appeals to the ECJ from CFI decisions on appeals from the new judicial panels. We will return to this below.

3. THE STRUCTURE OF THE COMMUNITY COURTS

From the foregoing section, it will be clear that the Nice reforms will have significant consequences for the structure of the Community Court system. On a basic level, the CFI is now acknowledged separately in the EC Treaty. Article 220 EC explicitly includes the CFI ('within its jurisdiction') as one of the courts that is to ensure that the law is observed in the interpretation and application of the Treaty and this is underlined by the new Articles 224 and 225 EC. Under these provisions, the CFI's jurisdiction and basic composition are detailed, which might suggest a greater recognition of the separate existence of the CFI, rather than simply as an appendage 'attached to the ECJ' as under the old Article 225(1) EC. There have also been responses to some of the issues discussed above in the Synthesis and we will deal with each of these in turn.

(1) *'One Member State, one judge'*

A clear principle on this issue has now been inserted into the Treaty as far as the ECJ is concerned. Article 221 EC provides that the 'Court of Justice shall consist of one judge from each Member State'. This formulation is welcome, as it is clearly drafted with an eye to future enlargement: now, there will be no need to alter the rules concerning the number of judges on every new accession. Furthermore, this ensures that an increasing number of judges will be available to deal with the new cases that will surely be generated by the arrival of any new Member State. We do not share the view that it is wrong to make an express link between the number of judges and the number of Member States: for the Court to have legitimacy, it is essential that the jurisdictions of all of the Member States be represented within it. These increased numbers, however, could have made the plenary formation of the Court too large and unwieldy to operate effectively. The new provisions also seek to provide guidance on this matter. Under the redrafted Article 221 EC, the normal rule will now be that the Court will sit in Chambers, with the alternative possibility of sitting as a 'Grand Chamber' or in plenary formation (the latter where the Statute so provides): this is a reversal of the previously applicable general rule. This change is a welcome recognition of already established practice as well as a logical response to the difficulties of managing an increasingly heavy caseload.

The details of this measure can be found in Articles 16 and 17 of the Protocol on the Statute of the Court of Justice. A Chamber will be the normal formation, consisting of either three or five judges, where the quorum will be three. However, in cases involving a Member State or a Community Institution as a party (i.e. as an applicant or defendant only), they can require the Court to sit as a Grand Chamber of eleven judges, where the quorum will be nine. Only in exceptional cases will the plenary formation be used: Article 16 of the Statute requires this in cases under Article 195(2), 213, 216 and 247(7) EC, which cover the dismissal of the Ombudsman of the European Parliament, the dismissal of or removal of pension or other benefits from a European Commissioner, serious misconduct by a member of the Commission and the dismissal of or removal of pension or other benefits from a member of the Court of Auditors respectively, all of which have been of little practical significance. Article 16 further allows the Grand Chamber to refer a case to the plenary session when it considers it to be 'of great importance', although only after hearing the Advocate General on the question. Thus, the clear basic rule is that the Court itself must decide whether the issue is one of sufficient importance to merit such a plenary hearing, which is an important step in securing the flexibility of the Court's jurisdictional arrangements.

Currently, these bits of fine-tuning do not seem to be of much practical significance, as they largely reflect current practice and are a logical response to the guaranteed continuation of each Member State having one judge at the ECJ. However, in the longer term, the composition of the Grand Chamber may be rather significant. After all, in a European Union of 25 Member States, it would become possible for two Grand Chambers to sit simultaneously.[15] This could be a further significant improvement on the Court's ability to deal with many important cases at once and is a possibility whose potential should be welcomed.

As to size of the CFI, Article 224 EC provides that the 'Court of First Instance shall comprise at least one judge from each Member State', the precise number to be fixed by the Statute. The possibility of increasing the number of CFI judges, without the need to amend the Treaty, is thus explicitly recognised. That is a welcome acknowledgement of the request by the Courts to secure greater judicial resources for the CFI to deal with its increasing workload. For the time being, however, the Statute provides for only 15 judges for the CFI,[16] in spite of the recent consensus on the need to increase its numbers by a further 6 judges: clearly, the precise modalities of this increase are still the subject of political dispute, but the CFI's need for more personnel is becoming ever more keenly felt, so rapid progress here in the Council is vital.

---

[15] Although this would require the amendment of the rule that the President of the Court must preside over the Grand Chamber, since this rule is contained in the Statute, such a change would require simply the unanimous approval of the Council (Article 245 EC). We will return to the issue of such amendments to the current rules in what follows in this chapter.

[16] Article 48 of the Statute.

(2) *Specialisation*

While the focus on Chambers noted in the preceding section might impact somewhat on this area, no concrete arrangements are currently in place for using Chambers in specialised areas of Community law. A much more significant development in this area has been made by the introduction of the provisions enabling the establishment of Judicial panels, Articles 220 and 225a EC. Article 225a requires the Council to act unanimously to establish such panels and both the Court and the Commission are granted the right of legislative initiative in this area, with the concomitant obligation on the Council to consult whichever of the two did not make the proposal, as well as consulting the European Parliament. Appointment to such a panel requires independence and the ability required for appointment to judicial office; the Council will need to agree unanimously on such appointments. The rules of procedure of any such panels must be drawn up in agreement with the ECJ and can be approved by a qualified majority vote in the Council. Most importantly, the determinations of such panels in their 'specific areas' may be subject to appeal to the CFI on points of law only, unless the Decision establishing the panel also provides for appeals on matters of fact.

This new provision reflects the wide consensus reached on the need for a new way of dealing with cases involving Community staff. Indeed, the Conference has called on the ECJ and the Commission 'to prepare as swiftly as possible a draft decision establishing a judicial panel which is competent to deliver judgments at first instance on disputes between the Community and its servants', suggesting the firm intention to make very early use of these new powers. Other potential areas that have been mooted for such coverage are the various EC-level IP rights, perhaps particularly the possibility of an EC Patent (although it is clear that the European Patent Office in Munich under the current Patent Convention will not give in to such a development without a fight!), but for now this must remain mere speculation.[17]

A potentially more difficult issue arises by virtue of Article 225 EC: the CFI is clearly granted jurisdiction to hear appeals from such judicial panels. However, there may 'exceptionally' be a review of the CFI's decision by the ECJ 'where there is a serious risk of the uniformity or consistency of Community

---

[17] Although, in an interesting unilateral statement made by Luxembourg, a hint is given that the IP rights are indeed the next main contenders for this treatment. Luxembourg made clear that, if judicial panels were to be set up to replace the OHIM Boards of Appeal (which were established pursuant to the Community Trade Mark Regulation), it would not seek to claim the seat of such panels. Presumably, this was to appease Spanish fears, but it also provides a clear indication of things to come.

law being affected' (Article 225(2) EC). Article 62 of the Statute explains that it will be for the First Advocate General to determine (within one month of the delivery of the CFI's judgment) whether or not there is such a serious risk: if he does so consider, then he may propose that the ECJ should review the decision of the CFI. The ECJ must decide within one month of its receipt of that proposal whether or not it will review the decision. It is clear that these stringent time limits are intended to mitigate the risk of serious extensions to what might already have been a rather lengthy court process on the European level in such cases, while the involvement of the First Advocate General is included to avoid tying up too much of the President of the Court's time in making such determinations. Overall, this filtering system is designed to deal with the problem in staff cases that, since costs are not awarded against staff in such proceedings, there is a tendency for the aggrieved servant of the Community to go on appealing any decision as far as possible. Some Member States were nevertheless still concerned that allowing such appeals would amount to a negation of the benefits of removing the burden of staff cases from the ECJ in particular and were in favour of appeals to the CFI as a court of last instance (perhaps subject to an appeal 'in the interests of the law' to the ECJ, on application by the Commission and without affecting the actual result reached in the case itself). Suffice it to say that the detailed operation of this appeal to the ECJ remains to be worked out and much will depend upon how practice in this area develops.

(3)   *The role of the Advocate General*

Article 222 EC maintains eight Advocates General to serve the Court of Justice, although a unanimous Council vote on a proposal from the ECJ could increase that number in future, as under the previous Article 222. The details concerning the partial replacement of Advocates General (and judges) every three years have been moved to the Statute from the old Article 223 EC, allowing the potential for greater flexibility in determining these conditions in the future without the need for Treaty amendments. Unfortunately, an annoying inaccuracy in the wording of the Treaty has been perpetuated, as Article 222 still refers to the 'submissions' of the Advocate General, instead of the Opinion that is actually delivered, independently of the parties' submissions. However, a significant change is the recognition under the new Article 222 that there is not necessarily a requirement that an Advocate General must deliver an Opinion in all cases before the ECJ. The Statute now provides that, after hearing the Advocate General on the subject, the Court may decide to dispense with such an Opinion where it considers that the case 'raises no new point of law'. This is clearly aimed at saving resources in obvious cases, avoiding the need for an extra

Opinion to be translated and published: provided that the procedure is used sensibly, it has much to commend it.

In a similar vein, the reduced possibilities of appeal from the CFI to the ECJ (due to the filtering mechanism of a 'serious risk of the uniformity or consistency of Community law being affected') may also serve to reduce the overall contribution of the Advocates General to the process of the development of Community law, even though the First Advocate General is involved in the operation of that very filter. Ultimately, this more efficient use of the available resources is necessary, yet it is difficult not to feel a certain unease at casting aside the useful and informative Opinion in too many cases. Certainly, the current proposals may not have any significant impact in this area given its case-by-case operation, but care should be taken lest this amounts to the first step on a slippery slope towards the total abolition of the role without clear consideration of the costs of such a move.

4. PROCEDURAL MATTERS

In this sphere, the most significant developments from the Nice IGC concern the changes to the way in which future amendments to the procedural rules governing the Courts will be possible. Previously, the Court's Rules of Procedure required the unanimous approval of the Council under the old Article 245 EC, while the Statute was in a Protocol to the Treaty and thus could be altered only by the same process as any other Treaty amendment. This inflexibility was worsened by the fact that there was no clear division of matters falling under the Statute and the Rules of Procedure, so that even the possibility of making such amendments within the normal EC political process was often skewed due the location of the various rules. Now, under the new Article 223 EC, the Council need only agree by qualified majority vote to change the Rules of Procedure and a similar rule applies both to the CFI (Article 224 EC) and will apply to any Rules of Procedure that may be adopted for the new judicial panels (Article 225a EC). Furthermore, the Statute is declared by the new Article 245 EC to be open to amendment by the Council by unanimous vote, with the exception of Title I (concerning the conditions of service of the members of the ECJ), thus removing the need for an IGC to secure any alterations. A similar right of initiative and consultation procedure applies here as under Article 225a concerning the new judicial panels, giving both the Court and the Commission a central role.

These developments are to be welcomed, as they provide an increased measure of flexibility to respond to difficulties that may arise in the operation of the Community judicial system, while providing a framework within which a future hierarchy of rules could be worked out, ensuring the adequate safeguards for certain provisions considered fundamental to the working of the Courts. It should be noted, however, that the rule of unanimity is to be retained with regard to the Courts' linguistic regime. Previously, the Rules of Procedure regulated the question of which languages were used in the Court. Had this remained the case, the matter would now be amenable to qualified majority voting in the Council. However, through the combined effect of Article 290 EC and Article 64 of the Statute, the linguistic regime is to be transferred to the Statute: until the relevant provisions have been adopted, Article 64 of the Statute explicitly provides that the existing rules may only be amended or repealed by the procedure for amending the Statute. This arrangement is clearly motivated by a desire to protect certain languages that some Member States may feel might be under threat, in response, for example, to the pressures of future enlargements of the Union.

At all events, it must not be forgotten that quite significant progress has also been made without the need for any Treaty revisions: the Court's recent proposals in this regard are to be welcomed and commended to the Council. Indeed, the Council has recently adopted a number of amendments to the Rules of Procedure of the ECJ,[18] in response to the ECJ proposal of mid-1999. The text of these amendments includes a number of changes to those proposals,[19] which entered into force on 1 July 2000.[20] Meanwhile, some of the proposed amendments, including to the jurisdiction of the CFI, have been incorporated into the legal framework by the Treaty of Nice itself. The IGC amendments to the procedure for altering these rules augurs well, if the Council can approach these matters in a manner similar to that shown in dealing with the current round of changes.

Overall, these procedural developments are really as much as could have been expected from this IGC. Significant progress has been made in readying the system to adapt itself as is required to the future challenges of the European Community and this is warmly to be welcomed. However, the precise shape and detail of these future changes is still very much uncertain, so the character of the European judicial system 'to come' still rests in the hands of the Member States

---

[18] Amendments to the Rules of Procedure of the Court of Justice [2000] O.J. L122/43, of 24 May 2000.

[19] See the explanatory note appended to the published amendments in the documents section (*infra*, Part Four (1)).

[20] See n. 14, *supra*, Article 2.

and their response to the needs and requests of the Courts, their representatives and interlocutors.

5. CONCLUSIONS

Perhaps the best overall assessment of the contribution of the Nice IGC to the reform of the European judicial system is provided in the title of the editorial of the Common Market Law Review when commenting on the Amsterdam Treaty as a whole: 'neither a bang nor a whimper'.[21] In many respects, given the early scepticism at the potential for change at the Nice IGC, this assessment must be seen as something of a victory for those who argued in favour of the need for judicial reform. The serious attention paid to these issues by the Courts and the Commission has proved difficult to ignore and while the changes actually introduced do not make many fundamental changes to the system, they do put in place a framework within which further progress can undoubtedly be made.

The most obviously significant reforms concern the power to set up new judicial panels in certain areas and the possibility to transfer certain areas of the preliminary rulings jurisdiction to the CFI. If properly prosecuted, these measures have much potential for dealing with the caseload crisis with which the Courts are currently faced. However, the precise mechanisms for operating these innovations have yet to be worked out and there is still the danger that over-zealous supervisory instincts could lead to many cases ending up at the ECJ's door anyway, thus undermining the progress that could be made. Both of these reforms could also have a growing impact upon the role of the Advocate General in the European judicial system, which is another underlying aspect that must not be forgotten in the debate on efficiency and the best use of limited resources. The possible benefits of the introduction of the idea of a Grand Chamber in the ECJ may well not be seen until the enlargement process has reached a more developed stage, but the confirmation of the use of Chambers as the Court's normal formation is a welcome recognition of practice and its attempts to deal with the increasing caseload. In this regard, the current wrangling that appears to be taking place concerning the proposal for six new judges for the CFI needs to be resolved urgently.

For the future, the changes to the way in which the Courts' procedural rules can be altered are potentially extremely important, as they have increased the flexibility available to the Council in this sphere (increasing the availability of QMV) and have made the process almost completely independent from any

---

[21] (1997) 34 C.M.L.Rev 767.

IGCs to come on Treaty amendment (by allowing amendment of the Statute by the Council, albeit by unanimity). Exactly how these powers will be used is a matter for conjecture, but the attention that the Council has paid to these issues does augur well for future reforms of the judicial system. The momentum thus created must be carried through from the Nice IGC in the coming months and years to solve the problems facing the European judicial system as the challenges facing it within an ever-changing Europe become greater and more complex.

B. *Annotated Texts*[*]

Introductory note. The EC, ECSC and Euratom Treaties all contain a set of provisions relating to the Court of Justice, and all have annexed to them a Protocol on the Statute of the Court. An Article laying down basic principles on the Court of First Instance was inserted into each of the Treaties by the SEA: these are, as amended by the TEU, respectively, Article 225 (ex Article 168a) EC, Article 32d ECSC and Article 140a Euratom. Their provisions were implemented by Council Decision 88/591/ECSC, EEC, Euratom of 24 October 1988 establishing a Court of First Instance of the European Communities.[1] The Decision also added a number of Articles on the CFI to each of the Statutes. The legal framework of the judicial system found in those provisions is extensively altered by the Treaty of Nice. There are amendments to the relevant provisions of the EC and Euratom Treaties, and their respective Protocols on the Statute of the Court of Justice are repealed and replaced by a single statute, to be annexed to those two Treaties and the TEU.[2] Except for the transitional arrangement mentioned below, Decision 88/591 is repealed (an instance of the use of constitution-making power to abrogate a legislative measure).[3] One of the consequences of these changes is the enhancement of the status of the CFI. The basic rules governing its composition, organisation and jurisdiction are now laid down, like those of the ECJ, by primary texts.

The ECSC Treaty is due to expire in July 2002. Under transitional provisions in the Treaty of Nice, the following Articles of the ECSC Statute of the Court are repealed: Articles 1 to 20, Articles 44 and 45, Article 46, second and third paragraphs, Articles 47 to 49, and Articles 51, 52 and 54 and 55.[4] Without prejudice to the Articles of the ECSC Statute which remain in force, the new Statute is made applicable to ECSC matters.[5] Also, Article 3 of Decision 88/591 continues to apply to the exercise of ECSC jurisdiction by the CFI.[6]

---

[*] The Treaty of Nice was published in the Official Journal of 10 March 2001 ([2001] OJ C80/1); all of the material that follows is drawn from this publication.

[1] OJ No. L319 of 25 November 1988, p. 1. The published version of the Decision contained many errors. A corrected version was published in OJ 1989 C 215/1.

[2] It is appropriate that the new Statute be annexed to the TEU since the ECJ has jurisdiction under that Treaty, still more limited than under the Community Treaties but of increasing importance.

[3] Treaty of Nice, Art. 10.   [4] Treaty of Nice, Art. 8.

[5] Treaty of Nice, Art. 9.   [6] Treaty of Nice, Art.10.

Articles or parts of Articles contained in the EC Treaty itself or in the Statute, which the Treaty of Nice leaves intact, are here presented in **Sans serif**. Any new text, or pieces of text which are to be moved from their present location, are presented in **Sans serif italics**. An indication is given, in **bold**, where text has been deleted or displaced.

I. EC TREATY ARTICLES

General note. The Articles annotated here are those contained in the section of the EC Treaty on the Court of Justice[7] which are the subject of amendments by the Treaty of Nice. There are corresponding amendments to the Euratom Treaty, in so far as necessary.[8] It was evidently not thought worthwhile altering the ECSC Treaty.

Article 220

The Court of Justice and the Court of First Instance, each within its jurisdiction, shall ensure that in the interpretation and application of this Treaty the law is observed.

In addition, judicial panels may be attached to the Court of First Instance under the conditions laid down in Article 225a in order to exercise, in certain specific areas, the judicial competence laid down in this Treaty.

Commentary. This is the provision which defines the fundamental role of the Community Courts – that of ensuring that, in the constitutional order resulting from the EC Treaty, the rule of law is upheld. The Article has been used by the Court of Justice as the source of its authority to give effect to the general principles of law, including the protection of human rights.

One amendment to the Article is that the Court of First Instance now receives explicit mention alongside the Court of Justice, as having the same role which each of them is to fulfil in its respective jurisdiction. This amounts to formal recognition of the CFI as a judicial organ of the Communities with its own distinct identity: *cf.* the reference in the present Article 225(1) to the CFI as being "attached to the Court of Justice".

---

[7] Section 4 of Chapter 1 of Title I of Part Five, EC Treaty. This comprises Arts. 220 to 245 (ex Arts. 164 to 188) EC.

[8] In view of the more limited scope of the Euratom Treaty, there is, for instance, no call for a provision like Art. 229a on disputes relating to Community industrial property rights. See the footnote to the heading, "Court of Justice and Court of First Instance" in the provisional text of the Treaty of Nice, SN 533/00.

A further amendment is the addition of the second paragraph, referring to the possibility of creating "judicial panels" (Fr. *chambres jurisdictionnelles*), which are to be attached to the CFI. The legal basis is the new Article 225a (see below). The conception is of tribunals which will be judicial, and not administrative, in character, though with limited and specialised jurisdiction.[9]

Article 221

The Court of Justice shall consist of one judge per Member State.

The Court of Justice shall sit in chambers or in a Grand Chamber, in accordance with the rules laid down for that purpose in the Statute of the Court of Justice.

When provided for in the Statute, the Court of Justice may also sit as a full Court.

Commentary. The opening paragraph of Article 221 has hitherto specified the number of Judges of the ECJ, thus needing to be revised on the occasion of each enlargement of the Union. The explicit acceptance of the principle that there be one judge from each Member State might be regrettable in theory; but it is a realistic acknowledgement of practice, and of the need for the Court to have legitimacy in the eyes of all the subjects of EU law. The Judges should be seen as representatives, not of the Member States, but of the legal traditions from which they come.

The rule of one Judge per Member State means that, from time to time as enlargements take place, there may be an even number on the Court. In the past that has been thought (mistakenly) to be inconsistent with the rule that decisions can only be taken validly when an uneven number of judges is sitting in deliberation:[10] hence, for example, the muddle over the 1995 enlargement, when it was initially decided that one of the Member States (*in casu,* Italy) should have an additional Judge, to bring the expected number of Judges (including a Norwegian) up to 17; the post had to be converted to one of Advocate General, when Norway failed to ratify the Treaty of Accession.[11] The solution, of course, lies in the rules as to quorums: even for a full Court, it suffices that 11 Judges be sitting.[12]

[9] The use of the term "judicial competence", rather than "jurisdiction" is not thought to be significant. The French version of Art. 220 speaks of "compétences" in both paragraphs. Moreover, Art. 225a, second para. refers to the "jurisdiction" conferred on a given judicial panel.

[10] Statute, Art. 17. See below.

[11] See Council Dec. 95/1/EC, Euratom, ECSC OJ 1995 L1/1, Art. 11 and the provision of Art. 222 EC as to the appointment of a ninth Advocate General until 6 October 2000.

[12] Statute, Art. 17. See below.

The second and third paragraphs of Article 221, as amended by the Treaty of Nice, refer to the organisation of the Court in chambers, and to the new concept of a Grand Chamber, as well as to the possibility of the Court's sitting as a full Court. The further definition of these various options is left to the Statute, giving greater flexibility.[13] The point to emphasise here is the reversal of the rule found in the present Article 221, that the Court *shall* sit in plenary session but *may* form chambers: the amendment makes clear that sitting in chambers represents the norm, and plenary sessions very much the exception.

Consistently with the position of principle taken in the first paragraph of the amended Article 221, the Council's power to increase the number of Judges, as provided for by the present fourth paragraphs, is abolished.

Article 222

The Court of Justice shall be assisted by eight Advocates-General. [sentence deleted] Should the Court of Justice so request, the Council, acting unanimously, may increase the number of Advocates-General [words deleted].

It shall be the duty of the Advocate-General, acting with complete impartiality and independence, to make, in open court, reasoned submissions on cases which, in accordance with the Statute of the Court of Justice, require his involvement.

[paragraph displaced]

Commentary. For the time being, there are to be eight Advocates General. The power of the Council to increase their number is moved, from the third, back to the first paragraph of the Article. The final words of the present third paragraph have been deleted, because increases in the number of Advocates General will no longer necessitate the amendment of Article 223, once the provisions on rotation have been moved into the Statute. The provision relating to the ninth Advocate General, being now spent, is deleted.

The principal change in Article 222 is that it is no longer assumed to be necessary, to assist the Court of Justice in performing its task, that an Advocate General give an opinion in every case. It is left to the Statute to identify the conditions calling for the involvement of an Advocate General in proceedings before the Court.[14]

---

[13] Statute, Art. 16. See below.
[14] Statute, Art. 20, fifth para. See below.

Article 223

The Judges and Advocates-General of the Court of Justice shall be chosen from persons whose independence is beyond doubt and who possess the qualifications required for appointment to the highest judicial offices in their respective countries or who are jurisconsults of recognised competence; they shall be appointed by common accord of the governments of the Member States for a term of six years.

Every three years there shall be a partial replacement of the Judges and Advocates-General, in accordance with the conditions laid down in the Statute of the Court of Justice.

The Judges shall elect the President of the Court of Justice from among their number for a term of three years. He may be re-elected.

Retiring Judges and Advocates-General may be reappointed.

The Court of Justice shall appoint its Registrar and lay down the rules governing his service.

The Court of Justice shall establish its Rules of Procedure. Those rules shall require the approval of the Council, acting by qualified majority.

Commentary. The Article contains both substantive and cosmetic amendments. In the first paragraph, the words "of the Court of Justice", qualifying the reference to the Judges and Advocates General, have been added (presumably) because the new Article 224 contains similar provisions relating to the CFI. More interestingly, there is no change in the mode of appointment by common accord of the governments of the Member States, which is also retained for the Members of the CFI in the new Article 224; in contrast, the appointment of the President and Members of the Commission will, pursuant to Article 214 (ex Article 158) EC as amended, in future be made by the Council acting by a qualified majority. This is not the place to analyse the new procedure of Article 214. The writers merely note that, in a formal sense at least, the relative status of the Council and the Commission will be altered, when the Members of the latter body are appointees of the former. Was it a fortunate oversight or a deliberate policy choice to maintain for the Members of the European Courts the status of bodies whose members are nominated at the level of the Union's constitution-making authority?

The provisions on partial replacement in the second and third paragraphs of the present Article 223 are brought together in the second paragraph of the Article as amended, with the details, as to the numbers of Judges and Advocates

General which will be affected every three years, transferred into the Statute.[15]

The third and fourth paragraphs of the amended Article reproduce, in inverse order, the fourth and fifth paragraphs of the present text.

The fifth paragraph incorporates the present Article 224, thus creating a space in the Treaty for the insertion of new provisions on the CFI.

The sixth paragraph incorporates provisions presently found in Article 245, third paragraph, with one important difference: the Council's approval of future amendments to the Rules of Procedure of the ECJ will be given by qualified majority instead of by unanimity.

Article 224
(New Article)

The Court of First Instance shall comprise at least one judge per Member State. The number of Judges shall be determined by the Statute of the Court of Justice. The Statute may provide for the Court of First Instance to be assisted by Advocates-General.

The members of the Court of First Instance shall be chosen from persons whose independence is beyond doubt and who possess the ability required for appointment to high judicial office; they shall be appointed by common accord of the governments of the Member States for a term of six years. The membership shall be partially renewed every three years. Retiring members shall be eligible for reappointment.

The Judges shall elect the President of the Court of First Instance from among their number for a term of three years. He may be re-elected.

The Court of First Instance shall appoint its Registrar and lay down the rules governing his service.

The Court of First Instance shall establish its Rules of Procedure in agreement with the Court of Justice. Those Rules shall require the approval of the Council, acting by qualified majority.

Unless the Statute of the Court of Justice provides otherwise, the provisions of this Treaty relating to the Court of Justice shall apply to the Court of First Instance.

Commentary. This new Article lays down basic provisions on the composition and organisation of the Court of First Instance.

The wording of the first paragraph indicates that the size of the CFI may be

---

[15] Statute, Art. 9. See below.

increased beyond the minimum of one judge per Member State. For the time being, Article 48 of the Statute fixes the number of Judges at 15. The task of Advocates General in the CFI is defined by Article 49 of the Statute.

There is a change, as compared with the present Article 225(3), in the terms of eligibility for appointment to the CFI. The second paragraph of Article 224 says that the persons concerned must "possess the ability required for appointment to *high* judicial office" (emphasis added). This is a formalisation of the actual practice of most Member States. It is consistent with the objective of enhancing the status of the CFI, and also provides a point of differentiation from the future judicial panels (see Article 225a, below).

As with the ECJ, the Council's approval of future amendments to the Rules of Procedure of the CFI will require a qualified majority instead of unanimity.

Article 225
(New Article)

1. The Court of First Instance shall have jurisdiction to hear and determine at first instance actions or proceedings referred to in Articles 230, 232, 235, 236 and 238, with the exception of those assigned to a judicial panel and those reserved in the Statute for the Court of Justice. The Statute may provide for the Court of First Instance to have jurisdiction for other classes of action or proceeding.

   Decisions given by the Court of First Instance under this paragraph may be subject to a right of appeal to the Court of Justice on points of law only, under the conditions and within the limits laid down by the Statute.

2. The Court of First Instance shall have jurisdiction to hear and determine actions or proceedings brought against decisions of the judicial panels set up under Article 225a.

   Decisions given by the Court of First Instance under this paragraph may exceptionally be subject to review by the Court of Justice, under the conditions and within the limits laid down by the Statute, where there is a serious risk of the unity or consistency of Community law being affected.

3. The Court of First Instance shall have jurisdiction to hear and determine questions referred for a preliminary ruling under Article 234, in specific areas laid down by the Statute.

   Where the Court of First Instance considers that the case requires a decision of principle likely to affect the unity or consistency of Community law, it may refer the case to the Court of Justice for a ruling.

Decisions given by the Court of First Instance on questions referred for a preliminary ruling may exceptionally be subject to review by the Court of Justice, under the conditions and within the limits laid down by the Statute, where there is a serious risk of the unity or consistency of Community law being affected.

Commentary. The present Article 225 is to be replaced by this new Article defining the jurisdiction of the CFI, and rights of appeal from the latter to the ECJ.

Paragraph (1) of the Article establishes, in its first subparagraph, the simple principle that the CFI is to have jurisdiction at first instance in the five kinds of direct action which are specified, with the exception of proceedings assigned to a judicial panel or reserved in the Statute for the ECJ. The heads of jurisdiction are: actions for the annulment of acts of the Community institutions (Article 230); actions in respect of a failure by an institution to act (Article 232); actions for damages in respect of harm caused by an institution or its servants (Article 235 and Article 288, second paragraph); staff cases (Article 236); and proceedings arising under arbitration clauses in contracts (Article 238). The first of the exceptions will become operative when the Council exercises its power under Article 225a to create judicial panels (see below). The other exception is given effect by Article 51 of the Statute. This preserves the jurisdiction of the ECJ in actions under any of the five heads identified by Article 225 (1), which are brought by a Community institution, by the European Central Bank or by a Member State. Thus the idea that all direct actions, including enforcement actions pursuant to Articles 226 and 227 EC, might start in the CFI, has not been taken up. However, there is power under the final sentence of the paragraph for the jurisdiction of the CFI to be enlarged through amendment of the Statute; and strong encouragement is given to the ECJ and the Commission to undertake a comprehensive review of the division of competence between the two Community Courts, by a Declaration of the IGC.[16]

The second subparagraph of Article 225(1) refers to the general right of appeal to the ECJ against decisions of the CFI in direct actions of the kind to which the paragraph relates. Articles 56 to 61 of the Statute lay down the conditions and limits to which such appeals are subject.

Paragraph (2) of Article 225 confers on the CFI jurisdiction to entertain

---

[16] Decl. No. 12 to the Final Act of the IGC:

"The conference calls on the Court of Justice and the Commission to give overall consideration as soon as possible to the division of jurisdiction between the Court of Justice and the Court of First Instance, in particular in the area of direct actions, and to submit suitable proposals for examination by the competent bodies as soon as the Treaty of Nice enters into force."

appeals against decisions of the new judicial panels. The benefit in terms of jurisdictional efficacy, which is expected to be gained from the establishment of panels in certain specialised areas, may in some degree be compromised by the possibility of further review by the ECJ, though this should take place only exceptionally, "where there is a serious risk of the unity or consistency of Community law being affected". Elements of the procedure which is to govern such review have been supplied by Article 62 of the Statute; but these remain incomplete, as the IGC acknowledged in a Declaration which calls for the "essential provisions" of the procedure to be defined in the Statute.[17]

Paragraph (3) of the Article represents one of the major innovations in the judicial system of the EU resulting from the Treaty of Nice. It confers on the CFI jurisdiction to give preliminary rulings on questions which are referred under Article 234 EC in specific areas laid down by the Statute. For the time being, this remains a potentiality, since the new single Statute contained in the Protocol agreed at Nice does not itself specify any such areas. The review to be undertaken pursuant to the Declaration cited in footnote 16, above, though concerned more particularly with the division of competence in respect of direct actions, will provide an opportunity for considering the possible transfer of Article 234 jurisdiction to the CFI, beginnings perhaps with questions relating to Community trade marks.

The second subparagraph of paragraph (3) enables the CFI, of its own motion, to send a case up to the ECJ if it considers that a decision of principle, likely to affect the unity or consistency of Community law, is required. That seems a sensible procedural safeguard, liable to add only marginally to the delay in ruling on the question referred.

The third subparagraph of Article 225(3) subjects decisions of the CFI on questions referred for a preliminary ruling to the possibility of review by the ECJ, under similar conditions to those provided for by paragraph (2) in respect of decisions on appeals from judicial panels. Such review appears even harder to justify in the present case, given the aim of reducing unacceptably long delays in dealing with references. The IGC showed it was conscious of the problem by adopting a Declaration encouraging the ECJ to have recourse to an emergency

---

[17] Decl. No. 13 to the Final Act of the IGC:

"The Conference considers that the essential provisions of the review procedure in Article 225(2) and (3) should be defined in the Statute of the Court of Justice. Those provisions should in particular specify:

- the role of the parties in proceedings before the Court of Justice, in order to safeguard their rights;
- the effect of the review procedure on the enforceability of the decision of the Court of First Instance;
- the effect of the Court of Justice decision on the dispute between the parties."

procedure in such cases.[18] Another way of meeting the concern would be if the implementing measures envisaged by the Declaration cited in footnote 17, above, were to provide for the ECJ's ruling to be one of principle only, not affecting the position of the parties to the main action.

It should finally be noted that the IGC has called for an evaluation of the measures implementing Article 225(2) and (3), within three years of their entry into force.[19]

Article 225a
(New Article)

The Council, acting unanimously on a proposal from the Commission and after consulting the European Parliament and the Court of Justice or at the request of the Court of Justice and after consulting the European Parliament and the Commission, may create judicial panels to hear and determine at first instance certain classes of action or proceeding brought in specific areas.

The Decision establishing a judicial panel shall lay down the rules on the organisation of the panel and the extent of the jurisdiction conferred upon it.

Decisions given by judicial panels may be subject to a right of appeal on points of law only or, when provided for in the decision establishing the panel, a right of appeal also on matters of fact, before the Court of First Instance.

The members of the judicial panels shall be chosen from persons whose independence is beyond doubt and who possess the ability required for appointment to judicial office. They shall be appointed by the Council, acting unanimously.

The judicial panels shall establish their Rules of Procedure in agreement with the Court of Justice. Those Rules shall require the approval of the Council, acting by qualified majority.

Unless the Decision establishing the judicial panels provides otherwise, the provisions of this Treaty relating to the Court of Justice and the provisions of the Statute of the Court of Justice shall apply to the judicial panels.

---

[18] Declaration No. 15 to the Final Act of the IGC:
"The Conference considers that, in exceptional cases in which the Court of Justice decides to review a decision of the Court of First Instance on a question referred for a preliminary ruling, it should act under an emergency procedure."

[19] Declaration No. 14 to the Final Act of the IGC:
"The Conference considers that when the Council adopts the provisions of the Statute which are necessary to implement Article 225 (2) and (3), it should put a procedure in place to ensure that the practical operation of those provisions is evaluated no later than three years after the entry into force of the Treaty of Nice."

Commentary. The conferment on the Council of power to create judicial panels is another major innovation. As in the case of the transfer to the CFI of jurisdiction to give preliminary rulings, the amendment agreed at Nice was only to insert an enabling provision into the Treaty. It is left to the competent institutions to determine, on a case by case basis, the rules on the organisation of panels, and the scope of their jurisdiction. The IGC indicated its wish that a draft decision establishing a judicial panel to deal with staff cases be prepared as swiftly as possible.[20]

As indicated by the third paragraph of Article 225a, there is to be a right of appeal from any judicial panel to the CFI on points of law, with the possibility of an appeal on the facts also, where the decision establishing the panel in question so provides.

Those eligible for appointment as members of a judicial panel must, besides being persons whose independence is beyond doubt, possess the ability for appointment to judicial office at some level (not necessarily "the highest", as for the ECJ, or a "high" level, as now for the CFI). The wording would, for instance, cover Barristers in England and Wales who satisfy the requirements for becoming a Recorder.

Like those of the ECJ and the CFI, the Rules of Procedure of judicial panels will require the approval of the Council acting by qualified majority.

Article 229a
(New Article)

Without prejudice to the other provisions of this Treaty, the Council, acting unanimously on a proposal from the Commission and after consulting the European Parliament, may adopt provisions to confer jurisdiction, to the extent that it shall determine, on the Court of Justice in disputes relating to the application of acts adopted on the basis of this Treaty which create Community industrial property rights. The Council shall recommend those provisions to the Member States for adoption in accordance with their respective constitutional requirements.

Commentary. The Council is here empowered to confer on the Court of Justice jurisdiction in disputes between individuals or companies relating to the application of acts creating Community industrial property rights. That would save the holder of a Community right from having to litigate infringements in the courts of different Member States. The novelty of the jurisdiction explains why

---

[20] Declaration No. 16 to the Final Act of the IGC:

"The Conference asks the Court of Justice and the Commission to prepare as swiftly as possible a draft decision establishing a judicial panel which has jurisdiction to deliver judgments at first instance on disputes between the Community and its servants."

the power of the Council is to be exercised in accordance with the "organic law" procedure, requiring national ratification of the measure. The reference to the Court of Justice must be understood, pursuant to Article 224, sixth paragraph and Articile 225a, sixth paragraph, as embracing the possibility of conferment of the new jurisdiction on the CFI or on a judicial panel. That such was the intention of the IGC is confirmed by a Declaration.[21]

Article 230

The Court of Justice shall review the legality of acts adopted jointly by the European Parliament and the Council, of acts of the Council, of the Commission and of the ECB, other than recommendations and opinions, and of acts of the European Parliament intended to produce legal effects vis-à-vis third parties.

It shall for this purpose have jurisdiction in actions brought by a Member State, the European Parliament, the Council or the Commission on grounds of lack of competence, infringement of an essential procedural requirement, infringement of this Treaty or of any rule of law relating to its application, or misuse of powers.

The Court of Justice shall have jurisdiction under the same conditions in actions brought [words deleted] by the Court of Auditors and by the ECB for the purpose of protecting their prerogatives.

Any natural or legal person may, under the same conditions, institute proceedings against a decision addressed to that person or against a decision which, although in the form of a regulation or a decision addressed to another person, is of direct and individual concern to the former.

The proceedings provided for in this Article shall be instituted within two months of the publication of the measure, or of its notification to the plaintiff, or, in the absence thereof, of the day on which it came to the knowledge of the latter, as the case may be.

Commentary. The IGC has not responded to those academic critics who have been arguing for a relaxation of the locus standi conditions for private parties bringing actions for annulment under Article 230 (ex Article 173). The only change to Article 230 is that the European Parliament has been given the full status of a "privileged applicant", alongside Member States, the Council and the

---

[21] Declaration No. 17 to the Final Act of the IGC:
"The Conference considers that Article 229a does not prejudge the choice of the judicial framework which may be set up to deal with disputes relating to the application of acts adopted on the basis of the Treaty establishing the European Community which create Community industrial property rights."

Commission. The Parliament is thus no longer required, as a condition of the admissibility of an action, to satisfy the Court of Justice that it is seeking to protect its own prerogatives. That condition remains applicable to the Court of Auditors and to the ECB.

Article 245

The Statute of the Court of Justice shall be laid down in a separate Protocol.

The Council, acting unanimously at the request of the Court of Justice and after consulting the European Parliament and the Commission, or at the request of the Commission and after consulting the European Parliament and the Court of Justice, may amend the provisions of the Statute with the exception of Title I.

[paragraph displaced]

Commentary. Under the present Article 245 (ex Article 188), the only part of the Statute which can be amended by an act of the Council is Title III, which contains provisions on Procedure. The new rule will allow all of the Statute so to be amended, except for the fundamental provisions on the status of the Judges and Advocates General contained in Title I. There is also a procedural change, enabling the Commission to take the initiative, as well as the ECJ, by putting forward a request (not a proposal) to the Council.

As noted above, the existing third paragraph of Article 245, on the Rules of Procedure of the ECJ, is moved to the final paragraph of amended Article 223.

II. THE NEW SINGLE STATUTE

General note. The whole text of the Protocol on the Statute of the Court of Justice, which replaces the three separate existing Protocols, is reproduced here. Many of the Articles are identical in substance as compared with the present EC Statute, and these are printed without any commentary, though changes of numbering are noted. Provisions imported into the single Statute from the present Euratom Statute are presented, like new Articles or parts of Articles, in **sans serif italics**. References to "the Community" have systematically been changed to "the Communities", since the Statute now applies to Euratom as well as to the EC: we do not comment upon that change in any detail.

THE HIGH CONTRACTING PARTIES

DESIRING to lay down the Statute of the Court provided for in Article 245 of the Treaty establishing the European Community and in Article 160 of the Treaty establishing the European Atomic Energy Community.

HAVE AGREED upon the following provisions, which shall be annexed to the Treaty on European Union, the Treaty establishing the European Community and the Treaty establishing the European Atomic Energy Community:

Article 1

The Court of Justice shall be constituted and shall function in accordance with the provisions of the Treaty on European Union (EU Treaty), of the Treaty establishing the European Community (EC Treaty), of the Treaty establishing the European Energy Community (EAEC Treaty) and of this Statute.

Commentary. The Preamble and Article 1 proclaim the applicability of the new Statute under the three Treaties (the TEU, the EC Treaty and the Euratom Treaty) which, once the ECSC Treaty has expired, will be the source of jurisdiction for the EU's Courts.

TITLE I
JUDGES AND ADVOCATES-GENERAL

Article 2

Before taking up his duties each Judge shall, in open court, take an oath to perform his duties impartially and conscientiously and to preserve the secrecy of the deliberations of the Court.

Article 3

The Judges shall be immune from legal proceedings. After they have ceased to hold office, they shall continue to enjoy immunity in respect of acts performed by them in their official capacity, including words spoken or written.

The Court, sitting as a full Court, may waive the immunity.

Where immunity has been waived and criminal proceedings are instituted against a Judge, he shall be tried, in any of the Member States, only by the court competent to judge the members of the highest national judiciary.

Articles 12 to 15 and Article 18 of the Protocol on the privileges and immunities of the European Communities shall apply to the Judges, Advocates-General, Registrar and Assistant Rapporteurs of the Court, without prejudice to the provisions relating to immunity from legal proceedings of Judges which are set out in the preceding paragraphs.

Commentary. The fourth paragraph of the Article is an addition. It must be read with Article 47 as regards the Judges and the Registrar of the Court of First Instance. Cf. Article 21 of the Protocol on privileges and immunities of the European Community, which is to be amended so as to include a reference to the latter; under present arrangements, Article 21 is extended to the Judges and Registrar of the CFI by Article 2 (5) of Decision 88/591. The insertion of the fourth paragraph into Article 3 does not alter the substance of the law, but aligns the text of the new Statute on the Protocol.

Article 4

The Judges may not hold any political or administrative office.

They may not engage in any occupation, whether gainful or not, unless exemption is exceptionally granted by the Council.

When taking up their duties, they shall give a solemn undertaking that, both during and after their term of office, they will respect the obligations arising there-from, in particular the duty to behave with integrity and discretion as regards the acceptance, after they have ceased to hold office, of certain appointments or benefits.

Any doubt on this point shall be settled by decision of the Court.

Article 5

Apart from normal replacement, or death, the duties of a Judge shall end when he resigns.

Where a Judge resigns, his letter of resignation shall be addressed to the President of the Court for transmission to the President of the Council. Upon this notification a vacancy shall arise on the bench.

Save where Article 6 applies, a Judge shall continue to hold office until his successor takes up his duties.

Article 6

A Judge may be deprived of his office or of his right to a pension or other benefits in its stead only if, in the unanimous opinion of the Judges and Advocates-General of the Court, he no longer fulfils the requisite conditions or meets the obligations arising from his office. The Judge concerned shall not take part in any such deliberations.

The Registrar of the Court shall communicate the decision of the Court to the President of the European Parliament and to the President of the Commission and shall notify it to the President of the Council.

In the case of a decision depriving a Judge of his office, a vacancy shall arise on the bench upon this latter notification.

Article 7

A Judge who is to replace a member of the Court whose term of office has not expired shall be appointed for the remainder of his predecessor's term.

Article 8

The provisions of Articles 2 to 7 shall apply to the Advocates-General.

TITLE II
ORGANISATION

Article 9
(New Article)

When, every three years, the Judges are partially replaced, eight and seven Judges shall be replaced alternately.

When, every three years, the Advocates-General are partially replaced, four Advocates-General shall be replaced on each occasion.

Commentary. These detailed provisions on the numbers of Judges and Advocates General to be replaced periodically have been transferred to the Statute from Article 223 EC. They can thus in future be altered by a Council decision, instead of requiring amendment of the Treaty. See the commentary on Article 223, above.

Article 10
(EC Statute, Article 9)

The Registrar shall take an oath before the Court to perform his duties impartially and conscientiously and to preserve the secrecy of the deliberations of the Court.

Article 11
(EC Statute, Article 10)

The Court shall arrange for replacement of the Registrar on occasions when he is prevented from attending the Court.

Article12
(EC Statute, Article 11)

Officials and other servants shall be attached to the Court to enable it to function. They shall be responsible to the Registrar under the authority of the President.

Article 13
(EC Statute, Article 12)

On a proposal from the Court, the Council may, acting unanimously, provide for the appointment of Assistant Rapporteurs and lay down the rules governing their service. The Assistant Rapporteurs may be required, under conditions laid down in the Rules of Procedure, to participate in preparatory inquiries in cases pending before the Court and to cooperate with the Judge who acts as Rapporteur.

The Assistant Rapporteurs shall be chosen from persons whose independence is beyond doubt and who possess the necessary legal qualifications; they shall be appointed by the Council. They shall take an oath before the Court to perform their duties impartially and conscientiously and to preserve the secrecy of the deliberations of the Court.

Article 14
(EC Statute, Article 13)

The Judges, the Advocates-General and the Registrar shall be required to reside at the place where the Court has its seat.

Article 15
(EC Statute, Article 14)

The Court shall remain permanently in session. The duration of the judicial vacations shall be determined by the Court with due regard to the needs of its business.

Article 16
(New Article)

The Court shall form chambers consisting of three and five Judges. The Judges shall elect the Presidents of the chambers from among their number. The Presidents of the chambers of five Judges shall be elected for three years. They may be re-elected once.

The Grand Chamber shall consist of eleven Judges. It shall be presided over by the President of the Court. The Presidents of the Chambers of five Judges and other Judges appointed in accordance with the conditions laid down in the Rules of Procedure shall also form part of the Grand Chamber.

The Court shall sit in a Grand Chamber when a Member State or an institution of the Communities that is party to the proceedings so requests.

The Court shall sit as a full Court where cases are brought before it pursuant to Articles 195(2), Article 213, Article 216 or Article 247(7) of the EC Treaty or Article 107d(2), Article 126(2), Article 129 and Article 160b(7) of the EAEC Treaty.

Moreover, where it considers that a case before it is of exceptional importance, the Court may decide, after hearing the Advocate-General, to refer the case to the full Court.

Commentary. This Article contains new provisions on the composition and organisation of the Chambers of the ECJ, and on plenary sessions. They replace the provisions of the second and third paragraphs of the present Article 220 EC. See the commentary on that Article, above.

The establishment of the Grand Chamber is a concrete consequence of the shift to the principle that the ECJ normally sits in one of its Chamber formations, and only exceptionally as a full Court. It is true that, pursuant to Article 16, third paragraph, the Grand Chamber must sit (as presently must the plenary session) if a Member State or a Community institution which is party to the proceedings so requests; and that the quorum for the Grand Chamber is fixed by Article 17, third paragraph (see below) as nine Judges (the same number as presently for decisions of the full Court). However, that does not mean the change is cosmetic. There will no longer be scope for the argument that all, or as many as practicable, of the Judges ought, in principle, to hear cases raising novel or difficult points of law. Consistency and continuity is to be ensured by creating for the Grand Chamber what the Due Report describes as a "permanent core" of Members:[22] this will consist of the President of the Court and the Presidents of the five-Judge Chambers, the authority of the latter being enhanced through their election for terms of three years.

The only cases in which plenary sessions are made mandatory by the fourth paragraph of Article 16 are those involving the removal of individuals from office or other punishments: re. the Ombudsman (Article 195 (2); re. Commissioners (Articles 213 and 216); re. Members of the Court of Auditors (Article 247 (7)). The Court itself (but no one else) may also decide, after

---

[22] See pp. 197 to 198, above. The suggestion is made in relation to plenary sessions.

hearing the Advocate General, to refer a case it considers "of exceptional importance" to the full Court.

The Article contains no reference to seven-Judge Chambers (*cf.* the present Article 221, second paragraph EC). The possibility of establishing such Chambers has thus been abandoned; presumably, because they are not seen as having any advantage over the combination of five-Judge Chambers and the Grand Chamber.

Article 17
(EC Statute, Article 15)

Decisions of the Court shall be valid only when an uneven number of its members is sitting in the deliberations.

Decisions of the chambers consisting of either three or five Judges shall be valid only if they are taken by three Judges.

Decisions of the Grand Chamber shall be valid only if nine Judges are sitting.

Decisions of the full Court shall be valid only if eleven Judges are sitting.

In the event of one of the Judges of a chamber being prevented from attending, a Judge of another chamber may be called upon to sit in accordance with the conditions laid down in the Rules of Procedure.

Commentary. The Article is presented here in bold italics, since it has been thoroughly reorganised, though its substance remains very largely as in the present Article 15 of the Statute.

One change is the deletion of the reference to seven-Judge Chambers.

It was noted above that the quorum for the Grand Chamber is 9. That for the full Court goes up to eleven.

Article 18
(EC Statute, Article 16)

No Judge or Advocate-General may take part in the disposal of any case in which he has previously taken part as agent or adviser or has acted for one of the parties, or in which he has been called upon to pronounce as a member of a court or tribunal, of a commission of inquiry or in any other capacity.

If, for some special reason, any Judge or Advocate-General considers that he should not take part in the judgment or examination of a particular case, he shall so inform the President. If, for some special reason, the President considers that any Judge or Advocate-General should not sit or make submissions in a particular case, he shall notify him accordingly.

Any difficulty arising as to the application of this Article shall be settled by decision of the Court.

A party may not apply for a change in the composition of the Court or of one of its chambers on the grounds of either the nationality of a Judge or the absence from the Court or from the chamber of a Judge of the nationality of that party.

TITLE III
PROCEDURE

Article 19
(EC Statute, Article 17)

The Member States and the institutions of the Community shall be represented before the Court by an agent appointed for each case; the agent may be assisted by an adviser or by a lawyer.

The States, other than the Member States, which are parties to the Agreement on the European Economic Area and also the EFTA Surveillance Authority referred to in that Agreement, shall be represented in same manner.

Other parties must be represented by a lawyer.

Only a lawyer authorised to practise before a court of a Member State or of another State which is a party to the Agreement on the European Economic Area may represent or assist a party before the Court.

Such agents, advisers and lawyers shall, when they appear before the Court, enjoy the rights and immunities necessary to the independent exercise of their duties, under conditions laid down in the Rules of Procedure.

As regards such advisers and lawyers who appear before it, the Court shall have the powers normally accorded to courts of law, under conditions laid down in the Rules of Procedure.

University teachers being nationals of a Member State whose law accords them a right of audience shall have the same rights before the Court as are accorded by this Article to lawyers.

Article 20
(EC Statute, Article 18)

The procedure before the Court shall consist of two parts: written and oral.

The written procedure shall consist of the communication to the parties and to the institutions of the Communities whose decisions are in dispute, of applications, statements of case, defences and observations, and of replies, if any, as well as of all papers and documents in support or of certified copies of them.

Communications shall be made by the Registrar in the order and within the time laid down in the Rules of Procedure.

The oral procedure shall consist of the reading of the report presented by a Judge acting as Rapporteur, the hearing by the Court of agents, advisers and lawyers and of the submissions of the Advocate-General, as well as the hearing, if any, of witnesses and experts.

Where it considers that the case raises no new point of law, the Court may decide, after hearing the Advocate-General, that the case shall be judged without a submission from the Advocate-General.

Commentary. This text includes a new fifth paragraph relating to the possibility for the Court to do without an Opinion from the Advocate General. Cf. Article 222 EC above, and the commentary thereon.

The rule is that an Opinion must be given unless the Court, after hearing the Advocate General, decides otherwise, because it considers that the case raises no new point of law.

Article 21
(EC Statute, Article 19)

A case shall be brought before the Court by a written application addressed to the Registrar. The application shall contain the applicant's name and permanent address and the description of the signatory, the name of the party or names of the parties against whom the application is made, the subject-matter of the dispute, the form of order sought and a brief statement of the pleas in law on which the application is based.

The application shall be accompanied, where appropriate, by the measure the annulment of which is sought or, in the circumstances referred to in Article 232 of the EC Treaty and Article 148 of the EAEC Treaty, by documentary evidence of the date on which an institution was, in accordance with those Articles, requested to act. If the documents are not submitted with the application, the Registrar shall ask the party concerned to produce them within a reasonable period, but in that event the rights of the party shall not lapse even if such documents are produced after the time-limit for bringing proceedings.

Article 22
(Euratom Statute, Article 21)

A case governed by Article 18 of the EAEC Treaty shall be brought before the Court by an appeal addressed to the Registrar. The appeal shall contain the name and permanent address of the applicant and the description of the signatory, a reference to the decision against which the appeal is brought, the names of the respondents, the subject-matter of the dispute, the submissions and a brief statement of the grounds on which the appeal is based.

The appeal shall be accompanied by a certified copy of the decision of the Arbitration Committee which is contested.

If the Court rejects the appeal, the decision of the Arbitration Committee shall become final.

If the Court annuls the decision of the Arbitration Committee, the matter may be re-opened, where appropriate, on the initiative of one of the parties in the case, before the Arbitration Committee. The latter shall conform to any decisions on points of law given by the Court.

Commentary. This Article had to be imported into the new Statute in its entirety, since the particular remedy is unique to the Euratom Treaty.

Article 23
(EC Statute, Article 20)

In the cases governed by Article 35(1) of the EU Treaty, by Article 234 of the EC Treaty and by Article 150 of the EAEC Treaty, the decision of the court or tribunal of a Member State which suspends its proceedings and refers a case to the Court shall be notified to the Court by the court or tribunal concerned. The decision shall then be notified by the Registrar of the Court to the parties, to the Member States and to the Commission, and also to the Council or to the European Central Bank if the act the validity or interpretation of which is in dispute originates from one of them, and to the European Parliament and the Council if the act the validity or interpretation of which is in dispute was adopted jointly by those two institutions.

Within two months of this notification, the parties, the Member States, the Commission and, where appropriate, the European Parliament, the Council and the European Central Bank, shall be entitled to submit statements of case or written observations to the Court.

In the cases governed by Article 234 of the EC Treaty, the decision of the national court or tribunal shall, moreover, be notified by the Registrar of the Court to the

States, other than the Member States, which are parties to the Agreement on the European Economic Area and also to the EFTA Surveillance Authority referred to in that Agreement which may, within two months of notification, where one of the fields of application of that Agreement is concerned, submit statements of case or written observations to the Court.

Commentary. The first sentence of the Article has been amended to take account of the new numbering of the EC Treaty and to include mentions of Article 35(1) TEU, which was introduced into the Treaty by the TA and provides for a system of references for preliminary rulings, under limitative conditions, in respect of certain Third Pillar acts, and of Article 150 Euratom, the provision of the Euratom Treaty corresponding to Article 234 EC. That change explains the addition to the third paragraph of an opening phrase referring to Article 234 EC, the EEA countries other than Member States of the EC not being concerned with the jurisdiction of the Court under Article 36 (1) TEU or Article 150 Euratom.

Article 24
(EC Statute, Article 21)

The Court may require the parties to produce all documents and to supply all information which the Court considers desirable. Formal note shall be taken of any refusal.

The Court may also require the Member States and the institutions not being parties to the case to supply all information which the Court considers necessary for the proceedings.

Article 25
(EC Statute, Article 22)

The Court may at any time entrust any individual, body, authority, committee or other organisation it chooses with the task of giving an expert opinion.

Article 26
(EC Statute, Article 23)

Witnesses may be heard under conditions laid down in the Rules of Procedure.

Article 27
(EC Statute, Article 24)

With respect to defaulting witnesses the Court shall have the powers generally granted to courts and tribunals and may impose pecuniary penalties under conditions laid down in the Rules of Procedure.

Article 28
(EC Statute, Article 25)

Witnesses and experts may be heard on oath taken in the form laid down in the Rules of Procedure or in the manner laid down by the law of the country of the witness or expert.

Article 29
(EC Statute, Article 26)

The Court may order that a witness or expert be heard by the judicial authority of his place of permanent residence.

The order shall be sent for implementation to the competent judicial authority under conditions laid down in the Rules of Procedure. The documents drawn up in compliance with the letters rogatory shall be returned to the Court under the same conditions.

The Court shall defray the expenses, without prejudice to the right to charge them, where appropriate, to the parties.

Article 30
(EC Statute, Article 27)

A Member State shall treat any violation of an oath by a witness or expert in the same manner as if the offence had been committed before one of its courts with jurisdiction in civil proceedings. At the instance of the Court, the Member State concerned shall prosecute the offender before its competent court.

Article 31
(EC Statute, Article 28)

The hearing in court shall be public, unless the Court, of its own motion or on application by the parties, decides otherwise for serious reasons.

Article 32
(EC Statute, Article 29)

During the hearings the Court may examine the experts, the witnesses and the parties themselves. The latter, however, may address the Court only through their representatives.

Article 33
(EC Statute, Article 30)

Minutes shall be made of each hearing and signed by the President and the Registrar.

Article 34
(EC Statute, Article 31)

The case list shall be established by the President.

Article 35
(EC Statute, Article 32)

The deliberation of the Court shall be and shall remain secret.

Article 36
(EC Statute, Article 33)

Judgments shall state the reasons on which they are based. They shall contain the names of the Judges who took part in the deliberations.

Article 37
(EC Statute, Article 34)

Judgments shall be signed by the President and the Registrar. They shall be read in open court.

Article 38
(EC Statute, Article 35)

The Court shall adjudicate upon costs.

Article 39
(EC Statute, Article 36)

The President of the Court may, by way of summary procedure, which may, in so far as necessary, differ from some of the rules contained in this Statute and which shall be laid down in the Rules of Procedure, adjudicate upon applications to suspend execution, as provided for in Article 242 of the EC Treaty and Article 157 of the EAEC Treaty or to prescribe interim measures in pursuance of Article 243 of the EC Treaty or Article 158 of the EAEC Treaty, or to suspend enforcement in accordance with the last paragraph of Article 256 of the EC Treaty or the third paragraph of Article 164 of the EAEC Treaty.

Should the President be prevented from attending, his place shall be taken by another Judge under conditions laid down in the Rules of Procedure.

The ruling of the President or of the Judge replacing him shall be provisional and shall in no way prejudice the decision of the Court on the substance of the case.

Commentary. The first paragraph of the Article has been amended to take account of the new numbering of the EC Treaty, and by the insertion of references to the relevant provisions of the Euratom Treaty.

Article 40
(EC Statute, Article 37)

Member States and institutions of the Communities may intervene in cases before the Court.

The same right shall be open to any other person establishing an interest in the result of any case submitted to the Court, save in cases between Member States, between institutions of the Communities or between Member States and institutions of the Communities.

Without prejudice to the preceding paragraph, the States, other than the Member States, which are parties to the Agreement on the European Economic Area, and also the EFTA Surveillance Authority referred to in that Agreement, may intervene in cases before the Court where one of the fields of application of that Agreement is concerned.

An application to intervene shall be limited to supporting the form of order sought by one of the parties.

Article 41
(EC Statute, Article 38)

Where the defending party, after having been duly summoned, fails to file written submissions in defence, judgment shall be given against that party by default. An objection may be lodged against the judgment within one month of it being notified. The objection shall not have the effect of staying enforcement of the judgment by default unless the Court decides otherwise.

Article 42
(EC Statute, Article 39)

Member States, institutions of the Communities and any other natural or legal persons may, in cases and under conditions to be determined by the Rules of

Procedure, institute third-party proceedings to contest a judgment rendered without their being heard, where the judgment is prejudicial to their rights.

Article 43
(EC Statute, Article 40)

If the meaning or scope of a judgment is in doubt, the Court shall construe it on application by any party or any institution of the Communities establishing an interest therein.

Article 44
(EC Statute, Article 41)

An application for revision of a judgment may be made to the Court only on discovery of a fact which is of such a nature as to be a decisive factor, and which, when the judgment was given, was unknown to the Court and to the party claiming the revision.

The revision shall be opened by a judgment of the Court expressly recording the existence of a new fact, recognising that it is of such a character as to lay the case open to revision and declaring the application admissible on this ground.

No application for revision may be made after the lapse of 10 years from the date of the judgment.

Article 45
(EC Statute, Article 42)

Periods of grace based on considerations of distance shall be determined by the Rules of Procedure.

No right shall be prejudiced in consequence of the expiry of a time-limit if the party concerned proves the existence of unforeseeable circumstances or of force majeure.

Article 46
(EC Statute, Article 43)

Proceedings against the Communities in matters arising from non-contractual liability shall be barred after a period of five years from the occurrence of the event giving rise thereto. The period of limitation shall be interrupted if proceedings are instituted before the Court or if prior to such proceedings an application is made by the aggrieved party to the relevant institution of the Communities. In the latter event the proceedings must be instituted within the period of two months provided for in Article 230 of the EC Treaty and Article 146 of the EAEC Treaty; the provisions of the second paragraph of Article 232 of the EC Treaty and the second paragraph of Article 148 of the EAEC Treaty, respectively, shall apply where appropriate.

Commentary. The final sentence of the Article has been amended to take account of the new numbering of the EC Treaty, and to include references to relevant provisions of the Euratom Treaty.

TITLE IV
THE COURT OF FIRST INSTANCE OF
THE EUROPEAN COMMUNITIES

Article 47
(EC Statute, Article 44)

Articles 2 to 8, Article 14, Article 15, the first, second, fourth and fifth paragraphs of Article 17 and Article 18 of this Statute shall apply to the Court of First Instance and its members. The oath referred to in Article 2 shall be taken before the Court of Justice and the decisions referred to in Articles 3, 4 and 6 shall be adopted by that Court after hearing the Court of First Instance.

The fourth paragraph of Article 3 and Articles 10, 11 and 14 shall apply to the Registrar of the Court of First Instance mutatis mutandis.

Commentary. The present Article 44 refers to "Articles 2 to 8 and 13 to 16 of this Statute". The differences, as compared with Article 47, are due to changes in the numbering of Articles, the insertion of a new Article 16, and the inclusion in Article 17 of a reference to the Grand Chamber, which is not applicable to the CFI, since the matter is to be determined by the latter's Rules of Procedure. See Article 50, below.

A second paragraph has been added to the Article as part of the reorganisation of the primary texts relating to the CFI. Provisions governing the appointment and conditions of service of the CFI's Registrar are found in the present EC Statute, Article 45, which is omitted from the new Statute.

Article 48
(New Article)

The Court of First Instance shall consist of 15 Judges.

Commentary. This Article implements Article 224, first paragraph EC. See the commentary on that provision, above.

Article 49
(New Article)

The members of the Court of First Instance may be called upon to perform the task of an Advocate-General.

It shall be the duty of the Advocate-General, acting with complete impartiality and independence, to make, in open court, reasoned submissions on certain cases brought before the Court of First Instance in order to assist the Court of First Instance in the performance of its task.

The criteria for selecting such cases, as well as the procedures for designating the Advocates-General, shall be laid down in the Rules of Procedure of the Court of First Instance.

A member called upon to perform the task of Advocate-General in a case may not take part in the judgment of the case.

Commentary. This Article implements the last sentence of Article 224, first paragraph EC, by incorporating into the Statute the provisions presently found in Article 2(3) of Decision 88/591.

Article 50
(New Article)

The Court of First Instance shall sit in chambers of three or five Judges. The Judges shall elect the Presidents of the chambers from among their number. The Presidents of the chambers of five Judges shall be elected for three years. They may be re-elected once.

The composition of the chambers and the assignment of cases to them shall be governed by the Rules of Procedure. In certain cases governed by the Rules of Procedure, the Court of First Instance may sit as a full Court or be constituted by a single Judge.

The Rules of Procedure may also provide that the Court of First Instance may sit in a Grand Chamber in cases under the conditions specified therein.

Commentary. Provisions relating to the composition and organisation of the chambers of the CFI are presently found in Article 2(4) of Decision 88/591 and in Chapter 2 of the CFI's Rules of Procedure. The new Article 50 adopts the same rule regarding the Presidency of five-Judge chambers as Article 16, first paragraph in respect of the ECJ. The Statute assumes that the CFI may sit as a Grand Chamber, leaving it for the Rules of Procedure to settle the details.

Article 51
(New Article)

By way of exception to the rule laid down in Article 225(1) of the EC Treaty and Article 140a(1) of the EAEC Treaty, the Court of Justice shall have jurisdiction in actions brought by the Member States, by the institutions of the European Communities and by the European Central Bank.

Commentary. See the commentary on Article 225 EC, above.

Article 52
(EC Statute, Article 45, second paragraph)

The President of the Court of Justice and the President of the Court of First Instance shall determine, by common accord, the conditions under which officials and other servants attached to the Court of Justice shall render their services to the Court of First Instance to enable it to function. Certain officials or other servants shall be responsible to the Registrar of the Court of First Instance under the authority of the President of the Court of First Instance.

Article 53
(EC Statute, Article 46)

The procedure before the Court of First Instance shall be governed by Title III [words deleted].

Such further and more detailed provisions as may be necessary shall be laid down in its Rules of Procedure. [words deleted] The Rules of Procedure may derogate from the fourth paragraph of Article 40 and from Article 41 in order to take account of the specific features of litigation in the field of intellectual property.

Notwithstanding the fourth paragraph of Article 20, the Advocate-General may make his reasoned submissions in writing.

Commentary. The first sentence of the second paragraph contains, in the present versions of the three Statutes, references to the respective Treaty provisions empowering the CFI to establish its Rules of Procedure, which are omitted from the new single Statute.

The numbers of the Articles of the Statute referred to in the second and third paragraphs have changed.

Article 54
(EC Statute, Article 47)

Where an application or other procedural document addressed to the Court of First Instance is lodged by mistake with the Registrar of the Court of Justice, it shall be transmitted immediately by that Registrar to the Registrar of the Court of First Instance; likewise, where an application or other procedural document addressed to the Court of Justice is lodged by mistake with the Registrar of the Court of First Instance, it shall be transmitted immediately by that Registrar to the Registrar of the Court of Justice.

Where the Court of First Instance finds that it does not have jurisdiction to hear and determine an action in respect of which the Court of Justice has jurisdiction, it shall refer that action to the Court of Justice; likewise, where the Court of Justice finds that an action falls within the jurisdiction of the Court of First Instance, it shall refer that action to the Court of First Instance, whereupon that Court may not decline jurisdiction.

Where the Court of Justice and the Court of First Instance are seised of cases in which the same relief is sought, the same issue of interpretation is raised or the validity of the same act is called in question, the Court of First Instance may, after hearing the parties, stay the proceedings before it until such time as the Court of Justice shall have delivered judgment. Where applications are made for the same act to be declared void, the Court of First Instance may also decline jurisdiction in order that the Court of Justice may rule on such applications. In the cases referred to in this paragraph, the Court of Justice may also decide to stay the proceedings before it; in that event, the proceedings before the Court of First Instance shall continue.

Article 55
(EC Statute, Article 48)

Final decisions of the Court of First Instance, decisions disposing of the substantive issues in part only or disposing of a procedural issue concerning a plea of lack of competence or inadmissibility, shall be notified by the Registrar of the Court of First Instance to all parties as well as all Member States and the institutions of the Communities even if they did not intervene in the case before the Court of First Instance.

Article 56
(EC Statute, Article 49)

An appeal may be brought before the Court of Justice, within two months of the notification of the decision appealed against, against final decisions of the Court of First Instance and decisions of that Court disposing of the substantive issues in part only or disposing of a procedural issue concerning a plea of lack of competence or inadmissibility.

Such an appeal may be brought by any party which has been unsuccessful, in whole or in part, in its submissions. However, interveners other than the Member States and the institutions of the Communities may bring such an appeal only where the decision of the Court of First Instance directly affects them.

With the exception of cases relating to disputes between the Communities and their servants, an appeal may also be brought by Member States and institutions of the Communities which did not intervene in the proceedings before the Court of First Instance. Such Member States and institutions shall be in the same position as Member States or institutions which intervened at first instance.

Article 57
(EC Statute, Article 50)

Any person whose application to intervene has been dismissed by the Court of First Instance may appeal to the Court of Justice within two weeks from the notification of the decision dismissing the application.

The parties to the proceedings may appeal to the Court of Justice against any decision of the Court of First Instance made pursuant to Article 242 or Article 243 or the fourth paragraph of Article 256 of the EC Treaty or Article 157 or Article 158 or the third paragraph of Article 164 of the EAEC Treaty within two months from their notification.

The appeal referred to in the first two paragraphs of this Article shall be heard and determined under the procedure referred to in Article 39.

Commentary. The Article has been amended to take account of changes in the numbering of Articles, and by the addition of references to the relevant provisions of the Euratom Treaty.

Article 58
(EC Statute, Article 51)

An appeal to the Court of Justice shall be limited to points of law. It shall lie on the grounds of lack of competence of the Court of First Instance, a breach of procedure before it which adversely affects the interests of the appellant as well as the infringement of Community law by the Court of First Instance.

No appeal shall lie regarding only the amount of the costs or the party ordered to pay them.

Article 59
(EC Statute, Article 52)

Where an appeal is brought against a decision of the Court of First Instance, the procedure before the Court of Justice shall consist of a written part and an oral part. In accordance with conditions laid down in the Rules of Procedure, the Court of Justice, having heard the Advocate-General and the parties, may dispense with the oral procedure.

Article 60
(EC Statute, Article 53)

Without prejudice to Articles 242 and 243 of the EC Treaty or Articles 157 and 158 of the EAEC Treaty, an appeal shall not have suspensory effect.

By way of derogation from Article 244 of the EC Treaty and Article 159 of the EAEC Treaty, decisions of the Court of First Instance declaring a regulation to be void shall take effect only as from the date of expiry of the period referred to in the first paragraph of Article 56 of this Statute or, if an appeal shall have been brought within that period, as from the date of dismissal of the appeal, without prejudice, however, to the right of a party to apply to the Court, pursuant to Articles 242 and 243 of the EC Treaty or Articles 157 and 158 of the EAEC Treaty, for the suspension of the effects of the regulation which has been declared void or for the prescription of any other interim measure.

Commentary. The Article has been amended to take account of changes in the numbering of Articles, and by the addition of references to the relevant provisions of the Euratom Treaty.

Article 61
(EC Statute, Article 54)

If the appeal is well founded, the Court of Justice shall quash the decision of the Court of First Instance. It may itself give final judgment in the matter, where the state of the proceedings so permits, or refer the case back to the Court of First Instance for judgment.

Where a case is referred back to the Court of First Instance, that Court shall be bound by the decision of the Court of Justice on points of law.

When an appeal brought by a Member State or an institution of the Communities, which did not intervene in the proceedings before the Court of First Instance, is well founded, the Court of Justice may, if it considers this necessary, state which of the effects of the decision of the Court of First Instance which has been quashed shall be considered as definitive in respect of the parties to the litigation.

Article 62
(New Article)

In the cases provided for in Article 225(2) and (3) of the EC Treaty and Article 140a(2) and (3) of the EAEC Treaty, where the First Advocate-General considers that there is a serious risk of the unity or consistency of Community law being affected, he may propose that the Court of Justice review the decision of the Court of First Instance.

The proposal must be made within one month of delivery of the decision by the Court of First Instance. Within one month of receiving the proposal made by the First Advocate-General, the Court of Justice shall decide whether or not the decision should be reviewed.

Commentary. This Article partially implements Article 225(2) and (3) EC by establishing some of the elements of the procedure for the review of CFI decisions on, respectively, appeals from judicial panels and questions referred for a preliminary ruling. See the commentary on Article 225, above. The judgment as to whether there is a serious risk of the unity or consistency of Community law being affected, must initially be made by the First Advocate General, within a month of the delivery of the decision by the CFI. Machinery will have to be set in place in the Chambers of the First Advocate General to examine such decisions systematically and with expedition. If the First Advocate General proposes that the ECJ review the decision, the Court must decide within a month whether or not to proceed (but no time limit is prescribed for the completion of any review). See the Declaration cited in footnote 17, above, as to other "essential elements" that remain to be determined.

TITLE V
FINAL PROVISIONS

Article 63
(EC Statute, Article 55)

The Rules of Procedure of the Court of Justice and of the Court of First Instance shall contain any provisions necessary for applying and, where required, supplementing this Statute.

Commentary. The Article has been amended, without alteration of its substance, to take account of the replacement of the EC and Euratom Statutes by the new single Statute.

Article 64
(New Article)

Until the rules governing the language arrangements applicable at the Court of Justice and the Court of First Instance have been adopted in this Statute, the provisions of the Rules of Procedure of the Court of Justice and of the Rules of Procedure of the Court of First Instance governing language arrangements shall continue to apply. Those provisions may only be amended or repealed according to the procedure laid down for amending this Statute.

Commentary. The linguistic regime of the ECJ and the CFI is presently determined by their respective Rules of Procedure (Articles 29 to 31 of the ECJ Rules and Articles 35 to 37 of the CFI Rules). If that had remained so, it would have been possible for an alteration of the regime to be approved by the Council acting by a qualified majority, once Article 223, sixth paragraph and Article 224, fifth paragraph EC became applicable (see above). To preserve the unanimity rule in the matter of language, the reference to the Rules of Procedure of the ECJ in Article 290 (ex Article 217) EC has been replaced by a reference to the Statute. The new Article 64 is a transitional provision, which maintains the existing arrangements, pending the incorporation into the Statute of new arrangements, and requires that any alteration be made by the procedure applicable to amendments of the Statute (see Article 245 EC, above).

Final Note. Article 56 of the EC Statute empowers the Council to make any adjustments to the Statute necessitated by an increase in the number of Judges pursuant to Article 221 (ex Article 165), fourth paragraph EC. The Article has been rendered redundant by the new principle of one Judge per Member State, and it is therefore omitted from the new Statute.

Article 57 of the EC Statute relates to the initial choice of Judges and Advocates General whose term of office was to expire after three years. As an obsolete provision, this too is omitted.